PROSPER

Five Steps to Thriving in Business and in Life

KEN BURKE

Because of the dynamic nature of the Internet, any web addresses or links contained in this book may have changed since publication and may no longer be valid. The views expressed in this work are solely those of the author and do not necessarily reflect the views of the publisher, and the publisher hereby disclaims any responsibility for them.

The author of this book does not dispense medical advice or prescribe the use of any technique as a form of treatment for physical, emotional, or medical problems without the advice of a physician, either directly or indirectly. The intent of the author is only to offer information of a general nature to help you in your quest for emotional and spiritual well-being. In the event you use any of the information in this book for yourself, which is your constitutional right, the author and the publisher assume no responsibility for your actions.

Print information available on the last page.

ISBN: 978-0-578-99707-0

Library of Congress Control Number: 2020905805

TABLE OF CONTENTS

Step 1 - Accept Yourself

Step 2 - Manage Your Ego

Step 3 - Get Clear

Step 4 - Take Action

Step 5 - Give Gratitude

Conclusion

FOREWORD

Welcome to an incredible journey to move you forward on your path to living a prosperous life. I'm so excited and truly honored that you decided to join me. I believe your life is a gift, and if you have an opportunity to take action to maximize your experiences in life, you should take it. By sitting down and actively reading this book (not just reading, but taking action based on what you learn), you'll take a big step toward what you want out of life. I am proud of you for valuing your life and working to make it even more prosperous than it is today.

I can't tell you how excited I am to share my thoughts and tactics about life with you. I have been researching and living these ideas for over twenty years. This book is a manifestation of my passion for life and what I have learned along the way.

While writing this book, it felt like at times my brain was about to explode with the many ideas I want to share with you. You are in for a quite a ride.

A Bit About Me

In full disclosure, I am just a normal entrepreneur. I am super practical, so give me a how-to guide and I am happy. Give me a bunch of theory and I get bored (or lost in psychological speak). Given this, I set out to write a practical guide with lots of how-to information about living a prosperous life. The book works more as a roadmap to get from point A to point B. The good thing is, you get to define what point A and point B are.

I have been a student of life for quite a long time. I started reading books and going to lectures over 25 years ago. I have read hundreds of books on the subject over the years trying to analyze this thing we call life from many different aspects. Each new idea or distinction I come across is something I have tried to implement into my own life. Some have worked great, but some have been miserable failures (the good thing is, I will leave those out of this book). I have always been fascinated by how people live their lives. What makes people successful? How do you even define success? And why are some people happy while others are not? I am going to attempt to answer these questions and many others in this book.

I have been extremely blessed to live a prosperous life. My life is by no means perfect, nor do I believe it should be. I experience many of the same challenges as you, but my perspective on those challenges might be different than yours. I believe that it is not what happens to you in life that makes the difference; it is your response to what happens that makes the difference and can create a truly prosperous life.

I discovered how to be a more loving and kinder person. I am sure I still have lots of room for improvement here, but I am on the road, and it feels great.

How did this happen, you ask? How can I tap into that? The idea is simple but took me many years to learn (and I still have not mastered it yet). It is to love and accept myself. How many self-help books tell you to do this? It sounds so simple, but it is something so many of us are challenged with. In this book, we will look at self-acceptance and how you can discover and/or enhance this in your life. My hope is for you to walk away with a few insights on how you can apply self-acceptance and self-love to your life.

Discovering Happiness

A funny thing happened during this journey. I stumbled on how to live a joyful life. It certainly did not happen overnight; in fact, it is still happening each day. I guess some of those books and lectures finally started to sink in. More importantly, I began to change my perspectives on life, making new distinctions each day. I started to look at life through a different lens. This lens (or perspective) guides all my actions. I also use it to adjust my behavior when I think I might be off course. My lens is a great tool for me. This book attempts to help you in developing your own lens through which to look at life.

There are some key principles that are part of this lens:

- The concept of growth puts everything into perspective for me. Once I understood why we were are here, it all became so much easier. We are simply here on earth to grow and develop.

- I stopped trying to achieve things for the purpose of achieving things. I discovered that was not a good definition for success.

- I discovered the negative impacts of living from ego and work to eliminate their affects in my life.

- I became aware of my life purpose, my values, my goals, my direction, and my actions. I got clarity, and now I work to maintain that clarity every day.

- I learned how to take "real" action. Sounds strange that someone must learn how to take action, but we do.

- I experienced giving gratitude for all that I have each day.

- And most importantly, I learned to accept to love myself.

Guess what! I just gave you the entire book in eight bullet points. Well, I guess we are done so you can stop reading now. Maybe I should provide just a little more detail, but really, this is it. There is no magic to this stuff.

Now here is the trick: this stuff changes all the time, so you need to stay on top of it. Don't make it your full-time job to run your life, but be aware on a regular basis how you are living your life and make adjustments as you need to in each area of your life. My life is no more or less prosperous than yours, but what I do have is a really good perspective that I live by each day and a bunch of tools I use regularly to help me on my journey through life.

A Few Things Before We Get Started

As we get started, there are a few things to keep in mind. First, the ideas presented in this book are designed to stimulate your mind to look at things through a different lens. Be open to seeing things a bit differently (with a new perspective). These new perspectives are extremely valuable as you work to develop your prosperous life. It is amazing to me that just a change in your thinking or in the way you look at something can have such a dramatic change in your life. Better yet, once you realize this, change can happen in an instant. As fast as you can think a thought, you can change your life.

My hope for you in reading this book is that you walk away with at least one new idea or perspective on your life that will move you forward in a positive direction.

Second, become aware. Awareness is the single most powerful tool you can use. Just by becoming aware, you can make incredible changes in your life. I will give you a step-by-step guide of becoming aware with lots of examples. But it is really simple.

Third, take action. You have to actually do something. Creating a prosperous life takes effort. In fact, it might take a lot more work than just living your life as it comes. I assure you the effort you put in will reap tremendous rewards for you. My hope is not only that you walk away with at least one new idea, but that you take at least one action to move you closer to living your prosperous life.

Let's begin the journey.

To enhance your experience with this book, make sure to get the Companion Guide, which contains valuable worksheets and other helpful resources.

Visit KenBurke.com

CHAPTER 1

Introduction

Change Your Perspective, Change Your Life

One of the most important principles you can learn is that by changing your thoughts, you will change your life. I like to think of this concept as looking at life through a different lens. This isn't a new concept. It has been around the personal development community for many years. But it's still as relevant today as it has always been.

Changing the way you think can be challenging because you have been thinking that way for so many years. Your perspective on almost everything comes from your belief system, which has been evolving since you were born. You have beliefs that have been around twenty, thirty, forty, fifty years or more. And to compound that, these beliefs have been constantly reinforced. Your brain has proved them to be true, at least according to *you*.

Here is some good news. Even though you may have deeply held these beliefs for many years, you can change them in an instant. Yes, that's right. You have the power inside you to change your beliefs in a nanosecond, and it all starts with seeing things from a new perspective.

INTRODUCTION

What Is a Prosperous Life?

There is no question in my mind that the reason you are here on earth is to learn, grow, and develop to make yourself so you can serve the world at an even higher level. And living a prosperous life is all about your growth journey and how you drive that entire process while you experience love, joy, and fulfilment for yourself while you go through this incredible journey called your life.

Your life is the masterpiece you are creating during this lifetime. And while you are creating your masterpiece, do so with as much love for yourself and others as you can.

If you can grow and experience joy in your life, you are living a prosperous life. If you can truly fulfill your purpose and passion while loving yourself and others through the process, you are living a prosperous life. If you can take action each day toward creating the masterpiece that is your life while being happy throughout the process, you are living a prosperous life. If you can serve others by sharing your life, you are living a prosperous life.

This is your opportunity to truly live that life you have always dreamed of, so seize it. This book will walk you through the entire process of living the prosperous life I just talked about.

So, that is my definition of living a prosperous life. If it doesn't resonate with you, then throw it out and create one for yourself. All I care about is that you move your life forward while experiencing joy and fulfillment as you create the life you want.

Five Steps to a Prosperous Life

I'm very excited to share my techniques so you, too, can lead a prosperous life. Over the last twenty-five-plus years of studying and living these principles, I have organized them into five steps. This manageable framework is full of great exercises to help you apply what you are learning to your life. I can't stress enough the importance of doing these exercises. If you want to make your life prosperous, you can't do so by sitting passively by. This book isn't an intellectual exercise in how life could be if you understood these principles but rather a practical guide. When you participate rather than just observe, your perspective on your life will start to shift, and suddenly, you will start to see things differently and think differently. And when you start to think differently, you will do things differently. Here is a quick summary of the five steps to living a prosperous life.

Step 1: Accept Yourself

Nothing else in your life works until you fully accept yourself. This isn't an easy step for most people to take. However, by not accepting yourself, it will continue to be challenging to truly experience that happiness and fulfillment most of us are seeking.

I am going to give a new perspective on how to look at yourself in a different way and a set of tools that will make accepting yourself much easier.

Step 2: Manage Your Ego

Your ego is probably the single biggest stumbling block to manifesting all you want in life. Let's fix it. I'm going to open your eyes, so you are aware when your ego is getting in the way of what you truly want out of life. Then I will show you exactly how to overcome this nasty villain that keeps getting in your way.

Step 3: Get Clear

Once you are clear about what you want, living a prosperous life becomes so much easier. Let's get you really good at getting clear on exactly what you want in your life and on the road to manifesting it. I have created a bunch of tools that will guide you through this process.

Step 4: Take Action

To create your prosperous life, you need to take action to make that happen. Manifesting exactly what you want requires you to put energy and work into making it happen. You have everything necessary to manifest anything you want in your life. I am going to show you what stops you from taking action and give you the tools to overcome these roadblocks.

Step 5: Give Gratitude

Gratitude is just like the icing on the cake of your life. Giving gratitude throughout your life takes your happiness and fulfillment to an entirely new level. Trust me – you want this secret ingredient woven through everything you do. I'm going to provide you with a gratitude toolkit that will allow you to give gratitude with ease.

INTRODUCTION

A Few Things Before We Get Started

Shifting Your Perspective

The ideas presented in this book are designed to stimulate your mind to look at things through a different lens. Be open to seeing things with new perspectives. These new perspectives — or guiding principles, as I call them — are extremely valuable as you work to develop your prosperous life. A small change in your thinking or the way you look at something can have a dramatic change in your life. Once you realize this, change can happen in an instant. As quickly as you think a thought, you can change your life. My hope for you in reading this book is that you will walk away with at least one new idea or guiding principle that will move you forward in a positive direction. Just one new idea will have made the entire journey through this book worth it.

Growth

Understand the importance of growth. Throughout all five steps, I'll stress the importance of focusing on change and growth. This might sound obvious, but it's the difference between believing you're on the wrong path and believing you're on the right one. As you'll see, I'm going to try to convince you that you are exactly as you should be at this moment in time — a claim that works only if you can look at things from the perspective of growth.

Awareness

Just by becoming aware, you can make incredible changes in your life. I will give you a step-by-step guide on becoming aware with examples.

Understand Your Ego

I talk about ego a lot in this book, but what do I really mean when I say *ego*? When you hear the word *ego*, you might think about being egotistical. I use *ego* in a different way. Ego is the part of the brain that judges everything we do (or others do) and compares ourselves to everyone else in the world. If you want live a prosperous life, you must understand and learn to manage your ego; otherwise, it will eat away at all the positive things you are trying to do.

4

Growth Is Challenging

As you are learning, growing, and developing, you will experience challenges along the way and even some pain. I am going to give you a ton of tools to help minimize these challenges, but the reality is that anytime you are doing something new, you might stumble while you are learning. Have faith that when you come out on the other side, you will be okay.

You Aren't Always Supposed to Be Happy

I want to tell you right up front that you aren't supposed to be happy 100 percent of the time. Give yourself a break. Please don't have being happy 100 percent of the time your goal, because I believe that is unattainable. When I tell people this, I always get the same reaction: "What a relief."

You have to work at happiness and joy each and every day. I call this "practicing joy." You literally have to practice it in your conscious mind each day. Ask yourself, what do I need to do today to experience more happiness and joy in my life? Ask this question every day. I will teach you more about practicing joy in your life.

> *"You aren't supposed to be happy 100 percent of the time, so don't make that the goal."*

Create Lasting Change

I promise that if you follow each step, understand the principles I have presented, and carefully practice the exercises in this book, you will change your life for the better. You will be able to manifest anything you want in your life. It might not happen in a day, a week, or even a month, but it will happen if you are committed to it and approach it using the principles outlined. I embrace these with all my heart and practice them each day.

I have found that change and growth happen in small, bite-size pieces over a period of time, not all at once. Just like running a business or raising your children, it doesn't happen overnight. But when you look back, you say to yourself, "Look at how far I have come." As you grow, learn, and develop, you will create lasting change in your life.

INTRODUCTION

If you follow the principles I lay out in this book, you will absolutely experience more joy, happiness, and fulfillment in your life. Remember, it won't be 100 percent of the time, but it will be more — a lot more.

I am so excited to go on this journey with you and to help in whatever way I can to maximize your growth opportunities and to minimize any challenges you might face along the way.

CHAPTER 2

What Is a Prosperous Life?

Ask yourself, "Do I want to live an ordinary life or a prosperous life?" Most everyone would say, "Of course, I want to live a prosperous life!" If you aren't living a prosperous life already, then ask yourself the next question:

Why Aren't You?

Having lived both types of lives myself, I would suggest to you that it takes no more energy or work to live a prosperous life. In fact, I believe it was a lot more work trying to live an ordinary life. I recently read a statistic that stated 65 percent of people are too busy to enjoy their lives. Does this sound familiar?

I don't think this topic is black or white. I don't believe you are destined to live an uninspiring, ordinary life or that you are destined to live a prosperous life. We are all living both lives at the same time. We are all somewhere on the continuum of life, with ordinary at one end and prosperous on the other.

Just for fun, let's look at what it means to live an ordinary life versus a prosperous one. Which column is more in alignment with what you desire?

WHAT IS A PROSPEROUS LIFE?

Ordinary Life	Prosperous Life
Sporadic feelings of joy and happiness	Feeling joy and happiness whenever you want to
Conditional love for you and others	Feeling love for yourself or others whenever you want
Constant judgment for yourself and others	A life free of judgments for you or for anyone else in your life
Doubting your abilities	Never doubting your abilities
Feeling unclear on what you want in certain areas of your life	Being very clear about what you want in all areas of your life
Never feeling like you have enough money in your life	Never worrying about money again
Working at an uninspiring career to pay the bills	Consistently loving what you do
Ebbing and flowing your way through life	Living with passion
Just trying to get through the day	Contributing to the world in a meaningful way
Learning new things when you have to	Holding a burning desire to constantly learn new things
Questioning your faith regularly	Feeling confident about your spiritual beliefs
Saying thanks when required	Effortlessly giving gratitude in all situations
Feeling stuck	Seeing unlimited opportunities

At the end of the day, you have a choice of which kind of life you want to live. Since you get the privilege to decide where you want to be on the continuum, I suggest that you consider moving toward the prosperous side of life. Based on my experience, I can tell you it is so much better.

Exercise: What Does This Mean for You?

Consider the following:

1. What does your ordinary life look like? Did you identify anything in the left column above? Spend five minutes thinking about this. Feel free to jot a few things down on paper.

2. Now, imagine living a prosperous life. Do you identify anything you want in the right-hand column? Spend another five minutes contemplating this question.

3. Pick one thing you could change in your life that would move you closer to a prosperous life. If you feel inspired, pick another and maybe another.

Thirty Thousand Days

So now you might be asking, "How do I know when it's time to start that prosperous life? Maybe it will be when I get that new job or start that new relationship. Or maybe I can start when I become wealthy. I mean, there is no rush – I have a lifetime."

All this might be true, but I want you to look at this from another perspective. You have a limited number of days on this earth. I once heard it estimated at thirty thousand days, and the realization instantly smacked me upside the head. So ask yourself, "What the heck are you doing with each and every day?"

While thirty thousand days – or about 82.2 years – is a bit higher than our current life expectancy, I am an optimist, and I like round numbers. So why not?

Let's do a quick calculation. Take your current age and multiply it by 365 days. Then subtract that number from thirty thousand days. That is the approximate number of days you have left on this earth.

30,000 - (Your Age) = Days Left

Let's look at a quick example. Say you are forty years old. You have lived 14,600, so you have 15,400 days left.

WHAT IS A PROSPEROUS LIFE?

This simple calculation helps put your life in perspective. If you don't feel you are living a prosperous life now, it might be time to take action to change that. And you are the only one who can change it.

I look at each day I have left as a growth opportunity. I'm excited and very grateful to live each day. I look at that number not as a countdown but as the number of days I have left to be prosperous.

I would suggest to you that *now* is the ideal time to start living a prosperous life. Ask yourself, what are you doing with today? What can you do to start down the path to living a prosperous life? This should create a sense of urgency for you. I know it does for me.

Every morning I ask myself, what am I going to do with today to live a more prosperous life? Now I realize I'm a bit strange (being a personal development author and all), but this stuff really works. Personally, I can't stand the idea of wasting even a single day. I see every day adding something to my growth in life.

It doesn't matter how little or much your daily experiences bring you; it all contributes to your growth. We'll get into that in detail in just a moment, but first, here's a word of caution. Don't get obsessed with achievement. That isn't what I am talking about. A great day can be as simple as walking in the park and observing children playing on swings or a beautiful flower garden and having the feeling of gratitude for your amazing life. So look at each of your thirty thousand days as opportunities for growth. Are you ready to take advantage of those opportunities? Are you ready to focus on what is meaningful in your life?

Don't waste a single precious day.

Get the latest updates on the book including articles and videos

Visit KenBurke.com

CHAPTER 3

Twelve Guiding Principles for Your Life

I have been using guiding principles for most of my life to keep me on track and to move in the direction I want my life to go.

I have created twelve guiding principles for my life I want to share with you. I have internalized these principles, and I refer back to them all the time to make certain I am moving my life in the direction I want. And I want you to do the same. In fact, you might even want to write them down on a card and attach them to a mirror or your refrigerator; review them each morning until you have them fully internalized.

These twelve guiding principles are designed to help shape your perspective on how you live your life. My hope for you is that you will see life through the lens of these guiding principles. You will notice some of your core beliefs changing as you internalize these more productive beliefs. And changing your beliefs is key to changing your life.

TWELVE GUIDING PRINCIPLES FOR YOUR LIFE

Guiding Principle 1: Life Is All About Growth

If I could provide you with one concept, one perspective that at its very core can change your life, it's the concept of growth. It is the foundational principle from which everything emanates. If you want the purpose of your life, I can sum it up in one word: growth.

I really think that is the only reason we are here on earth. We are here to grow and develop as souls. Don't worry, I won't get into a bunch of New Age speak (well, maybe a little), but that is my extremely strong belief. This guiding principle has served me very well, and it has helped me put all other things into perspective.

During all you have left of those thirty thousand days, it is your responsibility to look for opportunities for growth. In many cases, growth comes, and you don't even know it. But if you are aware of growth happening in your life, you can use it to your advantage.

Consider a life where it is impossible for something bad to happen to you. When you are living from the perspective of growth, suddenly everything becomes an opportunity. You can't possibly fail or have anything really bad happen to you as long as you learn from the experience and grow (even if ever so slightly) into a better person.

When something happens like losing money or getting into a fight with your loved one or even the death of someone close to you, all you have to do is the following:

1. Become aware of it.

2. Determine how this is going to enable you to grow into a better, more self-realized person.

3. Figure out how you can use this in your life going forward.

This concept of growth is the foundation of this entire book (and I believe the foundation of our entire existence on this planet), so I really want you to truly comprehend and ideally embrace the concept.

Guiding Principle 2: Accept Yourself

Learning to accept yourself is the single most important thing you can do to lead a happy, productive, and fulfilling life. This seems like such an obvious statement that I shouldn't even need to mention it, yet it is by far the largest single challenge most people have to overcome to live a prosperous life.

For some reason, many people like to beat the crap out of themselves. I have met so many people who feel that to achieve success, they must continually tell themselves they aren't good enough. They suffer from constant wishes to be "better," but they will never (and I mean never) win this psychological game. This is the most harmful thinking I can think of.

If you ever find that you are beating yourself up, trying to be perfect, always looking for the negative in situations, or just feeling bad about yourself, then you need to examine your level of self-acceptance or how you continually judge yourself. Ideally, you would never feel this way about yourself. Yet we all let ourselves or others mess with our heads about feelings of not being good enough.

I am here to tell you that you are more than good enough. I think you are perfect at this moment in time. You are the way you should be right now. But it goes even further than that. Dare I use the "L" word? Yes, *love*. Simply stated, you need to love yourself first. But loving yourself is actually not as easy as it seems.

We will be spending lots of time in this book to help you change your perspective on self-acceptance and self-love. If you learn this and nothing else out of this book, it will be worth more than all the money in the world.

Guiding Principle 3: You Are Responsible for 100 Percent of Your Life

Have you ever played the victim? Have you ever blamed someone else for how you are feeling? Have you ever blamed someone for something going bad? Maybe you hold your partner responsible for the reason your relationship isn't working. How about your boss? Has he or she done something to ruin your life? If you can answer yes to any of these questions, then you aren't taking 100 percent responsibility for your life.

TWELVE GUIDING PRINCIPLES FOR YOUR LIFE

Shoot, you might be thinking, *Really? Do I really need to be responsible for 100 percent of my life? Isn't it much easier to just make someone else responsible for my pain or my challenging situations?* Absolutely, and unquestionably, the answer is no.

And I do mean 100 percent, period. Not 90 percent, not 99 percent. This single perspective gives you more power and control over your life than almost anything else. The second you stop blaming other people for your challenges, you will gain the power to do something about your life.

You might be saying, "Hey, Ken, wait just a minute. I am not responsible if the bus is fifteen minutes late and I am late for work. I am not responsible if someone reacts negatively toward me. I am not responsible if an earthquake hits and my home is destroyed." Yes, this is true, but you are responsible for how you react to these situations.

If you are responsible for everything in your life, then you have tremendous control over what happens in it. This doesn't mean you can control all the situations that come into your life, but you can control your responses. This is the key. You control your feelings, emotions, and responses to situations. You will be amazed that once you start to shift your belief toward this, things become much easier, and you become much more joyful.

Guiding Principle 4: Always Be Present

We spend much of our time each day dwelling on the past or thinking about the future. If you really think about it, though, the only thing you can impact is the present moment. You cannot impact the past — you can only learn from it. Your ego loves living in the past so it can judge you and others in your life. It is completely unproductive to judge your past or the pasts of others. Thinking of the past from a detached perspective, such that you can learn from it, is just fine. But the key isn't to get your emotions wrapped up in the learning process. This is where most people go wrong.

Likewise, obsessing about the future is also unproductive. Getting emotional about a future that hasn't yet happened will just lead you to judge it. It is certainly okay to think about the future and to plan out how you will live your life. But for you to live a prosperous life, you need to take action, and that action takes place in the present.

It is very hard for most people to just live in the present moment without drifting constantly to the past or to the future. I am just as guilty of doing this as you. But I can tell you, I find that my most creative moments and greatest insights come to me in the present moment. This happens when my brain can get still enough to allow those valuable thoughts to come in. These insights have made a huge difference in my life, and I want them to do the same for you.

Here is the good news: there are some great techniques to help quiet your brain long enough to let this happen. It's not possible to live your entire life in the present, of course, but you'll learn to grab those important moments when you can, and they will make a difference. And once you learn the techniques that work for you and start to use them, you will find being present will happen more often and more automatically.

Let me share a few techniques that work for me. Meditation is by far the best thing you can do to quiet your brain and become more present in the moment. Find a quiet spot and focus on your breathing for at least fifteen minutes and more if possible. I have also found that writing in my journal is very helpful in focusing on the present and getting those valuable insights. Another easy technique is to take a nice, long drive in the country or on a long stretch of road with very little traffic. More to come on this.

Guiding Principle 5: Don't Die with Your Music inside You

This is a quotation from one of my favorite authors, Dr. Wayne Dyer, who was a renowned personal development author. I strongly believe we are all here for a reason and that we were all given some special gifts. We have an obligation to figure out what those gifts are and to use them to the fullest extent possible. I believe you owe this to the world. It's like the cost of admission to life (not to put too much pressure on you or anything).

The key to making sure we don't die with our music inside us is clarity. Once we are clear on where we are going and can get alignment with everything in our lives, we can start to take massive action to get to where we want to go.

You might be saying, "Well, this sounds good, but I am not sure what my gifts really are." That is okay. Here is the good news: in this book, we are going to spend a lot of time working on discovering your gifts.

TWELVE GUIDING PRINCIPLES FOR YOUR LIFE

Guiding Principle 6: Stop Living from Your Ego

The second I say the word *ego* to people, I usually get a very defensive reaction. "I am not egotistical. What are you talking about?" I'm not necessarily accusing you of being egotistical. I am talking about living from your ego, which unfortunately most people do.

The term *ego* is used to describe those beliefs you have that tear away at living a prosperous life. Ego is just a judgment (or opinion) about yourself or someone else. You define your life and who you are through destructive judgments that serve only to tear you or others down. Living from your ego is defining who you are by the following:

1. You are what you have.
2. You are what you do (like your career).
3. You are how much money you have.
4. You are your position in your social group.
5. You are what you have achieved.
6. You are the relationships you have.

The reality is that you are none of these things. You aren't your job, money, possessions, or relationships. When you strive for these things just so you can feed your ego, life becomes pointless. It is really hard to be happy because you can never satisfy the ego, so you keep striving and never actually arrive. Your entire life becomes a game of trying to feed your ego more. More of what? More of everything. And why? Well, just for the mere fact of having more. It is a game you can't win. This is no way to live life and certainly no way to live a prosperous one.

The key is to be aware of when you are living from ego and when you are not. We will be spending lots of time on this topic, but right now, just start contemplating when you might be living from ego. When you start seeing how your ego drives your actions, you can quickly change your behavior.

Guiding Principle 7: Stop All Your Judgments Immediately

For some reason, judgments of everything and everybody — my parents, friends, coworkers, even myself — came very easily for me. While I would rather have had other things come easily to me, like being a great athlete or being super smart, I got handed judgments, and I made them constantly.

Today it's one of the biggest areas of growth I have experienced. While I still have a ways to go, at least now I'm usually aware when I am in judgment mode. Now I see that my judgmental nature was a growth opportunity, and I look at it as a blessing, not a curse.

Judgments are a manifestation of the ego at work. You are so critical of yourself or others that these judgments can stop you right in your tracks and limit your success, happiness, and joy.

Just like with ego, all I want you to do for now is become aware of when you are judging a situation, another person, or most importantly, yourself. The signpost for when you are marching down the road of a judgment is when you render an opinion about something or someone. A judgment might be something like the following:

- I am too fat or too thin.

- I am not pretty enough.

- I am not smart enough.

- He or she is wrong.

- He or she is stupid.

- He or she is overweight.

When one of these judgments arises, just be aware of it. Later in the book, we will figure out what to do with them.

Guiding Principle 8: Detach from the Outcome

Most people connect whatever actions they are taking with some type of outcome, which could be making more money, feeling happiness, or achieving something. The problem is, if you don't get the outcome you desired, then you don't think the journey was worth it. The truth is, the journey (all those actions you took to try to achieve the outcome) was the true gift you received. It is all about the journey, not the destination, like we have all been conditioned to think. The journey is where all the growth comes from.

Guiding Principle 9: You Must Take Action If You Want Something to Happen in Your Life

Surprise! To get what you want in life, you can't just dream about it or wish it into reality. I know many people have heard about the power of intention (or manifesting). The wrong interpretation of that is, "If I think hard enough about something, it will magically appear in my life." What people don't realize is that there is a part-two to this belief. Taking action toward your intention will allow you to create what you want in your life. Please don't forget the second part, or you dream will most likely remain only a dream.

Guiding Principle 10: You Are Not Supposed to Be Happy All the Time

Life isn't supposed to be a bowl of cherries all the time. Sometimes it's just a bowl of pits. You might be thinking, *You mean, I don't have to be happy all the time like all those self-help books seem to say? Thank goodness someone finally said it.*

The second you give yourself permission not to be happy every second of every day, you will feel a huge relief. It isn't realistic to think you can have 100 percent control over all your emotions and have the ability to look only at the good things in life.

However, you can experience more happiness and joy if you develop a better set of tools to manage your life and to guide it toward that prosperous end of the continuum — rather than to simply react as things happen.

Guiding Principle 11: Balance Doing vs. Being

It isn't hard to live a prosperous life, but it does require that you be mindful of what is going on and consciously navigate your way. But life isn't about just doing. Doing for the sake of doing doesn't lead to a prosperous life.

Some "experts" say you should just simply *be*. Just let things happen without ever really doing anything. No pressures, no worries, no concerns for anything. Everything just pops into your life in a cosmic way.

In my experience, there is a lot of truth to this. But the best results come from balancing doing and being. I am a businessman and an entrepreneur who was programmed from birth to always be doing. When I stopped obsessing over doing and found a balance between doing and being, I got a lot more done, became much happier, and saw more success and fulfillment. We aren't human doers, after all; we are human beings.

Guiding Principle 12: Always Be Grateful

Something that so often gets overlooked but is so critical to living a prosperous life is gratitude. Life is such a gift, and you are given so much each day that you must acknowledge it, appreciate it, and embrace it.

There is no trick to being grateful. While I will share lots of tools and tips later in the book, all you really need to do is just become aware of what you have, and a feeling will come over you that feels a bit like taking a deep breath and exhaling. I know when I'm feeling grateful because a certain feeling of peace comes over me. It really boils down to just being aware of what I have.

Also, you must be grateful not only for all the good things that happen but also for all the things you would consider to be bad. ("What?! Grateful for the bad things? Is this guy crazy?") But both good and bad experiences create growth, and since growth is the most valuable thing, you should embrace them both.

Another interesting by-product of gratitude is that the more you give, the more you get back. It really happens. When you truly appreciate what you have, you get more of it.

CHAPTER 4
Make Growth Your Foundation

Growth is the single-most important concept to help you understand your life. By focusing on growth, you can start seeing your life from a better perspective. Every concept in this book revolves around the idea that our core purpose is to learn, grow, and develop as souls.

Growth is at the center of every thought you have and action you take. And everything you do relates back to this very simple concept. Once you fully understand this, life seems to make more sense. And if you don't believe that now, you will by the time you finish this book.

Growth Is a Universal Law

I believe everything in existence is designed for growth, including you. Look at a few pieces of evidence:

- Most scientists say the universe has never really stopped growing.

- The cells in your body are continuously growing and reproducing themselves. Your body never stops growing and changing until you die.

- Technological advancements impact more and more of our lives every day.

MAKE GROWTH YOUR FOUNDATION

Growth Is the Purpose of Your Life

There is no question in my mind that the reason you are here on earth is to grow and develop. It is no more complicated than that. But what is the point? The point is twofold.

First, our ability to help and serve others expands as we grow. We can have a bigger impact in the world the more we grow because we have the capability to do so.

Second, we develop as people. We come into this world with many lessons to learn in this lifetime. If we don't learn them, then guess what? We get to come back and try again.

Third, our lessons aren't the same as other people's lessons. We all come into this world with different lessons. Do you ever wonder why some people don't really seem to have money problems, while others have tons of them? Or maybe for some people, relationships are so natural, while other people are continually challenged to make their relationships work.

Looking at Your Life through the Growth Lens

If you start looking at life through the growth lens, everything becomes so much easier. Your perspective completely changes. For example, failure is no longer a possibility. And better yet, the fear of failure (most people's biggest fear) will disappear. Let's say that someone you are in a relationship with breaks up or divorces you. You are devastated at the thought that he or she won't be part of your life.

Sure, the divorce will hurt for a while, but look at this through the growth lens. First, look at how much this person has enriched your life (especially if the relationship is a challenging one). Ask yourself, "Did I learn anything from this relationship?" That simple question will put things in perspective. If you learned something from the relationship, then you grew. And oh, by the way, the difficult relationships are the ones you learn from the most. You wouldn't have been in that relationship unless you needed to learn something. Also, realize that it's nearly impossible to go through this experience in your life and not learn something.

Second, remind yourself that every relationship you have is designed to teach you something about yourself. In fact, that is the purpose of all relationships. This is a really important point. It's not about the other person; it is all about you. People come into your life for a reason – to help you grow. Figure out why that person is in your life, and you might just stumble on the lessons you are supposed to learn.

If you can't see growth happening in your life, this doesn't mean growth isn't occurring. You might just not be aware of it yet. In the next chapter and throughout this book, we'll discuss techniques for building your awareness so you can begin to notice it and benefit from it.

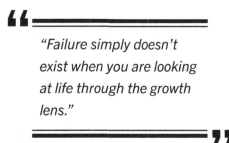

"Failure simply doesn't exist when you are looking at life through the growth lens."

Exercise: Becoming Aware of Your Growth Lens

Think of a situation in your recent past or something you are currently going through that has made you feel like a failure. With that in mind, try the following exercise.

- Take three deep breaths and close your eyes.

- Sit quietly for a few minutes to relax your mind.

- Ask yourself, "What lessons did I learn from this situation or experience?"

- Stay in the meditation until you can come up with three lessons (regardless of how small or big they are).

- Give thanks to the people involved who have helped teach you these lessons. This might be hard, but it's a really important step. It's harder to grow if you have resentments (or even worse, hatred) in your heart. This negativity will serve you no purpose. Trust me. And remember, these people are your greatest teachers.

- When you are done, take three deep breaths and come out of the meditation.

You have just experienced the realization of growth. You are now a different person than you were before the experience. Do this exercise anytime you are feeling like a failure about something.

Looking at Loss through a Growth Lens

One of the things people hate more than anything else is losing what they have already acquired. Because we are all programmed for growth, it makes us feel bad when we have to take a step back. These losses can take many forms:

MAKE GROWTH YOUR FOUNDATION

- A long-term relationship

- A demotion or job loss

- Money

- Physical appearance through aging, weight gain, and so forth

- The death of a loved one

When you feel yourself getting frustrated or angry about such a loss, understand that it might be coming into your life to teach you a lesson and to encourage a little growth. Turn the loss into a positive by figuring out what lessons it holds for you. What do you have to learn? How can you become a better person from this loss?

Do you wonder why loss is such a big deal? Well, the answer lies in a little thing called "ego." Your ego hates to lose. It carries around a scorecard it uses to measure every aspect of your life and to compare it to everyone else's scorecard. If it finds you deficient in some way, your wonderful ego makes you feel bad. In fact, it can even make you feel like you have lost something when you really haven't simply by comparing your scorecard to someone else's. Comparing yourself to others is a destructive game, one you can't win.

Loss is never easy, and I'm not trying to minimize it, but you must adjust your perspective about it to make it purposeful in your life. You already know I am a bit strange, but when I experience a loss, I get very introspective and appreciative of all the things I do have in life. In many cases, I then get excited about how I can turn the loss into something that can provide new understandings. Maybe you can be a bit weird with me.

Growth from Positive Experiences

Growth can also come from positive experiences, such as graduating from college, having a baby, getting married, or getting a promotion. When something great happens to you, ask yourself, what lessons can I learn from this success? Why did this positive experience happen to me? How is this experience helping me grow and develop?

Make certain you give thanks to whomever or whatever helped bring this into your life, even if you are just giving thanks to God or the universe. For you to maximize this positive experience, you need to express your gratitude for it. We will talk lots more about gratitude later in the book.

The Success Game

Many people get the concept of growth and success confused a bit. Just because you are successful doesn't mean you are effectively growing. In fact, what I find is that some people play a game in their minds, called the "Success Game," that might create an illusion of growth, success, and even happiness, but the reality is, you can't win this game.

The Success Game says, "As soon as I achieve this, I will be _____ [fill in the blank with something like *successful, fulfilled,* or *happy*]." The problem with that common logic is that when you achieve whatever you were striving for, you say, "So what is next? There must be more." And when your mind figures out for that specific achievement, there is no more, it's a let-down. You may even be depressed. Now what does your mind do? It looks for something else to achieve. The cycle repeats, and you get further away from living a happy and joyful life.

The Success Game is like living life on a treadmill. It is a vicious cycle, in which you are always striving and never actually getting "there." And where is "there" anyway? You aren't sure where "there" really is. Because once you get "there," you start looking for a new "there." You end up never happy with what you have, including your relationships or who you are. Let's look at some examples:

Money

Money is the most common Success Game. Think of a time when you started making more money, or maybe you even got a windfall, like an inheritance. What happened to you? You initially felt great about things and were even quite happy. But unfortunately, this feeling is usually short lived. You got used to the money and found that you needed more of it. The same motivation that made you desire the money in the first place makes you desire more money in the future. And more money. Just look at those guys on Wall Street. Is the money they have at any moment in time enough? No. Not in the Success Game.

Relationships

Are you the type of person who jumps from one love relationship to another and is never happy with your current situation? Once you get comfortable with the current relationship, do you look up and say, "I can do better ... this person isn't perfect"? Your mind starts to search for the next great person to bring into your life. Once you have that person, what happens? You find some flaws (because everyone has them), and your mind starts to look for the next "better" person. And the process never really stops. My father suffered from this condition and had five wives over the course of his life.

It's impossible to be happy playing the Success Game, but I can't tell you how many people I have seen playing it. Heck, I used to play it all the time.

Become Aware

Anytime you find yourself playing the Success Game, just become aware of it. If you find yourself using negative motivation — telling yourself you aren't good enough, which forces you to take action to get you to achieve something — just become aware of it. Or maybe you say, "Once I have this or do this, I will be happy." This is a very dangerous way of thinking. Catch yourself and understand how unproductive this is in your life. As you start to change your belief system, you will stop using this negative motivation to achieve things. It simply doesn't work.

" _____

"Live for the growth and not for the achievement that feeds your ego."

_____ "

How can you change this game? Stop living for some imagined achievement that may or may not happen. You are growing each day of your life. Don't get me wrong; there is nothing wrong with achieving things, but you must understand your motivation. If you are achieving something to feed your ego, you will never be satisfied and happy. If, however, your motivation is to grow and develop, then you will be satisfied and happy each day of your life.

Exercise: Discovering Your Success Game

Step 1: Becoming Aware

Let's determine whether you are playing the Success Game.

a. Identify an area in your life where you are trying to succeed but don't feel like you have gotten there yet. Could it be a promotion you're striving for? Maybe it is making more money. Maybe it's a relationship, something you want to learn, or losing weight and getting into shape.

b. Ask yourself whether you are using negative motivation to get yourself to achieve this success or happiness. Do you beat yourself up over the thing you identified above?

c. Ask yourself, do you believe you will be successful or happy if you achieve this? If the answer is yes, then you are playing the Success Game.

d. Finally, ask yourself what your motivation is for wanting to achieve something. Is your motivation coming from your ego or from your desire to grow, develop, or serve someone?

Step 2: Changing the Game

The second step is to change the game you are playing.

a. If you determine that you are coming from ego and not from your desire to grow, first acknowledge this fact. Just knowing your motivation is coming from ego is a huge step forward.

b. Once you have identified that you are coming from ego, ask yourself what belief is behind this. Why is your ego driving you in this way?

c. Next, identify how this belief is serving you. Is it helping you grow or stopping you from growing? Is it making you feel good or bad?

d. Finally, change your belief, and you will change your motivation. How can you change your thinking to help yourself grow and develop? Create a new belief that replaces the ego-driven belief with one that serves you better and helps you grow instead of stopping your growth.

For example, let's say you feel you are overweight, and you believe that once you get slimmer, you'll be happy. You also believe that once you lose that weight, people will like you more or think you are more beautiful. Or maybe if you lose weight, you will get promoted and make more money.

This says your motivation is to lose weight because of what other people think of you. But as soon as you lose that weight, your ego will jump to the next imperfection (or possibly you now want to be even slimmer). Maybe next you will need a nose job or a face-lift to go with your new thin body. This thinking never stops, and you never become happy. Trust me, I have been through this exact scenario, and until I changed my thinking (my beliefs) around the way I looked, nothing changed.

How does this belief serve you in your life? Is this belief bringing more joy and happiness into your life? Or is this belief dragging you down and making you feel bad?

Now let's change this way of thinking to something that is much more supportive of your growth. First, decide you want to lose weight for yourself and not for someone else. No one else matters but you. Your motivation to lose weight isn't so people will find you attractive and like you more, but rather it might be because you will feel better physically. Or it might be about your looks but change your thinking so it's about how *you* feel about your looks, not about how someone else feels. Once you feel attractive to yourself and, most importantly, don't care what others think about your attractiveness, then you are there. You have made it. The issue isn't about them; it is about you.

I'd suggest that the fact that you are overweight and faced with this so-called challenge is nothing more than the universe giving you an opportunity to grow. Maybe your lesson is to prove that you can achieve positive change in your life, to see the real beauty inside, to give yourself confidence, or to stop feeling stigmatized. But understand that you are overweight for a reason, and you must learn what that is. Find the lesson and start to grow from it. Being overweight might be the best gift the universe ever gave you. How about that for a perspective on being overweight?

Once you decide to start the growth process, I assure you the weight will start to fall off. And it will stay off. The issue is all about your motivation and why you are doing what you are doing. I held the belief that I was overweight for most of my life. As soon as I changed my belief about it, the weight came off.

A New Way of Thinking

I want to challenge you to change how you think about yourself going forward. First, you must accept the belief that we are all here on earth to learn, grow, and develop as humans. In fact, everything that happens to you is designed to provide you with that growth. *Everything!* Second, you must accept the belief that there is absolutely nothing wrong with you. You are exactly as you need to be at this moment in time to learn the lessons you need to learn in this lifetime. So, instead of beating yourself up for being a certain way, allow the universe to guide you through this process.

At this moment in time, there is nothing wrong with you. You aren't flawed or bad in any way. Whether you are poor, sick, overweight, in a bad relationship, or in a job you hate, you are as you should be and as the universe intended you to be. Each challenge you face is an opportunity for growth. So it might sound a bit crazy, but instead of looking at the challenges in your life as negative things, look at them as huge opportunities for you to learn and grow.

Once you change the perspective by which you look at your challenges in life, you are absolutely on the road to accepting yourself and living a prosperous life.

Exercise: Change Your Thinking about You

1. When you feel you are out of sync with the belief that you are perfect at this moment in time, *stop* and take three deep breaths. Just close your eyes and remind yourself that there really is nothing wrong with you and the way you're responding to your challenges.

2. If you find your mind drifting to past regrets or future concerns, just bring yourself back to the present. To get present, I make sure my eyes are closed and that I am focused on my breathing and nothing else. Try to keep your brain from processing thoughts. Listening to soft music can help if you are struggling with this.

3. Remind yourself that your so-called flaws or challenges are just growth opportunities. And at this moment in time, you are just as you are supposed to be.

Growth Never Stops

Once you start looking at life through the growth lens, you will soon realize it never stops; in fact, it creates lots more work for you. I think this is a good thing, because this growth is constantly changing you. It requires you to pay attention to it and create some new behaviors that will allow you to maximize your opportunities to live a prosperous life. The framework below will help you manage this continuous growth process.

MAKE GROWTH YOUR FOUNDATION

Acknowledge Your Growth

Just realize that growth is happening to you all the time. Sometimes small growth events occur, and sometimes massive growth occurs. Acknowledge the changes and acknowledge how others are dealing with your growth. Are they still treating you like they did before the growth occurred? In many cases, the answer will be yes. It takes people some time to catch up to you. That is okay – give them a break and maybe even a little help so they can realize the new you. In the process, maybe they'll even learn a little about their own growth lenses.

Embrace Your Growth

I don't believe there is any such thing as bad growth. If you are learning from your actions, then all growth is good. Embrace this growth and know it is valuable. Be grateful for it.

Clarify Your Growth

As you are growing and looking at your life through the growth lens, you must also constantly reevaluate aspects of your life. Ask yourself whether your old belief system is still serving you. Do you still want the same things? Are your relationships still serving the same purposes? It is critical to reassess your goals and to clarify the things you want next in your life. This process of obtaining new clarity as you grow never stops.

Act on It

It isn't enough just to get some new clarity in your life and file it away. Keep the ball rolling toward new growth opportunities. Use your new clarity to make new decisions. Taking action will ultimately set you on a new growth path.

Your Life Journal

I have been keeping a life journal for many years, and I suggest you do the same. It is an incredible tool. Try to find thirty minutes to sit down and write about how you are growing and changing. Jot down the lessons you are learning along the way. Writing in my journal has been life-changing for me. It gives me a place to connect with my thoughts, and through this, I learn a ton about myself. But for this to work, you need to make writing in your journal a habit. I make sure I write at least a few pages every week. Some weeks, I write lots more. It all depends on what is going on in my life.

Roadblocks to Growth

I want you to be aware of a number of things that can slow down or stop your growth process. Once you become aware of them, you will be able to spot and resolve them quickly.

Roadblock 1: Fear

This is probably the biggest one. Fear stops you from taking action, and if you don't take action to resolve whatever challenges you have, growing is extremely hard. This is where most people get stuck. There are so many fears we as humans have, but the most common one is fear of failure. We don't take action because we might fail at whatever we are doing. This could lead to loss of money, a relationship, or status, just to name a few. My philosophy is, whether we learn from what we do, we really can't lose anything or damage our ego. A good tool to use is to simply ask yourself what is stopping you from taking action. If it is fear, ask what the fear is. Once you bring this into your mind space, you can deal with it.

Roadblock 2: Judgments

When you judge either yourself or others, you distract your mind from any growth opportunities. Judgments are just opinions about you or someone else. These opinions are highly unproductive in your life. Work to eliminate as many judgments as you can from your life. They slow your down on your growth journey.

Roadblock 3: Lack of Clarity

If you are not clear on where you are going, optimizing your growth opportunities can be difficult. Are you uncertain, confused, or unclear about what you want out of life? Do you overthink things and can't make a decision on what to do next? Are you wondering why everyone else has so much more than you do and why you can't seem to get there? Answering yes to any of these questions might suggest you have a lack of clarity on what you want out of life. The more clarity you have on what you want, the more growth you will experience in your life.

CHAPTER 5

Make Awareness Your Superpower

One of the most important tools I can give you is the ability to become aware of your thoughts and behaviors in any situation. Awareness is the foundation to just about every exercise in this book. I want you to become really good at becoming aware.

Let's get started. I have broken this process down into three parts.

Part 1: Observation

The first part is observing your life from an objective, detached, nonjudgmental point of view. Just step back and see what you are doing and thinking. This might sound easy on the surface, but it can get more complex. Let's start with a few simple techniques to help you.

Stop and Breathe

When you find yourself reacting to something or someone, getting angry, or judging a situation or a person, stop yourself and take three deep breaths. While this technique seems simple, the key is to know when you are reacting to something in an ineffective way.

MAKE AWARENESS YOUR SUPERPOWER

Take it one step further and spend five to ten minutes in a very basic meditation. Here is how: Take a seat in a comfortable, quiet spot; close your eyes, and start breathing. And I mean the real kind of breathing, not the fake breathing you do most of the time. Take that breath deep into your lungs. Focus on your breathing rather than the eighty thousand things inside your mind.

The Snap

Wear a rubber band around your wrist and give yourself a snap when you find yourself reacting. As with the stop-and-breathe technique, the snap will stop you in your tracks and remind you to refocus with a physical signal.

Your Third Eye

When you sense that you are reacting and don't have control over your emotions, simply picture your awareness jumping up to your third eye (the mystical eye in the center of your forehead). See whatever you are reacting to from a neutral space in your mind's eye. You will instantly become aware that you are reacting so you can stop yourself before you go any further.

Get Out of Your Body

Okay, this one might sound a bit wacky, but stay with me for a moment. When I need to become aware, sometimes my spirit literally jumps out of my body and observes the situation from right above my head. You can do this by simply taking three deep breaths, closing your eyes, and picturing yourself coming out of your body and sitting on a platform about three feet above your head. Weird, huh? But it works.

Next, it is good to just sit with that awareness for a little while. Don't judge it. Don't attach to it. Just let it be. Whatever the situation, whatever the thoughts, or whoever the person, allow yourself to observe it from a neutral spot. Another term for awareness is becoming or being mindful. If this is all you do to become aware, you are light-years ahead of where you used to be. Implementing part 2 and part 3 will only make your awareness more impactful.

Part 2: Judgments and Attachments

There are a few big detractors to awareness. You need to consciously watch for these because they will sneak up on you. The first is judgments. Judgments are deadly for many reasons. If you ever find yourself rendering an opinion about someone or something, that is a judgment. The first step is to simply become aware of that judgment; this will cause its power to diminish or to completely go away.

Right now, think of a judgment you might have. This should be easy because most of us have literally thousands each day. Maybe you have an opinion about how someone is dressed or how someone treated a waiter. Your workplace is filled with judgments. *Why did my boss make that dumb decision? Why is my coworker so lazy?* The key here is to stop yourself from rendering (and sharing) your opinion.

When I start to formulate an opinion about someone or something, I become aware that I am beginning to create a judgment, so I literally stop myself from going any further, since I don't want judgments to fill my life. The second big detractor is attachments. We can become so emotionally focused on a situation or on the people involved that it's hard to become fully aware. Our brains keep going right back to what we are attached to. Right now, all I want you to do is to become aware of whether you are attached to something or someone.

Ask yourself a few questions:

1. Are you reacting emotionally to a situation or a person?

2. Do you feel as if your reaction is out of your control? Many times, we kid ourselves into believing we are in control when we really are not.

3. Are you currently neutral to the situation or person? You are neutral if you have no concern about the outcome of the situation. Once you remove your attachment to the outcome, your emotional charge will disappear. This allows you to think clearly and logically about the situation rather than emotionally.

Part 3: The Triggering of Awareness

To become more fully aware of a situation, it helps to have a trigger that tells you to become aware in the first place. But what triggers do you look for?

MAKE AWARENESS YOUR SUPERPOWER

When you experience a negative emotion like anger, greed, jealously, sadness, or frustration, this is usually a good indicator that you need to become aware. Another signpost to look for is when you find yourself reacting to a situation.

Initially, this will take some effort to remember to do each time you are reacting to something, but after a while, you won't even need to think about it. Your brain will just jump right into awareness mode and run this routine without having to think too much about it.

Why do I teach this technique first? You will be using this tool throughout this entire book, not to mention your entire life. I am going to come back to this very valuable tool over and over again. You will get plenty of practice by the time you finish this book.

Exercise: Becoming Aware

In any given situation, simply ask yourself how God would act. (Think of God as representing all possible goodness. If you don't like the word *God*, replace it with *goodness*.)

1. Then ask yourself, "Am I moving closer to (or away from) God and how He might act?"

2. Measure how close or far away you are from God. If you are moving closer to God, then how close are you? Use a one-to-ten scale, with ten being as close to God as possible. Or if you are moving further away from God, use a scale from minus one to minute ten, where minus ten is as far away from God as you could be.

3. If your actions (or reactions) have you moving away from God, then just become aware of that fact. This clarity is invaluable.

4. Now, if you want to take action to change your course, please go right ahead. But this exercise is just about becoming aware of where you are. We will get to massive actions you can take later in the book.

Example: Let's say you are currently having money challenges with your partner. He or she is spending more money than you feel comfortable with. You react by getting into an argument and by personally attacking him or her. In this situation, are you moving closer to or away from God with your reactions? We would all agree the answer is "away." Now, evaluate your reaction. Maybe it is a minus five or a minus six.

Ask yourself, "How would God react to this situation?" Become aware of this answer and think about how you can change your direction and react more like God would. This strategy might move you into more positive territory.

I love this exercise. Do it right now. Pick something you are struggling with or reacting to. Maybe it's a challenge in your job, a horrible boss you react to in a negative way, or an intimate relationship. Are you moving closer to God or away from Him?

Change Your Thoughts, Change Your Life

Now that you better understand how awareness works, you can start applying it to your life. Awareness is the first step to most any change you want to achieve in your life because it gives you the opportunity to change the way you think (change your thoughts). And once you change your thoughts, you can change any aspect of your life. That is right! Changing your life is controlled 100 percent by your brain.

In whatever area of your life you want to change to develop further, you will start to see change once you look at that situation from a new perspective. I like to say you start looking at life with a different lens.

Changing the way you think can be challenging because you have been thinking that way for so many years. Your perspective on almost everything comes from your belief system, which has been evolving since you were born. You have beliefs that have been around twenty, thirty, forty, or fifty years or more. And to compound that fact, these beliefs have been constantly reinforced in your life. Your brain has proved them to be true, at least according to you.

Here is some good news. Even though these beliefs might be deeply held for many years, you can change them in an instant. Yes, that is right. You have the power inside you to change a belief in a nanosecond, and it all starts with thinking a new thought.

The key to this entire book is trying to get you to look at your life from a different point of view (or out of a different lens). And once you start to do that, whatever you want your life to become can happen. But whatever is true doesn't come until you allow yourself to look at life from a different lens; until you do that, change won't happen. The key to changing your thoughts is awareness. It all starts with awareness. Once you are aware of how you currently think and of the beliefs you hold, then you can work on changing them. The first step to almost every exercise in this book starts with becoming aware of how you think now. Then we can work on changing it to the way you want to think to change your life for the better.

Choose a New Belief

Establish a new more positive and productive belief that will lead you to the change you desire. This step is usually very easy for people because it's what they have been dreaming about. Maybe it's the desire for more money, so the new belief might be that you deserve to be rich. Funny enough, maybe people don't believe they deserve to be rich (seems strange but true). Whatever the new belief is, make sure you are crystal clear on it.

Now Take Action

Once you have awareness and a new belief to replace the old one, you can start taking action toward your new future. It isn't enough to just change your thoughts. That is just the beginning. Next, you need to take action toward whatever you want to manifest. If you don't want some kind of action that moves you closer to your goal, then you won't reinforce that new belief, and you will regress back to your old ways (looking at life through your old lens, not your new one). Taking action is just as important as initially becoming aware of what you want to change.

Most people in the world never even get to the awareness step, but you are the exception. The mere fact that you are reading this book means you are willing to become aware and open to changing your thoughts. But where most people in this category fall down is the taking-action part. Don't let that happen to you. Be part of the limited group of people who go all the way and take that all-important step to manifest anything they want, and then you will live the prosperous life you deserve.

To enhance your experience with this book, make sure to get the Companion Guide, which contains valuable worksheets and other helpful resources.

Visit **KenBurke.com**

STEP 1

Accept Yourself

CHAPTER 6
Determine Your Level of Self-Acceptance

Accepting all aspects of yourself is the foundation of all growth. You can accept yourself in a nanosecond. All it takes is a thought and your belief in that thought.

Here is the reality: self-acceptance is something everyone struggles with, even me. Even the most confident and cocky people you know suffer from accepting themselves; in fact, they suffer more than most. The belief that there is something wrong with us comes from childhood and is reinforced throughout our lives. Every time someone criticized you or when you were hard on yourself caused your negative beliefs to become stronger. Unless you have proactively worked to combat these beliefs, they are still there, impacting your daily life.

It's now time to reverse this unhealthy thinking. The truth is, there is absolutely nothing wrong with you. You are perfect just the way you are. This doesn't mean you can't improve your life; we are all here to grow, and if you allow yourself to do just that, you're on the perfect track. Sure, you are going to run into challenges while you are growing, but instead of beating yourself up, embrace them. These challenges are your opportunities for growth.

STEP 1 – ACCEPT YOURSELF

Self-Acceptance Defined

Self-acceptance is all about loving who you are in this instant, not who you might be in the future. This doesn't mean self-love in the sense of narcissism or thinking you're better than anyone else but rather that you accept yourself unconditionally as you are today while also embracing your efforts to work to your full potential to live a prosperous life. In other words, love who you are … unconditionally. This means without any judgment.

Many things can get in the way of your ability to love yourself, and the main culprit is ego. Your ego lives in a world of negativity, which tells your soul that you aren't good enough. Your ego judges and criticizes you constantly. Your ego wants to compete with the world, reminding you that someone else out there is better than you, so you better work harder and be better. And if that isn't enough, you might also have critics judging you.

The key to self-acceptance is disregarding your ego completely. Get rid of those judgments about not being good enough and ignore all the critics. We are going to explore this further when we look at all the roadblocks to self-acceptance.

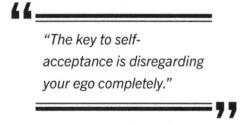

"The key to self-acceptance is disregarding your ego completely."

Here is one of the most important universal laws I live by: If you do not have total love for yourself, there is no way you can totally love someone else. For you to give love, you must have love inside you. It all starts with you. But the good news is that you can make the choice to stop the negative thoughts about yourself.

My Challenges with Self-Acceptance

I have been challenged with self-acceptance for most of my life. For the first twenty-six years of my life, I beat the crap out of myself in just about every aspect of my life. All through school, I thought I was pretty stupid. I suffer from both dyslexia and attention deficit disorder (ADD), and I struggled through grade school, high school, and even college. I used negative motivation to tell myself I wasn't good enough, and I believed I just had to work harder than everyone else. While I managed to get good grades, this was certainly not a fun way to live. It wasn't until I graduated magna cum laude with an MBA from a top business school that I realized I wasn't all that stupid after all.

Does this sound familiar to you? Do you have an example like this in your life?

Why Is Self-Acceptance So Important?

There are three main reasons why mastering self-acceptance is so important:

1. Self-acceptance optimizes your growth. Achieving true and optimal growth is difficult unless you have a high degree of acceptance for yourself. Your growth journey can be made easier or harder, depending on your level of self-acceptance. When you accept yourself, things will absolutely flow more smoothly.

2. You can't truly accept others if you don't accept yourself. I think this universal law is worth the price of admission itself. Hear me on this: *You accept another person only to the degree that you accept yourself.* Period. It's hard to give something you don't have. If you wonder why many relationships fail, this is it. Self-acceptance is the common denominator in so many situations. We are all here to grow. If you fix your self-acceptance, your relationships will flourish.

Accepting yourself brings more joy to your life. Self-acceptance is inextricably linked with experiencing true joy and happiness. The degree to which you accept yourself will dictate the degree to which you will experience true happiness in your life. I experience tons of happiness and joy daily because I know I am okay regardless of what circumstances come into my life. If I accept (and love) myself, I know I'll still have *me*—even if I lose all my money or my house, or even if I have challenges in my relationships. I also have enough self-acceptance that I know I can create anything I want as fast as I can think it. It's a pretty great space to live from.

Exercise: Becoming Aware of Your Own Self-Acceptance

Let's start by figuring out to what degree you accept yourself. There are probably some areas of your life where you absolutely accept and love yourself. That's great. But I'm sure you also have some challenging areas where you struggle to accept yourself. Let's become aware of them and focus on ways we can increase the level of self-acceptance in each area.

To start on this journey of self-acceptance, let's start with a quick evaluation of where you are right now. The exercise below is a simple and effective tool you can use anytime. Once we've established a place to begin, we'll work to raise that level of self-acceptance in each of these areas and keep it up. The result will be more satisfaction, joy, and happiness every day.

STEP 1 – ACCEPT YOURSELF

Generally, the scores among the different questions in the exercise are correlated but not always. Observe the differences. These answers indicate your areas of potential growth.

Exercise: The Self-Acceptance Thermostat

All you have to do for each area of your life is simply rate your level of self-acceptance. Breaking this exercise down into each life area provides you with more information than just looking over your overall self-acceptance (although that is good to do as well).

The quality of questions you ask yourself will determine the quality of your life and provide you with a higher level of clarity. To help you, simply answer the following question for each life area:

On a scale of one to ten (with ten being the highest), what level of love and acceptance do you have for yourself in this area of your life?

Career: _____

Love relationships: _____

Friends or family relationships: _____

Financial situation: _____

Physical looks or body: _____

Spiritual path: _____

Learning and growth path: _____

Finally, ask yourself, "Overall, how much love and acceptance do I currently have for myself?"

_____

Remember, there are no wrong or right answers here. I am not going to say that if your score is ten, you are great and have nothing to worry about. These levels are all relative. As we grow, these levels will fluctuate, and that is okay. A certain area of your life with a lower rate might indicates the need to pay more of your attention there and possibly work on more growth in that area.

Okay, we aren't quite done yet. Let's do the same exercise but ask a slightly different question. Ask yourself, on a scale from one to ten, "What is your level of satisfaction for each of your life areas?"

Career: _____

Love relationships: _____

Friend or family relationships: _____

Financial situation: _____

Physical looks or body: _____

Spiritual path: _____

Learning and growth path: _____

Finally, ask yourself, "What is my current level of overall satisfaction level with my life?" _____

Great. Now let's ask one last variation on the question. For each of the life areas, what is your level of happiness or joy?

Career: _____

Love relationships: _____

Friends or family relationships: _____

Financial situation: _____

Physical looks or body: _____

Spiritual path: _____

Learning and growth path: _____

Finally, ask yourself, "What is the level of happiness and joy I currently have for myself?" _____

This exercise is meant to help you focus on the areas of your life that need some attention. Please don't get too caught up in the actual numbers; rather, use this to figure where you need to take action to move your life forward in a positive direction. We will be doing more exercises to get very clear on exactly what actions you need to take and in what order you should take them.

I would recommend that you revisit this exercise at the end of the book and see whether anything has changed. You don't need to have tens across the board all the time. In fact, if that were the case, it would be rather odd because we always have things we are working on to grow.

In the future, return to this exercise regularly. Self-acceptance is something you need to monitor all the time. Your feelings about yourself will likely change regularly. If something bad happens at work or if you get into a fight with your partner, you may not feel so good about yourself. If you can become aware of this issue immediately, you'll be in a better position to change your perspective on how you can enhance your self-acceptance.

Accepting Yourself Is a Choice

I hope you'll agree that you *and only you* have complete control over your level of self-acceptance. If you don't control this, who do you think does? You might not be able to control whether others accept you, but you completely control whether you do. You can accept yourself in an instant — in a second. Literally in just one second, you can decide to accept yourself and then consciously reinforce that decision with awareness.

> *"I hope you'll agree that you and only you have complete control over your level of self-acceptance."*

While most of us have areas we're not completely happy with, that doesn't mean we should stop loving ourselves. Simply become aware of those areas. Then change your perspective about areas that you dislike or disown; look at them as opportunities for growth instead. Living from this perspective, you'll find that there really is nothing wrong with you.

You Are Perfect

I have said it before, and I'll say it again: you are just as you should be at this moment in time. There is nothing wrong with you. Just because you aren't where you want to be, or just because you have challenges in your life, doesn't mean you shouldn't fully accept yourself. Your greatest lessons come from your challenges, so accept them as learning opportunities.

One of the big (if not *the* biggest) aims of this book is to help you look at what you perceive as problems with yourself or challenges in your life through a different lens (a growth lens). Understand the following:

- We all have parts of ourselves we completely accept.

- We all have other parts of ourselves we partially accept.

- We all have other parts we absolutely don't accept.

This is completely normal. But the secret is, these are all choices. You have the power to make the choice, right this second, that you are perfect just the way you are at this moment in time.

But again, don't worry if lots of things came to mind with the second and third prompts above. I want you to become aware of these areas; we'll work on them together. Personally, I first had to fully believe that I'm on earth to grow and learn. Next, I realized I am always just how God intends me to be so I can receive the lessons I need to grow. With this mindset, how could there possibly be anything wrong with me, even if I am in a "bad" situation or am "failing" at something?

You are just as you should be. Remember this and work to embrace it.

CHAPTER 7

Roadblocks to Self-Acceptance

To help you understand the concept of self-acceptance, it is very helpful to look at those things that hold us back from accepting and loving ourselves. If you find yourself engaging with these thoughts and behaviors, then you should take them into account when contemplating self-acceptance. More importantly, these signposts also give you keen guidance into what thoughts and behaviors you might want to consider changing in your life.

For me, these signposts work as triggers in my life to tell my brain to watch out since I might be doing something that isn't supporting acceptance in my life.

As you read through these roadblocks, determine whether living with these behaviors is acceptable to you. Consider the intensity level of each of these behaviors in your life. Just becoming aware of these different roadblocks can help you change your thoughts and behaviors.

Roadblock 1: Judging Yourself

It is in our nature to judge things. Self-judgments are simply opinions we hold about ourselves. Unfortunately, judging anyone, including yourself, is bad, even destructive.

STEP 1 – ACCEPT YOURSELF

We constantly form opinions about ourselves. To help you identify a judgment, think of it as just an opinion. A self-judgment is really just an opinion you have of yourself. Now we have opinions about ourselves constantly. Anytime you start a sentence with, "I am _____," you're likely forming a self-judgment. Anytime you render a negative opinion about yourself, it is destructive to your being.

In what ways do you judge yourself? Do you find yourself feeling or saying to yourself the following?

- I am too fat.

- I am too thin.

- I am ugly.

- I am not sexy enough.

- I am not rich enough.

- I am not successful enough.

- I am not smart enough.

- I am too shy.

- I am too pushy.

- I am a bully.

- I am a perfectionist.

- I am bad in relationships.

Now think about how your self-judgments make you feel. Why in the world would you impose this kind of thinking on yourself? Some people feel they must think this way because it is the only way they will get better. Other people might feel that if they don't judge themselves negatively, others will perceive them as arrogant. Let them hold that belief about you – but don't accept it as *your* belief.

Accepting yourself is hard when you're judging yourself. When you start using negative judgments, become aware of them and understand that they eat away at your self-acceptance.

Try to stop this self-judgment. At first, it might take some effort, but after a while, your brain will stop this thinking on its own. Trust me, it works.

Exercise: Evaluate Your Self-Judgments

Write down five negative self-judgments you've used in the last thirty days — or maybe even in the last thirty minutes. For each negative self-judgment, write down the positive thought or judgment you can replace it with. I share some of my personal self-judgments in this sample.

Negative Self-Judgment	Positive Thought or Judgment
I am too fat.	I love who I am on the inside and can work toward a better outside.
I am not going to be able to build a successful business.	There is no question that I can build a successful business because I have done it before.
I'm not qualified to teach people how to be successful.	I have a PhD in life, and I have so much insight to give people all around the world.
I am not smart enough to learn a new language.	I can learn anything I set my mind to.
I'm not interesting or funny enough to make and keep new friends.	There are many people who appreciate and love me already, and I will find new friends.

Try This

We know like energy attracts like energy. If you are constantly putting out this negative judgment energy, you will attract more negative judgment energy into your life. It's that simple. Every time you realize a judgment, I want you to imagine this energy coming into your space and body. We also know this negative energy has a huge impact on your body and being. So the more you attract, the worse off you are. This goes against everything we have been talking about regarding growth. This negative energy not only slows down or stops your growth; it deteriorates your physical body, makes you unhealthy, causes even more stress in your life, and makes the people around you negative (just to name a few side effects). This is what is happening when you bring negative judgments into your life. I suggest that if you associate these actual negative side effects with your judgments, your brain will soon stop this kind of thinking.

Can you imagine how much happier you would be without all these negative judgments in your life? Just think for a moment. It is a life where you don't judge yourself. I can tell you it is an amazing life.

Roadblock 2: Judging Others

Close cousins to your own negative judgments are the negative judgments you bestow on others. It's no surprise that outwardly directed judgments are just as harmful. In fact, your judgments of others destroys *you* even more. They are worse because the negative energy they create comes right back to bite you in the ass.

There is an important link between judging yourself and judging others. You might be saying, "Okay, I judge others, but I really don't judge myself." Or you might say, "Yes, I judge myself, but I rarely judge others." Typically, someone will do both to the same degree. If you're judgmental of others, you're likely judging yourself just as much, if not more. When you judge yourself, you're beating the crap out of yourself. Imagine what you're doing to the other person.

Now here is an even bigger point. This was an "aha!" moment for me. All this judging comes from your ego, which works to tear you down. Sometimes it feels kind of good to judge someone else, at least on the surface. *She is fat. He isn't very smart. She doesn't know what she is doing.* Or one of my favorites: *He is just plain wrong.* When you gossip with your friends or complain about something, it can feel like relief to vent and rip the other person to shreds, especially people who are close to you. The closer they are, the more judgments you make about them.

Why does this happen? Simple. You feed your ego every time you render a judgment on yourself or others. Your ego feels better in the moment but living from ego long-term doesn't feel all that good. It isn't a path to a happier life. In fact, each time you feed your ego, you become less happy with who you are and what you are doing. With as much work as I have done on myself, my ego still regularly rears its ugly head in my life.

When I started my business, I was completely obsessed with its success, and I tied my ego and my own self-worth to how well the company was doing. When something bad happened in the company, like losing an account, I felt horrible. Then what I thought was the worst possible thing happened to me: my venture-backed board of directors replaced me as the CEO of the company. This disappointment felt about as bad as anything could. After growing a successful company over twelve years and building it up from nothing, these guys decided to replace me for reasons my ego couldn't understand.

After about a year, I was able to detach my ego from the success of the company through a pretty challenging process. It's difficult to detach from many things, and in this case, it was particularly hard. I'd given birth to the business and worked tirelessly for many years, and the emotional ties I had to it were very strong, so it took several years for me to detach myself from it. The new CEO, who was highly egocentric, destroyed my company in eighteen months. The universe couldn't have given me a better teacher. The incredible lesson from all this was that I was able to detach my financial success and achievements from the success of the company. I used to tell myself that even if the company was worthless when it sold, I still would have gotten a multimillion-dollar education. And I was right. I got the best education I could have asked for. Living from ego makes growing very difficult if not impossible. When you are judging, you are putting a huge barrier in front of any personal growth.

How can you fix your judgments? Take these three steps:

1. Become aware that you are judging. This will be the fastest way to stop it. Remember what I talked about earlier in the book about awareness.

2. Associate that judgment with negative impacts on your life. Remember all the negative things you're doing to your life by holding that judgment (for example, slowing or stopping your growth, living from ego rather than from your true self, attracting negative energy into your life, or destroying happiness).

3. Flip the judgment. Turn the negative judgment into a positive thought you can use to move forward. Example, flip "I am unsuccessful" to "I am successful in what I am doing right now, and I am working on my success every day."

Exercise: Evaluate Your Outward Judgments

As we did with the self-judgment exercise above, replace negative outward judgments with positive thoughts or judgments. Write down five outward judgments you've used in the last thirty days on other people. Specify on whom you used each judgment. Replace each with a positive thought or judgment.

STEP 1 – ACCEPT YOURSELF

Target of Judgment (Who?)	Negative Outward Judgment	Positive Thought or Judgment

Check out **KenBurke.com** for the Companion Guide that contains
useful worksheets for this exercise.

Roadblock 3: Living through the "Good" Opinions of Others

This is one of my favorites — and one I've been working on a long time. You'll be surprised to find how freeing it is when you stop reacting to others' opinions. I put the term "good" in quotes because many times their opinions aren't really all that good. Living through the "good" opinions of others happens when you're always trying to consider what someone else's opinion of you is and then adapt to it. It is an absolute impossibility that makes it really hard to accept yourself.

For example, you may put on a certain outfit or get a certain haircut to evoke a opinion from someone. If he or she doesn't respond the way you anticipated he or she would, it hurts. Instead of reacting to others' opinions of you, do things on your own terms — for yourself. Just have the haircut you like, regardless of how you think others will respond.

You're living through the "good" opinions of others if you're wondering, *What will they think of me?* or *Will they like me?* Who the hell cares? When you accept the "good" opinions of others, you're living though someone else's lens. That lens carries their belief system, values, life experiences, and everything else that makes them who they are. *They aren't you.* So how can you possibly live through their lens?

Now I do believe others' opinions can provide helpful information for you. It is data you can choose to use about yourself. If it feels right for you, then use it. There is nothing wrong with getting constructive feedback. It can be very helpful to your overall growth and the choices you make. Below are a few things to look at when processing the opinions of others.

1. Check the motivations of people making the comment. Ask yourself the following:

   - Why are they providing me with this opinion?

   - What perspective are they coming from?

   - How are their values different from mine?

2. Is this opinion in alignment with your beliefs and values? Does it feel right in your gut? If not, consider just deleting it.

3. Consider how emotionally attached you are to the opinion. Here's the trick: when others provide one of their "good" opinions, those often create an emotional charge in you. This emotional charge makes you react, sometimes intensely.

Those closest to us (parents, a spouse, children) are the ones we usually react to most intensely. Nobody is better at providing an emotional charge in me than my Italian mom. She felt obligated to comment on my weight on a regular basis when I was young. This is something I am very sensitive to because I was a chubby kid. But her comments have persisted well into my adult life. Every time I see her, I am either too fat or too thin. And, of course, when my mom (or anyone else) comments negatively on my looks, she makes me feel like crap.

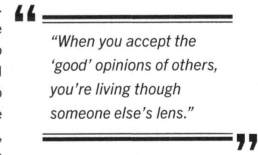

"When you accept the 'good' opinions of others, you're living though someone else's lens."

When you get an emotionally charged opinion from someone, the best way you can deal with it is to immediately detach your emotions from it. (Detachment is a great tool we will talk about in-depth later. For now, just step back, take a few deep breaths, and step away from the comment. Don't react or bark back.)

Roadblock 4: Comparing Yourself to Others

Do you compare yourself to others? Your ego rears its ugly head again when you run into this roadblock. If you ask yourself questions like these, accepting yourself becomes hard:

- Is he or she more successful than I am?

- Is he or she better looking than I am?

- Is he or she smarter than I am?

- Is he or she a better athlete than I am?

Evaluating your self-worth by comparing yourself to others is a road to nowhere. The reality is, there will always be someone better looking, smarter, faster, or richer than you. And if you are number one in a specific area of life, just wait because someone will surpass you.

Comparing yourself to others will lead you down a road where your ego starts telling you that you aren't doing enough, and you need to push harder to get better. This might sound great, but it's using negative motivation to propel yourself forward. This isn't the healthiest way to live. And with this way of thinking, you will never get there (wherever there is). As soon as you beat someone at the comparison game, you will just find another person whom you perceive to be better than you, and you'll start the comparison cycle all over again. It's a vicious cycle.

> *"Evaluating your self-worth by comparing yourself to others is a road to nowhere."*

Remember that your growth starts with where you are today, not where you were last week, last month, or last year. Look at who you are at this moment in time and plan your life going forward, not looking back. If you feel the need to compare, then compare yourself *with yourself*. If you feel compelled to have a yardstick to measure your progress, measure against a point in your past and see how you have improved.

Do you see how comparing yourself to others really doesn't provide you with any useful information? That other person is living his or her own life, not yours. The person has his or her own mission, life, and lessons to learn. If you find yourself in the comparison game, keep these in mind:

1. Become aware that you are comparing. The instant you become aware that you are playing the comparison game, you can get to work on fixing it.

2. Understand how destructive this can be. Recognize that you are really not helping yourself on your growth path.

3. Remember detachment. Detach yourself from this comparison. Don't react emotionally to the comparison. Just look at it as information that may provide clarity about your growth path.

Roadblock 5: Using Negative Motivation

This is using self-talk that says, "I am not good enough until I achieve a certain level of success." Many people fall into this trap, and what a trap it is!

In my twenties, I put an incredible amount of pressure on myself to be "successful." I thought if I had millions of dollars, the money would make me happy. I came from a rather poor family, and money was always an issue; it seemed to be a pathway toward success and happiness. (Remember, the quotation marks are around "successful" because that word can mean whatever you define it to be: wealth, beauty, physical appearance, relationships, and so forth.)

You may be using negative motivation if you find yourself saying the following:

*   Until I have $_____, I won't be successful.

*   Until I have the perfect body (or lose _____ pounds), I won't be happy or successful.

*   I am not good enough until I fix this relationship.

*   I am not worthy of a great career until I finish college.

*   I cannot be happy until I find my life partner.

How Do You Define Success?

As you think about motivation, think back to your personal definition of success. As we discussed in the book's introduction, success can mean many different things. Everyone has a different definition of success. Often people use someone else's definition of success instead of their own. It is critical that you do not use someone else's (or society's) definition of success. Only you can define what success means to you.

One of my closest friends is a top employee at a highly successful high-tech company; she defines her success by how well she does at her job and how much money she makes.

Through my travels, I've been to Brazil numerous times and have made some wonderful friends there; many of them are financially poor but live extremely happy lives, surrounded by family and friends. These are two drastically different examples of success. What's your definition of success?

This entire approach rests on the belief that you are inferior or lacking in some way. If you use this tactic to motivate yourself, you will *never* achieve the success you're looking for. This is also why comparisons don't work. As soon as you achieve your goal, you'll use negative motivation again to strive for the next level of success. And once you achieve that level of success, you will do it again and again – another vicious cycle you'll never complete.

Now is the time to stop this bad pattern and to replace it with something much more productive. I'll say it again. *You are lacking nothing.* You are perfect just as you are at this moment in time. You are learning all the lessons you're supposed to be learning. Once you truly believe this, you'll stop using negative motivation.

Instead, use positive motivation. I don't mean for you to get hyped up in some false way or to try to force good thoughts to run through your brain. Using force to create positive motivation won't work. You will inevitably regress back to your old state. Instead, change your perspective on how you achieve success. The good news is that it is rather easy to do.

Exercise: Eliminate Negative Motivation to Create Long-Lasting Success

Replacing an ego-driven, negative approach to achievement with positive motivation will enrich your life and make your achievements much more rewarding and long lasting. This positive approach to achievement creates a snowball effect on your growth, happiness, and fulfillment. Each time you achieve, you'll be even better than before. It's a great way to live.

Begin by determining whether you're actually using negative motivation to achieve your success. Think of something you're striving for, and ask yourself the following:

- What propels me to achieve this specific thing? What is driving me?

- How do I think I will feel when I meet a goal? How long will that feeling last? Will that achievement satisfy me and make me feel great for the rest of my life? Or will I use the same negative motivation to push myself forward?

- When I achieved something in the past, did the great feeling of achievement wear off? Did I go back to my old habit of beating myself up because I hadn't yet manifested the next achievement?

Now, use the following steps to disassociate your achievement from your ego.

1. Check to see whether any of the reasons you want the achievement or success are associated with boosting your ego. You're coming from ego if your motivation is something like this: "People will think I am pretty if I lose weight," or, "People will want to be me if I am rich," or, "I will have more power over people if I get that new job or promotion."

2. Realize that if your motivation is coming from ego, you will never get long-lasting happiness and fulfillment. Your achievement may yield a short-term high from it, but that's all. Once you realize this, it's really hard for you to maintain an ego-boosting motivation.

3. Remember, you are perfect at this moment in time, regardless of this achievement. Fundamentally, regardless of what you achieve, you really are the same person inside. Losing weight, becoming wealthy, getting a promotion, or finding a new relationship won't make you happy if you aren't already happy with exactly where you are today.

4. Accept where you are today. Understand that if you accept yourself and are happy now, then when you achieve your next goal, you will continue to be happy and fulfilled. Stop using the delusion of a wonderful future; imagine a wonderful present instead.

5. Finally, associate your achievement with some positive motivation.

    a. What about this achievement can help you better serve others?

    b. How will this achievement allow you to grow as a person?

    c. How does this achievement make you a better person inside, not outside?

What about this achievement can help you better serve others? How will this achievement allow you to grow as a person? How does this achievement make you a better person inside?

Replacing an ego-driven, negative approach to achievement with using positive motivation that will enrich your life will make all your achievements so much more rewarding and long-lasting. You will find these achievements building on each other as opposed to being temporary until you start the negative cycle over again. This positive approach to achievements creates a snowball effect on your growth, happiness, and fulfillment. Each time you achieve, you feel even better than before. It is a great way to live your life.

Roadblock 6: Perfectionism

Perhaps you're someone who holds high or unrealistic expectations, or maybe you even demand perfection of yourself. Yikes! Overcoming perfectionism is a challenge for lots of people. The first challenge for perfectionists? Admitting they are perfectionists.

Perfectionists beat themselves up constantly for not being good enough. They are never satisfied with their achievements or with the achievements of others close to them. Perfectionists rarely achieve true happiness or feelings of fulfillment because by definition, whatever they are doing or striving for needs to be 100 percent perfect. How do you achieve anything with 100 percent perfection? If you think about it, can't just about anything be improved? The answer is yes.

You can never catch true perfectionism, so instead, you die trying. And through the process, you drive yourself nuts. Being a perfectionist is usually associated with having unrealistic expectations that are impossible to meet (since perfect really doesn't exist; rather, it's something you define in any given situation).

The people closest to you don't feel particularly good either, because you typically hold others to your unachievable high standards. I would never suggest that you should lower your standards. Instead, I encourage you to realize when your expectations are out of balance with reality. If your expectations cause frustration or unhappiness, or if they prevent you from loving yourself, then you need to adjust them.

Try This

Instead of having one great big expectation, break it into bite-size pieces. Start with a small expectation. Once you achieve that, slowly ratchet up the expectations until you have achieved your goal. This is a much better way to keep loving yourself in the process of achieving success.

I use this technique all the time in my businesses. For example, when I returned to my company, I had a goal of growing it from $30 million to back over $100 million. This would have been overwhelming, but I broke down what I needed to do into little, bite-size pieces. First, I secured some additional funding. Second, I restored great customer service. Next, we got our product on track with a new vision and lots of new features. Finally, we stimulated sales and marketing. Instead of becoming paralyzed by the fact that I had so much to do, I just took one step at a time and brought both my investors and employees along with me for the ride.

If you are frustrated with yourself for not achieving large-scale or difficult goals, look for ways to do the same thing. As you achieve each smaller goal, remember to check in with yourself to make sure you're still using positive motivation to achieve.

Roadblock 7: Living from Shame

Are you ashamed of certain parts of who you are, such as your income or job, education level, weight, sexual orientation, ethnicity, or another part of your identity? Or maybe you are ashamed of something you did in the past that you're holding onto.

Most of us have experienced shame over something we did. Hanging onto this shame allows it to control your life; it can even stop you from taking action. When you're ashamed of something, you feel bad about it, beat yourself up over it, and use it as an excuse not to take action. It's hard to love yourself when you're feeling ashamed.

There is absolutely nothing to be ashamed of in your life. Nothing. Shame is a manifestation of the ego. Shame is just the ego's way of protecting itself from things that otherwise might damage it. Remove the ego, and the shame will go away. Your ego can make you feel ashamed of something, but your true self can't be ashamed of anything.

Often this ego magnification is caused by comparing yourself with someone else. You make yourself feel bad because you aren't as good as someone else. Or you are different from someone else, whom you or the world has said is superior in some way. Here is what I have ᴚ

ᴧ that has really helped me. There are many ways to live a life, and none of them are or less superior; they are simply different. Embrace who you are.

Try This

Figure out what you are ashamed of and ask yourself, "What am I supposed to be learning about this?" Many people are ashamed of not having the perfect body. Maybe you are overweight or skinny, lacking muscle mass. Have you noticed how this shame is stopping you from taking action? Maybe you put off dating or finding a partner. This is your ego protecting itself from getting damaged because it might get rejected. If you are ashamed of something in your past, remember our basic principle: appreciate your past, for it has led you to the lessons you need today.

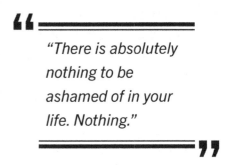

"There is absolutely nothing to be ashamed of in your life. Nothing."

Roadblock 8: Living from Obligation

Obligation can be a horrible feeling. I felt obligated to my company, even during the very bad times. The board replaced me with an ego-driven CEO, who was reckless with what I'd built and wanted nothing more than for me to be gone. I felt a strong obligation to myself, my employees, and my investors to stay at the company and make it work, even though I didn't want to. I felt like I was stuck and unable to walk away.

Do you live for the obligations you have to others? Do you disregard your own needs? Are you a martyr? If you answered yes to any of these questions, you are probably living your life from some degree of obligation. Everyone has obligations in his or her life, but the people who are living from obligation are slaves to them. These people tend to have many obligations they believe control their lives. As these obligations build up, people feel worse about themselves. Eventually, these obligations overtake their lives, and there is nothing left for themselves. The gas tank is empty.

For example, many moms do everything for their kids to the point that there is nothing left. Parenthood is a big obligation and responsibility, but if you are always running on empty, you likely aren't providing good quality time for your children. A mom who loves and cares for herself is going to be much more effective at caring for her kids.

Try This

You must find balance, even within chaos. Show yourself some love in whatever way will help you. Meditation, yoga, exercise, a trip to the movies, a weekend getaway, or even some extra sleep may do the trick. When you live from obligation, you need to push yourself to give back to yourself (I know this is easier said than done),. The more you recharge your batteries and give to yourself, the more you must give to others.

Roadblock 9: Identifying as a Victim

A close cousin to living from obligation is playing the victim. Being a victim is simply not taking responsibility for the things in your life. A victim points to everyone else but himself or herself for the challenges he or she faces. Someone or something else is causing the person's unhappiness, or so the victim believes. A victim blames the world for how he or she is feeling and for the situations he or she is in.

Yes, you guessed it — this is another tool the ego uses. It is always someone else causing the pain in your life when you are the one doing it to yourself. If your ego can blame other people for the problems in your life, it can feel good about itself and express discontent, even hatred, for others. The ego doesn't want you to accept yourself when it is so much easier to point the finger at someone or something else. Accepting yourself is incredibly difficult when you don't take responsibility for your life.

Try This

Take control over being a victim. Start by telling yourself that you're responsible for absolutely everything in your life. Realize that you create every situation in your life. You attract and accept each person in your life. The refreshing part is that when you take responsibility, you also take back control to change your negative experiences. Sure, you might have made a mistake, messed up, or hurt someone, but remember, these are learning experiences. Don't beat yourself up over them.

Let's pretend for a moment that you're in a bad marriage. You blame your spouse for everything wrong. Clearly it isn't your fault because you're usually right about everything (or your ego is usually right about everything). Instead of accepting yourself and taking responsibility for your current situation, you are angry and filled with hatred.

Meditation

Meditation is a great tool to get your mind back into the present and to stop obsessing over the past or the future. Sit quietly and focus on your breathing without your mind being cluttered with thoughts of things you have to get done or problems you need to solve. Give it a try. Focus on your breathing or maybe on some soft background music. If you try too hard, the thoughts you're trying to avoid may come rolling in. Once you get relaxed enough, you will have moments of silence within a thirty-minute session. And if you meditate regularly, those moments of silence will come more frequently. Trust me, I still have to work on this. My brain often jumps around like a hyperactive three-year-old child, so you can imagine how difficult it is for me to silence my thoughts.

A much better approach would be to realize *you* are the reason you are in this situation. Wouldn't it be much more productive to figure out what those lessons are rather than to simply let your ego blame your spouse? And since you are responsible for this bad marriage (gulp), you have full control to fix the situation. You have a choice about continuing with the current situation.

Roadblock 10: Living in the Past or in the Future

One of the hardest things for humans to do is to live in the present. Our brains (and egos) love to jump back in time and replay the past or jump ahead and let our minds contemplate life in the future. The only thing you can affect is now. You can't affect the past, because it has already happened, and believe it or not, you can't control something that hasn't happened yet, so living in the future is pointless. The place where you can totally accept yourself and love yourself without beating yourself up over the past or worrying about the future is in the here and now.

Remember, you are perfect at this moment in time, even with all your challenges and flaws. You are living your life at this moment exactly the way it was intended with all your lessons ready for you to learn. So, if you jump to the past, you will find all these things that didn't go right in your life. You will think about them and try to figure out why. You might even beat yourself up over things you have done in the past. You know all those stupid things you did. But, in fact, there are no stupid things you did in the past because all those so-called mistakes were teaching you lessons. Whatever you did in the past doesn't change anything about the current moment. All you can do is pick up from right now and go forward, minute by minute.

Exercise: Assess Your Roadblocks to Move beyond Them

Let's recap this chapter with an exercise that looks at each roadblock, its presence in your life, and its intensity. Once you really understand your roadblocks, this will help you eliminate the them and get closer to accepting yourself.

Step 1: Identifying Your Roadblocks

For each of the roadblocks we've covered, specify how it shows up in your life. What thoughts or behaviors do you see yourself exhibiting as they relate to each of these roadblocks? And if any of the roadblocks don't apply to you, just put a line through them.

Roadblock	Present in Your Life
Judging yourself	
Judging others	
Living via the "good" opinions of others	
Comparing yourself to others	
Using negative motivation	
Perfectionism	
Living from shame	
Living from obligation	
Playing the victim	
Living in the past or for the future	

STEP 1 – ACCEPT YOURSELF

Step 2: Taking Action

For the roadblocks present in your life, I want you to come up with a set of specific actions you will take to overcome or eliminate each one.

Roadblock	Present in Your Life
Judging yourself	
Judging others	
Living via the "good" opinions of others	
Comparing yourself to others	
Using negative motivation	
Perfectionism	
Living from shame	
Living from obligation	
Playing the victim	
Living in the past or for the future	

Check out **KenBurke.com** for the Companion Guide that contains useful worksheets for this exercise.

CHAPTER 8

Five Steps to Building Self-Acceptance

Here is one more tool that can help to eliminate those roadblocks and to build more love and acceptance for you. These steps will help you break patterns of negative, limiting beliefs and create new positive ones. You will feel such relief and an inner peace that you can't help but love yourself. This love will open you up to an entirely new world of attracting what you want. Remember, your thoughts determine your actions and ultimately the quality of your life. We are going to point those thoughts and beliefs in a more productive direction.

Step 1: Get Aware

Select one of the roadblocks you identified in the exercise above. I would suggest picking one you find particularly challenging. If you're having trouble, consider these questions:

- What causes pain in your life?

- What are your shortcomings?

- What do you find inadequate about yourself?

STEP 1 – ACCEPT YOURSELF

- What do you get frustrated with?

- What makes you get angry at yourself?

- What are the things that make you feel numb?

- What are you biggest fears in life?

Write it down instead of just thinking about it. Now close your eyes and take three deep breaths. Sit quietly for just a few minutes and focus on your breathing; when you're ready, allow yourself to really feel the feelings you attach to this perceived challenge. Keep breathing. What feelings (for example, frustration, anger, sadness, fear, anticipation, unhappiness) does this roadblock cause in your life? If there is pain associated with this, feel the pain. If there is anger associated, feel it. If there is sadness, feel the sadness. We will heal this shortly.

If you can't get to the feeling, keep breathing and work to clear your thoughts from your brain. Be still and sit quietly. If you still can't get there, then just come back to it later. Don't force it, because it won't work. The feelings have to come to you naturally.

Next, move from your head, where you are just thinking about the feelings, to your heart. Close your eyes again and take three deep breaths. Try to focus on your breathing. Ask yourself where you feel this roadblock in your body. Sometimes when you can identify how this is triggered in your body, it will help you identify the roadblock in the future.

Step 2: Feel It and Change Your Feelings about the Roadblock

Replace that limiting belief with a much more productive belief. State the new belief in the present. Replace "I will" with "I am." You can impact your life only in the present moment, so keep your brain from thinking about the past or jumping to the future.

If you need extra motivation to get rid of that limiting belief, ask yourself how it's helping you to live a prosperous life. How does it help you grow and develop? How does it help you become happier? You can choose in a second to delete it from your life and hold a new, positive belief in its place. Let's look at a few examples of this.

Limiting Belief	Productive Belief
I will always be poor.	I am creating abundant wealth in my life.
I will never have the body I want.	I am creating the body I feel great about each day.
I will never have a loving relationship.	I have the power to create a relationship-filled love.

Step 3: Grow through Your Limiting Beliefs

Anytime you think about one of these limiting beliefs, try to refocus your thoughts on what you are trying to accomplish. If that belief is getting in the way of your growth, get rid of it. Your growth is so much more important than some silly and unimportant limiting belief about yourself. Remember, you have no limits except the ones you put in front of you. You can literally accomplish anything you can imagine.

Step 4: Forgive Yourself

Why are we so hard on ourselves? Give yourself a break. Once you realize that beating yourself up is one of the most unproductive things you can do to yourself, you'll stop. Realize that you work against yourself and your achievements when you don't forgive yourself. By not forgiving yourself, you dramatically slow down your growth process.

If you are obsessed with something you did in the past, realize that the past isn't a predictor of the future. In fact, the past is meaningless as it relates to your future. You can learn from the past, but it is irrelevant beyond that.

Step 5: Give Gratitude

Giving gratitude is easy; it means giving love to others and yourself. Start by giving thanks for everything you have. Give thanks for the person you are right now. Look at how far you've come already. Give thanks for all you have learned so far. Give thanks for everything that has helped you. Give thanks to God and to yourself.

Bonus Exercise: No Judgment Days

As you know a big contributor to your own self-love and acceptance are the judgments about yourself and others you have each and every day (maybe each and every minute). My challenge to you is to have a no-judgment day. That means you go an entire day without a judgment rendered about either yourself or others. This exercise might be a big challenge, since some of us have a judgment a minute. If you can't do an entire day, just try starting off with one hour in the day. When you start providing an opinion about someone else or yourself, make sure you catch yourself. Reset that clock and start that exercise over again. If you can get through an entire day, then you are well on your way. Just the mere fact that you can train yourself to catch your judgments is a huge step forward. Give it a try.

If you find this step challenging, give gratitude to other people first. You'll get used to giving it out, and some will spill over to you. It is easier for some people to say thanks and to give love to others rather than to themselves.

This might sound strange, but even giving thanks for your limiting beliefs (the ones you *used* to have) is a great thing to do. Remember that inside those limiting beliefs are the seeds of great lessons that helped you to grow and to take your life to the next level. Embrace them for what they were and be happy they are now gone. There will be much more on this when we get to phase five, which is dedicated to the benefits of gratitude.

Exercise: Giving Gratitude Each Night

Each night before you go to sleep, take a minute to give thanks for who you are, for the people in your life, for the experiences you had that day, and for the growth you experienced. If you find this exercise challenging, just force yourself to say thank you, even if you don't fully believe in the words initially. You will feel gratitude more each time you do the exercise.

Self-Acceptance Is a Continuous Process

Developing self-acceptance is a continuous process. I check how I am doing with this on a weekly basis while I am writing in my journal. I suggest you do the same, at least once a month. Remember, there are so many things that come up each day to challenge us and to throw off our self-acceptance.

You will have ups and downs with self-acceptance, at least at first. The key here is just to become aware of where you are. If you are aware of it, then you have the power to change it for the better. Trust me, there will come a time when you will have little to no need to monitor your level of self-acceptance because it will just come so naturally to you.

I suggest that you go back and redo the monitoring exercise at the beginning of this chapter. Take it again to evaluate how you're feeling. I hope you'll find that your levels of acceptance, satisfaction, and happiness are moving up.

Refer back to the exercise.

Get the latest updates on the book including articles and videos

Visit **KenBurke.com**

STEP 2

Manage Your Ego

CHAPTER 9

Understanding How Your Ego Works

Ego runs through everything we do in life. It's hard to avoid it completely because it is so embedded into who we are, but we can learn how to identify when our actions are coming from ego. Managing your ego is one of the keys to unlocking ultimate happiness.

When you are constantly battling your ego, it's hard to feel joy and true happiness in your life. Sure, you might experience bursts of happiness, and those bursts are like a drug. You feel great for a little while, but the feeling will wear off if your motivation is simply to feed your ego. And just like with drugs, the downside isn't so pleasant. Freeing yourself from the ego roller-coaster ride can provide you with more sustained, long-term happiness.

Understand that when you are living from ego, it is nearly impossible to optimize your growth. Your ego is a huge detractor to growth. Instead of learning from life, your ego denies you these important lessons. The ego will fight not to be wrong and shift responsibility for anything bad onto someone else. Don't let your ego get in the way of your growth; you must learn how to properly manage it.

Managing your ego is no small task, and it could take years to really get the hang of this. Well, at least it did for me — twenty years — and I still haven't mastered it. But I work on it every day and have made huge strides in the right direction. I am so much happier being relatively free from ego-driven thoughts and actions. I can tell you, life is so much easier when you don't have to live though your ego. Conflicts and other struggles in our life just melt away.

Did I say "relatively free"? Yes. If you think you will rid yourself of 100 percent of your ego, think again. We aren't wired that way, so please don't expect that. But you can absolutely learn how to become aware when your thoughts and actions are coming from ego, and you can learn how to correct that issue. Over time, this process will become automatic, so you won't even really need to think too hard about it.

Some people believe you need ego to drive you toward success. I disagree. Then we'll identify ego-triggers, those behaviors that trigger your ego, and you will learn some tools to be able to quickly identify when you are living life from ego. Finally, we will look at effective techniques to manage your ego-driven life. Buckle up, because dealing with your ego can be quite a ride.

Keep a open mind while going through this chapter. It isn't easy to admit that you are living your life from ego. And the more you are, the harder it is to detect and manage. The ego is a funny little thing; it is going to fight you on this one – and fight hard. The more you are living your life from ego, the bigger its fight will be. Its life depends on it.

It's very possible that your ego won't even allow my words to enter your mind. It will be saying, "I am not egotistical. Clearly, this chapter isn't for me. It must be intended for someone else, so I will just skip it." Well, the truth is that we all have an ego, and to one degree or another, we all live our lives through ego. If you think this chapter doesn't apply to you, then you have an even bigger battle to wage with your ego.

My Personal Journey with Ego

When I first started learning about ego, I had this exact issue. I had no idea I had an ego. Remember, ego is not about being egotistical; rather, it is about how you define yourself to the world. I am defined by what I have, what I do, who I associate with, etc.

I was a nice, relatively humble boy growing up. In fact, I had huge self-confidence issues. I felt very smart going through school, but I had a learning disability with reading (later diagnosed as dyslexia), and I was pretty darn hyper and had a hard time focusing. (ADD wasn't a common diagnosis in those days.) I was also a chubby kid with acne, not athletically inclined, and not all that good-looking. To top it off, I was socially awkward. Sometimes I wonder how I ever got through my childhood.

I held these images of this awkward kid in my head for many years after high school. So how could someone like this be living from ego? My self-confidence was pretty much shot through my twenties and even thirties.

I always thought ego meant I was egotistical. I certainly didn't qualify as outwardly egoistical, since I had huge self-doubts and tons of self-judgments. I used to beat the crap out of myself for not being "successful" enough. I was hardly egotistical, but I was a case study of living from ego.

Ego has little to do with being egotistical. Instead, it is a way of thinking. Your ego is the lens through which you see yourself and others. It is what motivates your behavior.

Most of us don't walk around thinking we are "all that." Most of us are actually filled with tons of self-doubt and a whole lot of self-judgment. Many of us even have a hard time seeing any real success or achievements in our own lives. What do you think this leads to? Yes, you guessed it – unhappiness.

I had a severe case of living from ego for most of my life and had absolutely no idea. I couldn't figure out why I was never really happy. I felt that God had just dealt me a bad hand. Other people got all the advantages, and I was destined to struggle without them.

Then suddenly, I started to experience some success. I got into the University of Southern California and managed really good grades while working almost full-time in a professional management job, all at the age of twenty-two. I put myself through school, and then I got a great job at the *San Francisco Chronicle* after I graduated, making a bunch of money and driving my own company car. Later, I went back to school for my MBA (again putting myself through school), and lo and behold, I graduated with a near-perfect GPA. I guess I wasn't stupid after all.

After grad school, I started my own company at the ripe old age of twenty-nine. While it wasn't an instant success, it became one of the leading e-commerce software platforms in the industry. The company was growing rapidly, and I got my face on the cover of *Inc.* magazine. I raised a bunch of money from the industry's best-venture capitalists, which turned me into a millionaire before the age of forty.

STEP 2 – MANAGE YOUR EGO

Now, surely with all that success, there should be no question about my happiness. All that self-doubt and self-judgment should have just disappeared, but guess what? It didn't. I didn't understand why. I had enough money to buy many of the things I wanted. I had social status. I had considerable business success.

But what I didn't change was my internal motivation or the lens through which I saw my life. I was still living from ego, just like when I had been that awkward kid in high school. I still had a ton of self-doubt and self-judgment. In fact, I got really good at using negative motivation to try to move myself forward. Here was my logic: *If I keep telling myself I'm not good enough yet, I will push myself harder to be successful.* The more successful I became, the more I beat myself up for not being good enough. I thought this was an amazing technique for achieving more success.

My ego was so in control of my life that I had no shot at being happy, no matter how much success I experienced, because once I achieved some success, my ego said, "What have you done for me lately?" And the cycle continued. Sure, I felt bits of happiness after achieving something, but that happiness came to an end when my ego came back into the picture.

You see, I defined myself by my perceived success. I thought, *The more money I have, the better person I am. The more I'll be respected, and the more happiness I'll have.* Well, I was able to acquire the money and the "success," but I never felt successful.

I started reading lots more on ego and how it worked, and I completely changed the way I thought. Once I disconnected my happiness from my success, everything got a whole lot better. This took quite some time to figure out. I had to experience several life lessons – like my board of directors replacing me as the CEO of my own company. (It helps to have life events like that to get you to rethink things.)

My hope for you is that you don't have to go through all the crap I went through and that you will get these concepts much faster. I learned that I'm not defined by the things I have, by my status in society, or by my relationships. All those are illusions. At the end of the day, do you really need all your money, your successful career, or those status-building relationships?

I realized that things come in and out of my life constantly. If I am growing, this is going to happen, and there is nothing I can do about it. I learned to figure out when I'm living from ego and when I'm living from my true self. Now I can detect that pretty well (although not always) and adjust my behavior to be more aligned with my true self. This lesson changed my perspective on just about everything. In this chapter, I will share with you what I learned and the techniques you can use in your life to figure out when you are living from ego and how to better manage that darn ego of yours.

Understanding Your Ego

It is completely natural to live through your ego. We learn how to do this when we are babies, and guess whom we learn it from? Yes, from the people around us — namely, our parents.

We learn that we experience happiness when we get things like toys. We want more. Have you seen a young child at Christmas receiving gifts? As soon as he or she gets a gift, the child pushes it aside and reaches for the next gift. Somehow, the child thinks that the more things he or she gets, the happier he or she will be.

This tendency only gets worse as we grow up. We get into adulthood, and the toys just get bigger: cars, houses, fancy clothing, and money. Once we get the nice car, the big house, and loads of money, guess what? We want more. We want a nicer car because the nice car we bought a few years ago just isn't good enough.

How about the house you bought ten years ago? It was great ten years ago, but now all your friends have similar houses, and you have to be a bit better than your friends. It's time for an even bigger house with more extras. And no more shopping at Ross — you're heading to Nordstrom and Neiman Marcus or the boutique shops on Fifth Avenue. What will your friends think of you if you don't have that nice car, the perfect house, or the right look?

But it isn't all your fault (or even your parents' fault). Our society has developed around the concept that having more is a good thing. You can't open a magazine, turn on a TV, or even surf the internet without being bombarded with messages that attack the ego. Marketers know exactly how to speak to your ego to compel you to want more and better rather than to be content with what you have. Have you ever seen a TV commercial that says, "You really don't need this product. It really won't make you happy"? I doubt it. Well, think about having these societal messages programmed into your brain from a very early age. It's no easy task to undo all that "brainwashing" over those many years, and we wonder why people struggle with ego.

STEP 2 – MANAGE YOUR EGO

Was I really like that? Now that I realize it, I have no idea how I could have lived my life this way. It seems so foreign to me now, but just seven years ago, it was what controlled me. I can tell you from my experience that I am much, much happier now than I was back then. I can't even imagine going back to that place again.

Looking at Your Life through a Different Lens

When you are living an ego-filled life, you really have no idea that anything is wrong with you. You are just like most everyone else in the world, striving to become "successful." Many of us don't even have a good working definition of what success is for us (we will take this content on in the clarity section). Understand that you also could be (and most likely are) living an ego-filled life without knowing it.

For me, ego is a creature who lives right in front of my forehead. Before anything can get into my brain, it has to go through this "ego creature," who will interrupt, filter, and manipulate all inputs. The ego has a certain way it wants to see the world, and it communicates with your brain to make sure things are just as it likes. Now here is the thing that sucks: when you are a baby, this creature is pretty small, but as you get older, the world starts to get ahold of it, and it starts to grow. It gets better and better at interrupting and manipulating almost everything that goes into your thoughts. The result is your ego lens, that small part of the world the creature lets through because it can't handle the rest.

Once you adjust that lens to understand and identify when you are living from ego, then you can take action to change it. This is how I define growth. You're growing anytime you adjust your lens. Much like other kinds of growth, adjusting your lens to see ego in a different way isn't easy, but we'll take it step by step.

It begins with an understanding of the ego and some self-awareness. Combine this with knowledge about ego-triggers and you'll have the tools to identify when you are living through ego. From there, we'll discuss how to modify your thinking and behavior.

This is exactly what I did and still do. Anytime I think I am living from ego, I simply ask myself, "Are my actions motivated by ego, or are they coming from my spirit or true self?" This simple question changed my life.

It took me quite a bit of time before I was able to get good at detecting when I was living from ego, and I still don't get it right all the time. Don't worry if you don't get this right away — it will take some practice and getting used to. Eventually, though, you are going to get really good at identifying and manipulating your ego.

Characteristics of the Ego

Once you understand the ego's characteristics, you can begin to see how ego manifests in your life. And trust me, it is present in your life every day, unless you happen to be a Buddhist monk. Let's look at some of these characteristics.

Ego Hates to Lose

Have you ever lost at something that was important to you? How did that make you feel? Some people get downright angry or depressed when they lose. Where do you think that comes from? You guessed it — your ego. Because the ego is so caught up with what other people think (and that includes what you think about yourself), it has a really hard time with losing at anything. Take arguing with your partner. Have you ever argued just because you didn't want to lose, even though you knew your position was really quite weak or even wrong? Was that you arguing, or was it your ego? Ask yourself this next time you find yourself in a disagreement. One thing I have learned about arguing is that there really is no right or wrong in the world, just different ways of seeing things. That is where most arguments come from. When you lose at something and experience anger, sadness, or even depression from it, that is a great indication that you are coming from ego instead of from your true self. Ask yourself what lens you are looking at this situation through.

Ego Hates to Go Backward

As we start to acquire life achievements, the ego begins to define the "story of me." This story becomes very important because *we think* it is how the world sees us. The ego works incredibly hard to build this story into something big. The ego thinks, *The bigger, the better.*

When you encounter setbacks in your life, the ego doesn't handle them very well. Money is a big one for the ego. Let's say you saved $100,000 over the last ten years and really want to see that money grow, so you make a few risky investments. Well, those investments don't pay off, and you lose most of that $100,000. How would that make you feel? If the ego has anything to say about it, you might be very angry and quite depressed.

I know something about this. My software company was worth hundreds of millions of dollars at one point, but because of the greed of some of my investors, we chose not to sell. Instead, within two years, the business was worth close to zero. How do you think my ego reacted to that? The reality was hard at the beginning, but I realized that all that money was just an illusion and that the growth experience was much more valuable than the money I had lost. I learned so much more surviving while the company was going down and working to recover it than I would have ever learned with many millions in my bank account.

Think about something in your life where you have taken a step back. Maybe you worked on a new business that failed, or maybe it was a relationship or marriage that ended. How did you handle these situations? Were you devastated?

I have a friend who started up a cookie store called Mindy's Cookie Jar. She opened her business in a local shopping center, right next to a post office. She thought it was the perfect location; she would make millions selling cookies. She bought all the equipment, decorated the store beautifully, and made the best cookies I have ever tasted. However, her effort just wasn't enough. It turned out you had to sell lots of cookies to make a buck, and there just wasn't enough traffic to make the business work. Not only did she lose a bunch of money, but she also felt like she had lost several years of her life. She was a smart businesswoman, but she just couldn't get over the fact that this very simple business failed. She was crushed and even became quite depressed for many years afterward. It took her fifteen years before she tried to start up another business.

One of my biggest personal challenges with doing something new (like writing this book, for example) is the belief that if it fails, I will have wasted a huge amount of time. What my ego struggles with is the opportunity cost of investing time (a valuable asset) and not yielding the result I wished for. For me personally, I see time as my most important resource and my most coveted asset. If I think I'm going to waste time on doing something that won't yield an outcome, my ego is right there to stop me. For example, I had ego challenges with writing this book. I started and stopped several times. My ego tried to convince me that I might not be qualified to write a book such as this. Who am I to think I know anything about being prosperous? What if the book isn't a success and no one reads it? And do I really even want to be known as a self-help guy? It could be a huge waste of time – time I could have invested in something else.

Well, after all these struggles with my ego, I taught myself an invaluable lesson. The fact is, it would be impossible for me to waste time writing this book. I have already learned so much from going through the process, and at the end of the day, I can always decide whether I want to live my life as a self-help teacher or do something else. But if I hadn't started this book, I would never have known the answer to that question. I am learning and growing along my journey, so there really is no time wasted.

If your ego is always worried about taking a step backward, then your ego won't even allow you to try something new. It will allow you to try things only when it knows it can succeed. But growth is all about trying new things and learning along the way. Of course, you are going to have challenges; that is part of growth. If you try new things, you can't fail. Failing to try new things – and therefore never experiencing real growth – becomes the ultimate failure.

Ego Loves to Compare and Compete

For your ego to grow, it needs to find ways to compete; otherwise, how is it going be able to win? This competitiveness starts when we're young; the ego tells us boys we need to be faster and stronger, and it tells girls they need to prettier. I hate these stereotypes, but they help illustrate my point. Today we compete in business, sports, and relationships, just to name a few. And when we win, we are happy, and when we lose, we are sad and angry. Remember, the mission of the ego is to become bigger, so each time we win, we are feeding the ego just a bit more. It now can say, "Hey, world, look what I achieved."

Another thing that helps the ego grow is comparing it to something else. As long as it is ahead of someone or something, it is happy. "How am I doing against my coworkers?" "Do I make more than my friends or family members?" "Am I better looking than her or him?" And the list goes on and on. Once you realize you can't win the comparison game, life gets much easier.

Ego Grows as You Feed It

The more you live from ego rather than from your true self, the larger your ego gets, and the more likely you will continue to live from ego in the future. I am sure you can think of someone whose ego has gotten a bit out of control, whose arrogance is obvious and extreme. For most of us, though, the ego hasn't gotten that bad yet. Now is the time to check it. Ask yourself, *Is my ego growing? Is it controlling my decisions?*

STEP 2 – MANAGE YOUR EGO

Ego Loves Attention

Do you know someone who has to be the center of attention? You know that friend who, no matter what you talk about, always makes it about himself or herself? When the ego is getting attention, it is very happy. Your ego might be saying, "Hey, world, look at me." There are many obvious examples of this, like dressing head to toe in noticeable designer labels or driving a really fancy car. This person might be known as a showoff. But there are also many more subtle examples that exist in all our lives. I have a close relative who has been the center of attention since the day she was born, and all the energy in the room always goes to her. Every interaction is all about her, and she is a whirlwind of drama to boot. Sound familiar?

If you are afflicted with this tendency, it is rather hard to see it in yourself. You have been this way all your life, so it just seems normal to you. Shouldn't everything revolve around you? When you engage in conversation with your friends, do you always bring the conversation back to you and your life? Is the vast majority of any conversation you have about you and not about the other person? If this is the case, your ego just might be driving this need for attention. And if all else fails, just ask some of your close friends whether you are always the center of attention.

To resolve this, first become aware that your tendency is to seek attention. Once you are aware, resist the impulse to make every situation about you. Allow other people to take the spotlight. Listen more and talk less, allowing others to grab some of that attention.

Ego Loves to Judge

This is one of my favorites. Since the ego is into being better than everyone out there, it wouldn't be complete without judging everyone around it. That person is too fat, too dumb, or too smart. And the list goes on. Judgments are a great way to feed the ego, because they give the ego a way to compare itself against the world.

But the ego doesn't stop there. You aren't immune to the judgments of ego. Self-judgment is also a tool the ego uses to grow. Have you ever beat yourself up for making the wrong decision? Maybe you used negative motivation to try to push yourself forward to an achievement. Have you ever called yourself "stupid"? Maybe you think you aren't pretty enough. These are all self-judgments that manifest from the ego.

Ego Stunts Your Growth

Well, this is true not of physical growth but certainly of your personal growth. I know from my own personal experience that while I thought I was growing during my twenties and thirties, I really didn't make massive leaps in my personal growth until I started to understand my ego and how to better manage it. I did lots of growing at that time, but now I see it was more ego growth than growing my spirit. Sure, I was getting smarter by going to school (for a very long time), and sure, I built a business and made a few bucks along the way, but I wasn't really all that happy throughout the process. In fact, I have grown more now in my forties than during any time of my life. But more importantly, it has been healthy growth.

I often say, "If I had only known about managing my ego in my twenties, where would I be now?" Now that doesn't mean I would have achieved more. I just would have felt a whole lot better about what I achieved, and I would have lived life more at peace. But I try not to live life in the past. What is done is done. It might well be that your ego is slowing your growth as well. To better effectively manage your growth, we need to effectively manage your ego.

Ego Loves to Distort the Facts

Watch out — the ego will do what it needs to grow, including distorting your reality. I have seen this time and time again in the business world, where many executives make really bad business decisions for the sake of their egos. It can be nearly impossible for some of these executives to change their minds or admit they're wrong, even if all the facts and figures point in a different direction. Their egos would rather be right than do what is best in the interest of a company. This happens in other areas of life as well, such as in our home lives and relationships. It can be very easy for us to dismiss true information that threatens our egos at the expense of everyone around us.

Ego Loves to Create Conflict

Conflict allows the ego to do all the things it is good at, especially being right. Because for the ego to be right, someone needs to be wrong. And the ego loves that dynamic, because it makes it feel superior. Do you know someone who is always taking the opposite position from you regardless of the topic? Does that person always have to be right and literally won't stop until he or she wins? Maybe there are two or three people like this in your life. Maybe this person is you. Yikes!

We have to understand that conflict is really just a tool for the ego. Notice your behavior. When you have conflict with someone, is your ego driving your behavior? Ask yourself whether the conflict you are in is purposeful. Is it all that important for you to win the conflict? Does it really matter whether the other person sees your point of view? Remember, in many cases, it is just your point of view or opinion about something. That doesn't mean you are right or wrong; it means only that you have a point of view or opinion. There really is no right or wrong; they're complete illusions.

An Ego-Driven Mind-set

As we get a clearer understanding of how the ego "thinks" and "acts," let's find out whether you have an ego-driven mind-set. How do you define yourself as a person? How do you define success for yourself?

For some reason, most humans have a strong need to define themselves and their places in the world as they relate to everyone else. We use measuring sticks to compare ourselves with everyone else around us. This is how our egos get their identities. And the bigger the ego, the more it has a need to compare. It can't function without this perspective.

Do your actions come from your ego or from love for others? Your mind-set determines the actions you take each day. It gets to the core of what motivates you to do what you do. Remember, we all have an ego, but some of us are driven more aggressively by our egos than others are. Let's look at how the ego defines itself and see whether any of these definitions resonate with you.

You Are What You Have

The ego loves to define itself by its possessions. The core belief here is that the more things you have, the better you are. In fact, possessions become a drug the ego can never get enough of. As soon as the ego gets more, what does it do? It continues to compare itself with other egos that have even more. And the process goes on and on. You can never win this game. You just keep getting more, and the ego keeps increasing the stakes, comparing itself with something bigger and better.

Do you know people who define themselves by their possessions? How about you? Are you driven by the need for material possessions in your life? Sure, we all like things, but what is your motivation for wanting those things? Do you want more because you want to be superior to others? Or do you want certain things that bring you happiness because you enjoy them? Maybe things bring you comfort, safety, pleasure, and so forth. But if you just want things to accumulate, then you might need to do an ego check. You just might be controlled by your ego in this area of your life.

I certainly struggled with this problem earlier in life. I wanted the coolest car on the block. I wanted more money just because. I'm not sure I even knew why, but striving for more was always in my mind. Did I just want to be better than other people? Maybe.

You Are What You Do

This might be your career, the university you attended, your service in the military, or anything you do that leads to your accomplishments. These labels become very important when the ego is trying to define itself as a superior being.

What you do might be your passion, but it isn't who you are. It's just what you do. You should absolutely be proud of what you do and of your accomplishments but striving for these accomplishments merely to identify yourself with them isn't useful.

Remember, the ego always wants more, so what do you think the ego does when managing your career? The ego will drive you to a better job with higher pay and more status. Just because someone defines a career path as "better" than another doesn't make it right for you. A "better" job with more money and a higher-level title might not be in alignment with what you are good at or what gives you pleasure. Maybe a non-management, creative job is better for you than managing people in a higher-level position. Is your ego driving you toward a better job, or do you have a true desire to enjoy the work you do and to strive to get better at it?

Do you know people who start off a conversation with their job title? Do you know people whose entire identity is wrapped up in what they do for a living? How about that college student who had to get into the school with the best reputation or name? Do you define yourself by what you do?

STEP 2 – MANAGE YOUR EGO

You aren't what you do. You aren't the titles you have. You aren't the school you went to. You aren't the fame or notoriety you might have. What happens if you lose your title or fame? Are you destroyed?

You Are the Relationships You Have

The ego defines itself by whom it associates with. Maybe you know someone who has a higher status than you do. The ego might say, "The more friends or people you know, the better you are." Again, more is better. In today's world, some people get their identity from the number of friends they have on Facebook. Does their number of friends make them who they really are?

Let's get a little closer to home. Maybe you define yourself by the fact that you have a husband or wife. Or maybe your definition of yourself is that you are a mom or dad. Do you derive some status from these relationships? If so, then you might need to check to see whether your ego is driving this.

What happens if those relationships you so closely identify yourself with go away? Then what? The answer is you become unhappy in most cases.

You Are Your Achievements

Look at all those awards and trophies you have. These achievements are great, but do they define you? Do you wear these accomplishments as a label to define who you are? Do you brag about your achievements to others? If you answered yes, you are coming from ego.

I like to think my accomplishments are for me and no one else. I can share them, but instead of letting them define who I am, I can just enjoy the fact that I did them for myself. I also hope my achievements in some way have helped others. You really don't need to share your achievements with anyone because they aren't who you are. Achievements are just what you have done – that is all.

You Are Your Social Status

The ego loves nothing more than social status because it loves to be ahead of everyone else. It has a strong need to be recognized and held in high opinion by others. The funny thing is if the ego doesn't know the people it is trying to impress, this is just as important.

Do you consciously think about your social status? Do you take action to increase your social standing? Do you have to go to parties or certain events because of what other people will think if you don't?

Social status is just the ego saying other people's opinions matter to you. You can play this game all day long, but it's impossible to win. The ego loves to chase the good opinions of others, but you will drive yourself crazy trying to live up to them. The same holds true of your social status. You can chase status all day, but it will always elude you.

Social status has never resonated with me personally. I just never really cared about what my friends or social circles thought about me. But I do know ego-driven people who must be part of the right groups or go to the right parties only to increase their social status. Social status might be a by-product of all the other great work you are doing in your life, but it isn't something you should strive for.

The Big "Aha"

It took me a long time to figure out what I am about to tell you. Now, I know I am not the brightest bulb on the block, but this is a pretty simple concept. In all the reading and research I have done on ego, I was still struggling with one big question. If I work to get rid of my ego, does that mean I can't desire success or have money? Am I not allowed to want material things? Should I not try to attract a physically beautiful person? Should I not strive to achieve my goals?

The messages involving ego can be very confusing. All the books were telling me I shouldn't desire these things, but I just couldn't artificially suppress my desire to be successful and to have nice things. Am I supposed to live like a monk? Maybe I was just destined to be an ego-driven person.

I realized I just needed to check to see what my motivation was for desiring something. Now I ask myself, "What is my motivation here?" Determining what is motivating your behavior will give you a ton of information as to whether you are coming from ego or from your true self.

If your actions or desires are coming from the following, you are most likely coming from ego.

STEP 2 – MANAGE YOUR EGO

- You are acquiring things like faster cars and bigger houses so you can feel good about yourself.

- You are acquiring possessions so you can be better than other people in your life.

- You desire to have things because of the way they look to others.

- You want to be in a love relationship because of how others will think of you.

- You want a friend because he or she will make you look better or more important.

- You want to be rich because of how it will look, or you simply want to have more than others.

- You want success because you will have power or higher status over others.

- You want power over other people or things.

- You want success because you don't want to feel bad about yourself anymore.

- You want success because of all the material things it will bring you.

- You want to be famous because everyone will know your name and see all your greatness.

On the other hand, if your actions or desires come from the following, you are most likely coming from your true self and not from ego. Your true self is who you really are without an ego hanging over you.

- You want to be successful because you want to help people live better lives or to be a service to them.

- You want success because you want to give some of your financial wealth to others.

- You desire to be successful because this growth experience will bring you more joy and happiness in your life.

- You want to acquire things in your life because you want to share them with others.

- You want a certain item because it will bring you joy and allow you to live life at a higher level.

- You want fame because it will allow you to share your ideas with others or inspire others.

- You want friends or a love partner because you just want to love him or her and nothing else.

- You want friends or a love partner because you want to share all the good things inside you, including your ability to help him or her become a better person.

- You want success, a material thing, a friend, or just an experience because you want to learn and grow from it.

The simple question *Where is my motivation coming from?* can change everything for you. It changed everything for me. I ask this question all the time. I started to live life seeing things through a completely different lens. I also became much more aware of my ego-driven behavior and was able to separate that from non-ego-driven behavior. The awareness this question drives is key. Just by becoming aware enough to ask the question is a big step forward.

Understanding My Own Ego Challenges

I have had lots of ego challenges throughout my life. I have struggled with many of the same things you do. Sure, I wanted to be rich and successful. I wanted the big house, nice cars, and fancy vacations, and I wanted to be surrounded by nice things. But I never understood why I wanted these things. Acquiring lots of money and other material goods just seemed like the right thing to do. Wasn't that the purpose of life? Some people believe it is. But then I started looking at things through a new lens, and suddenly things became clearer to me. I could now figure out why I wanted what I wanted. How many of you identify with this challenge?

Many of us are afflicted with this condition. One of the reasons is Madison Avenue and the entertainment industry. The business world has programmed you during your entire life to think that *more is better*; it tries to make you desire its goods through advertising. What better way to tap into the most powerful thought center in your being – your ego? That's right, businesses have been directing much of their advertising directly at your ego. So maybe it isn't your fault that you have this disease. But now, it's time to take the control back from Madison Avenue. Don't beat yourself up if you have this disease because even with all I have learned about this stuff, I am still afflicted with it too.

I had a similar experience with my business. For as long as I can remember, I wanted to own my own business. I wanted it to be successful because I wanted to be successful. Then I began one, and it became a reflection of me in every way. If we got a new customer, I felt great, and if we lost a customer, I was devastated. It was an emotional roller coaster, because it was completely connected to my ego and my drive for money. I was so attached to the outcome of selling it and becoming wealthy. It took me a long time to understand this and to change my motivation. While the money would have been nice, my true motivation for staying at the company I had started was to continue my learning process and to grow. And once I stop learning or experiencing joy from my activities, I will stop them.

It's the same with this book. For me, writing it is all about helping people and nothing else. My motivation was clear from the start. This book isn't about me becoming a best-selling author (I have no interest in that) but rather about hopefully helping just one person see life through a different lens. The process of writing the book was such a great learning experience for me; working on it brought me great joy and happiness. The thought that I could help one person live a better life brought me enormous motivation to finish the book.

Check Your Ego

The good news is that you don't need to give up what you desire to live an ego-free life. All you need to do is check in regularly on what you desire and to make sure the motivation for why you are doing it stays in check. You might have to ask yourself this question daily about a variety of things, and the answer might not always be the one you want. It just means you need to work on that particular desire or experience until your motivation is in alignment with your true self. And if you can't get it there, then you need to evaluate whether that desire is something that should be in your life. And remember, you aren't going to be perfect with this ego stuff. Things will slip past you, and that is fine; just be aware of your actions and where that motivation is coming from.

Here is the difficult part: Now that you have awareness of your ego and have these tools, it makes things a bit harder, not easier. Why? Well, before becoming ego-aware, you were living in a cloud. You really didn't know why you were unhappy, frustrated, or even angry. Now that you are aware of your ego, things will change. Now you will pause to check your motivation on most everything you do. This needs to take only a moment, but it could slow down or completely alter a decision you might make. By adding the ego check test into your life, you might find that expensive car or big house is coming from ego and not from your true self. This might take a little extra time, but I am certain you will live a much more joy-filled life in the long term.

Exercise: The Ego Check Test

Let's take a moment to check some decisions you have made and to see whether they are coming from ego. It's critical that you are honest with yourself in this exercise.

Take five significant decisions or actions (the more recent, the better) you have made and determine whether your ego or your true self motivated them. Here are a few questions to prompt you:

- What was the last big purchase you made (house, car)?

- What people (friends) have you recently associated with?

- What job were you particularly proud of having?

- What have you recently accomplished?

- What material possessions do you hold dear?

- Whom have you had power over? How did you use that power?

Decision or Action	What Was Your Motivation?

All I want you to do for now is to get some practice with asking this question with things that are real to you. It is my hope that you will adopt this little technique in your daily life.

CHAPTER 10

Ego-Triggers: The Keys to Identifying Ego in Your Life

Ego-triggers are those things you do that engage your ego in a situation. When you see yourself engaging in one of the things below, it's a strong sign that you may be coming from ego in that situation. Now that you are aware, these ego-triggers will allow you to look at life through a different lens and possibly choose a different action. At a minimum, the ego-triggers will tell you to ask the question, "Am I living from ego in this situation?"

My objective is to just get you to see when you are living from ego rather than from your true self. Then I leave it up to you and your free will to either continue down the same path or to take corrective action. If you take corrective action, see how things are working for you a few days, weeks, or even months later. I think you will find that the ultimate outcome is more joy, happiness, and fulfillment.

Ego-trigger 1: Judging Others

Remember, I said earlier that the ego loves to judge. Your ego has an opinion on just about anything, and when you form and express an opinion, you're judging. It is a super-simple concept, yet it causes more pain, anger, and sadness in the world than anything I have ever seen. I'm not sure whether we were born with the innate ability to judge, but we certainly learn it at an early age, and it grows through life. Think of your parents; they are great at judging their children. Now they may do it from a "good" place, where they are only trying to help you, but they are also teaching you how to be a master at judging others.

As you have grown, have you found yourself as more judgmental of others? Do you have lots of opinions about how others should act in certain situations or even live their lives? Maybe you have opinions about how someone looks or acts. *He is too tall, too short, too fat, or too thin. She wears too much makeup, dresses funny, or doesn't take care of herself. He is a bully, and he's mean to others and really nice to others*. And the list goes on and on.

Judging others is about the deadliest thing to joy and happiness. It brings out the worst in people, can be incredibly harmful to the person you're judging, and generally comes from a very negative space. You don't need this kind of energy in your life.

As bad as it is to hurt another person, you are actually doing more damage to yourself than to those you're judging. Here is a zinger for you: *People who are really good at judging others are even better at judging themselves. The more you judge, the more you are allowing others to judge you.* You essentially open yourself up to being judged. And someone who loves to judge others equally hates to be judged.

I speak from experience on this one because as you probably know, I am a judger. I have had my challenges with judging others and myself for most of my life. I have worked hard over the last ten years to try to eliminate judging from my life. I can tell you, it isn't an easy thing to do. While it still pops up from time to time, I am much more aware of it now and can stop myself in many cases. After years of practice, you can get good at recognizing and stopping it to where not judging becomes almost automatic.

I often say to myself and others, "What gives you the right to judge others?" Only God or the universe has the right to judge. You were never given that right or power over others, so why do you continue to use it? This truth certainly puts things into perspective for me, so you might want to look at your judgments through the same lens.

Let's run through behaviors that are generally great indications that you are judging someone else.

Ego-trigger 2: Gossiping

If you find yourself gossiping to a friend or loved one about someone else, there is a very high probability that you are judging something about him or her. Gossiping is really nothing more than expressing an opinion about someone else, and usually it isn't a positive opinion.

Ego-trigger 3: Criticizing

Did you have a critical parent? I did, and criticizing was just a natural part of my family life. Maybe you have a spouse who loves to criticize your actions, and I am sure everyone has a friend or two who loves to criticize from time to time. Friends are the best at this. None of these people want to hurt you, but their egos want to provide you with advice and guidance. Usually (but not always) this criticism comes from a good place.

Ego-trigger 4: Complaining

Are you a complainer? Well, there are many people who are. If you find yourself complaining about someone or something, this is just your ego letting the world know it exists. The louder your complaining is, the more your ego is involved. Why are you complaining anyway? Do you really need to be complaining about things? Are things really that bad, or is your ego just creating drama so it can get power and attention? When you find yourself complaining, you might want to ask yourself those questions.

Ego-trigger 5: Resentments

Resentments are nothing more than the judgment that your expectations aren't being fulfilled. You create these resentments toward others (and yourself, in fact) because you think other people should be doing something or acting in a certain way, but they aren't. And when they don't live up to your opinions, then you start to resent them. Feeling resentments toward others is just your ego acting up and playing the judgment game, so become aware of whenever you experience these feelings.

STEP 2 – MANAGE YOUR EGO

Ego-trigger 6: Opinions

One of the first things I learned very early in my self-discovery journey was to give my opinion only when others asked for it. If people don't ask for my opinion, they generally don't want it. This means that even if you give it, they really aren't ready or don't want to hear it. You're just wasting your time and energy by doing this. If someone wants your opinion, he or she will ask you for it. But the ego actually says, "What if the person forgot to ask? I better just do it anyway." The ego loves to give its opinion on just about everything. It's like a dog chasing a ball. That's just its job. And the ego seems to gain energy the more it does this.

Keeping your opinions to yourself is incredibly hard for most of us. We are programmed to give our opinion because we learned at an early age to do so. And most opinions come from a good place. You are saying, "Hey, wait a minute. All I am trying to do is help this person." But in fact, all you are helping is your ego – to feel more superior because it has the answers (well, perceived answers anyway).

No one is better at giving his or her opinion than my Italian mother. She seems to have opinions on every aspect of my life, and she isn't afraid to share them every chance she gets. Now, over the years I have trained both of my parents not to do this, but my training doesn't always hold. If you find yourself spreading your opinion all over the place, that opinion is just your ego using its outside voice.

Ego-trigger 7: Judging Yourself

The evil cousin to judging others is judging yourself. Those who judge others are typically just as judgmental of themselves as they are of the outside world. Let's face it, the ego loves to beat the crap out of you. Remember, it loves drama and conflict, so it looks for opportunities to create drama and conflict inside you. This internal drama often becomes external drama, which is even more juice for the ego to thrive on.

Any opinions of yourself are a self-judgment, so you really need to get good at detecting these. All these are the self-talk you do inside your head each and every day – opinions like "You're too fat (or too thin)" or "You're not smart enough (not good enough, not talented enough, or not worthy enough)." Let's take a closer look at some of the ego-triggers you need to look out for in this area.

Opinions about Yourself

Just like with judging others, judging yourself is all about rendering opinions. You have tons of opinions about yourself. Most of these are unproductive and contribute very little to your life. It's certainly okay to be aware of how you are behaving, but the ego takes this judgment much too far, and those opinions go from just being good, positive data points on how you should live your life to being opinions that rip at the very fiber of your life.

Opinions about yourself can be very destructive if not managed properly. These thoughts come up constantly for many people each and every day. It is a hard way to go through life. As I've mentioned before, you are perfect exactly the way you are at this moment in time. Please give yourself a break and learn to accept yourself in the moment. I assure you that these unproductive opinions of yourself will go away.

The real problem comes in when we get attached to these opinions (or judgments) about ourselves. Getting attached to these judgments is the difference between just using these opinions as helpful data points and letting them actually define who you are. That is when the judgment has gone from useful information to a negative impact.

If you hear this chatter going on in your thoughts, become aware that these are all just judgments your ego is placing on you. Awareness is the key to battling these. Once you realize it's just a judgment that may or may not be true, you can work to manage it by reducing it to a simple data point that may be helpful to you.

Ego-trigger 8: Doubting Yourself

The ego loves to make you doubt yourself. It's just another way to create drama in your life. If you find yourself questioning every decision you make, this is just you doubting yourself. The ego is saying, "You aren't good enough (not pretty enough, not strong enough, and so forth)." And guess what? These are all just judgments you create about your abilities. Generally, self-doubts are unproductive and unnecessary in life.

STEP 2 – MANAGE YOUR EGO

Ego-trigger 9: Valuing the Opinion of Others

Caring about what others think of you is one of the biggest self-judgments that come from the ego. I assure you that there are many opinions floating out in the world about you. Have you ever asked yourself these questions?

- Will he or she like the way I look?
- Will he or she agree with what I am saying?
- Will he or she like me?
- Will he or she think I am smart?
- Will he or she think I am making the wrong decision?

While these are judgments directed to your ego by others, it is you who is internalizing these judgments and making them real. The damaging thing isn't whether people have these judgments about you but rather how you deal with them. In fact, these judgments may not even be real. The ego is a tricky little devil, likely to fly into a rage at even the idea of a possible judgment aimed at you. Regardless of whether these are actual judgments from others or just your perceptions, you need to deal with them in the same way. Any opinion coming from someone else is irrelevant to your true self.

Ego-trigger 10: Feeling Guilty

When you are experiencing guilt, you really need to ask yourself why. Guilt is just a judgment about what you are doing (or not doing). It comes from expectations, whether your own or that of others, about what you "should" or "should not" be doing. When you start hearing yourself say things like, "I should be doing this," or, "He thinks I should be doing that," you need to raise a red flag inside you. Get rid of the "should", and you can get rid of this unproductive guilt in your life. There is absolutely no reason to feel guilty for anything once you understand how to better manage the judgments inside you.

Ego-trigger 11: Feeling Inferior or Inadequate

This is probably one of the most popular judgments that comes out of the ego. Feeling inferior taps into our natural insecurity about ourselves. We are so fearful of the judgments of others that this sense of inadequacy enters into our beings and can take over our lives.

When you feel this, you're just placing judgments about your capabilities on yourself. Often you will feel inferior when you are trying something new or when you're in a situation where you feel other people are going to judge you. Your natural reaction is to start internalizing those judgments and to make them even stronger with your own judgments. Somehow this gives these judgments more validity. Stop the cycle and become aware of when you are starting to feel inferior or inadequate. These are just your own judgments, created by the perceived judgments of others. In many cases, those judgments you think are coming from others aren't really there at all. It's just your ego telling you they could be there.

This all gets back to what we talked about in the last chapter. Self-acceptance can go a long way toward combating all these self-judgments. Just becoming aware that you are judging yourself is a great start to combating your ego.

People often push themselves to be successful by beating themselves up. If I tell myself I'm not good enough in these areas of my life, then I will be motivated to do something to change things. Using negative motivation through judgments isn't a good technique to try to move your life in a positive direction. I assure you, there are better ways.

Have you used self-judgments as motivation to get yourself to do something? How about that dangerous self-talk that goes on inside your brain? I have used both many times in my life. When I was younger, I thought mentally beating the crap out of myself was the number-one tactic to becoming successful. If I told myself I wasn't good enough in certain areas of my life, then I worked on those and got better. Unfortunately, all that resulted was lots of unhappiness because I thought I was fat and stupid, unlovable, and so on. When I think about it now, it seems like the most ridiculous way to motivate myself. However, there are millions of people who use this technique (whether they are aware of it or not) to motivate themselves.

Ego-trigger 12: Competing

The ego loves to use competition to measure how good or bad you are. We are taught at a very early age that competing for what you want is a good thing. Kids playing sports is a prime example. They feel bad, even devastated, if they lose and exhilarated if they win. This pattern carries on into later life when they are competing for a job or even in business when they compete against other companies. And boy, can the situation get ugly.

STEP 2 – MANAGE YOUR EGO

When the ego is fully engaged, it can be downright nasty. Often the ego will make up the illusion that the people whom you are competing against are evil or bad in some way. Maybe they are even out to get you or to hurt you.

Anytime you find yourself competing against someone or something, you are coming from ego. Your ego has to be bigger, stronger, faster, smarter, richer, and so forth. Your ability to win or lose in the competition is somehow a measurement of who you are and your self-worth. In fact, nothing could be further from the truth. If you start associating your self-worth with whether you win or lose, then your life is going to be one big, emotional roller coaster.

Competing has another dimension to it, from which the ego loves to feed. Typically, when you are competing, you aren't the only one involved. The act of competing is often quite public, and your ego will be judged based on the outcome. "Wow, he won that tough competition. He must be great!" or "Wow, he lost. He really sucks." These judgments are part of the act of competing, and the ego puts lots of value on them.

Ask yourself, "What was the last competition I won? How did I feel? And what was the last competition I lost? How did that make me feel?" The more important question is, "Were my emotions around this controlled by the fact that I won or lost?" That is where the problem lies. If you felt great when you won and horrible when you lost, then you were attached to the outcome.

Now, competing is a fact of life in our society, so I am not suggesting you can remove yourself from every competitive situation. But what I am telling you is that you can detach from the outcome when you find yourself in a competitive situation. It is irrelevant to your true self whether you win or lose. All that really matters is that you grow from whatever competitive situation you are in. Growing and learning from the experience are the benefits, not whether you win or lose.

Anytime I am in a competitive situation, I always first check to see what my motivation is for competing. If my motivation is to win because I need an ego boost or because I want to feel good about myself, then I am probably in the game for the wrong reason. If I want to win because I want other people to think highly of me, then I am probably in the game for the wrong reason. Next, I tell myself that regardless of the outcome, I am grateful to be part of the experience, and I am grateful for any learning or growth I get. Sure, it is fun to win, but that isn't the point of the competition, contrary to popular belief. In fact, you will probably get more valuable life lessons if you lose.

Now this gets a bit tricky. I know some of you are asking, "But if I don't care about the outcome, then I won't have the drive to win and succeed." Detaching from the outcome isn't an easy thing to do without lots of practice, but it is one of the most helpful life tools I can teach you. Detaching from the outcome shouldn't take away your drive to be the best you can be. It means that if you don't win, you won't be emotionally devastated from the outcome. Your victory is in doing the best you can and in learning from the process. *Redefining your definition of success and looking at it from a new lens can dramatically change the way you look at competing.*

Ego-trigger 13: Comparing

A close cousin to competing is comparing yourself to others. Are you better or worse? Are you stronger or weaker? Poorer or richer? Prettier or uglier? Depending on the answer to these questions, the ego determines your self-worth. The ego lives for this.

Do you realize you can't win this game? The comparison game will drive you absolutely crazy and make you feel like crap in the process. The most obvious example of this is women who compare their bodies to the photoshopped bodies on covers of beauty magazines. You will never win this game, because they don't play fair and also because there is always going to be someone out there with a better body than yours. There are people who spend hours each day in the gym and watch every bite they eat. You can't compete, so don't let your ego make you feel bad about it.

Ego-trigger 14: Creating Conflict

Since your ego must always be right, it is constantly looking to pick fights with people. It's looking for reasons to be right and to feed itself.

Do you know people like this? They will fight with you over just about everything. If you have a viewpoint, they will take the opposite viewpoint just so there can be a conflict they can win. Maybe you know someone like this. The situation is no fun.

Or worse, maybe this is you. Do you look for conflicts, only to assert your opinions and to prove to the world that your opinion is the only right way of thinking? What an exhausting way to live. And while your ego keeps getting bigger, are you really moving forward in your life?

STEP 2 – MANAGE YOUR EGO

Anytime you find yourself in a conflict with someone, there is no question your ego is arguing for only one reason: to be right. Ask yourself, "Does it really matter if I am right or wrong in this situation? Who really cares?" Oh yes, your ego really cares, but does your true self really care? Not at all.

We are so conditioned to engage in conflict and to prove that we are right that it's hard to stop ourselves. Next time this happens, get instantly aware that this is your ego driving this conflict. Choose not to engage. Tell yourself it really doesn't matter whether they see your point of view. The ego thinks its job is to get others to see its point of view, but it isn't your job to change people. And guess what? Their egos aren't interested in changing. Their egos are perfectly happy keeping their points of view.

There is a saying Wayne Dyer taught me that I would like to share. He always said, "If you have the choice to be right or kind, always pick kind." I love that because it is so true.

Exercise: Identifying Your Ego-triggers

Part 1: Ranking Your Ego-triggers

I want you to contemplate each ego-trigger and rank how prevalent that trigger is in your life. The point of this exercise is to become aware of those ego-triggers that pop up in situation after situation.

Ego-trigger	Intensity Ranking (1 to 10)
1: Judging others	
2: Gossiping about others	
3: Criticizing others	
4: Complaining about others	
5: Resenting others	
6: Giving your opinions of others	
7: Judging yourself	

8: Doubting yourself	
9: Valuing the opinions of others	
10: Feeling guilty	
11: Feeling inferior or inadequate	
12: Competing	
13: Comparing	
14: Creating conflict	

I hope that exercise was eye-opening for you. Are you surprised by how much you are coming from ego and never realizing it? Were you honest in your rankings? If you are brave enough, try this. Ask someone close to you to complete this chart on your behalf. That is even more eye-opening.

Part 2: Discovering Your Ego-Triggers in Life

Next, I want you to take each ego-trigger and find a situation where it has appeared in your life. For most of us, we don't need to look too far (it might have been this morning, yesterday, or last week for most of these). Think about whom you judge, whom you gossip about, and whom you resent. For a bit more insight about your ego, in addition to identifying a real-life situation, for each situation ask yourself, "Why do I do this? Why am I judging this person? Why do I resent that person? Why do I criticize this person?" Just jot down the real-life situation where this ego-trigger appeared in your life.

Ego-Trigger	Example of a Real-Life Situation
Judging others	
Gossiping about others	
Criticizing others	
Complaining about others	

STEP 2 – MANAGE YOUR EGO

Resenting others	
Giving your opinions of others	
Judging yourself	
Doubting self	
Valuing the opinions of others	
Feeling guilty	
Feeling inferior or inadequate	
Competing	
Comparing	
Creating conflict	

Check out **KenBurke.com** for the Companion Guide that
contains useful worksheets for this exercise.

CHAPTER 11

Resolving Your Ego Conflicts

I want you to get really good at identifying your ego-triggers so you can resolve them quickly. The great news is that once you do this for a while, you can start to identify them instantly, and you'll be able to resolve them in seconds before they impact your actions. Just like anything else in life, the more you work on identifying ego-triggers, the better you will get, and the faster you can resolve them.

I have been practicing this strategy for years, and I have gotten pretty good at spotting ego-triggers and resolving them as they happen. But I am by no means perfect at this. I am sure the people around me would tell you that I miss ego-triggers all the time. And in many cases, I know I am coming from ego, but I'm unable to resolve the issue. It feels like a freight train heading for a brick wall. I know I need to stop it, but my brain just won't let me stop the words before they come out of my mouth. I'll hit the wall full speed and say to myself, "Damn, why did I let that happen?" But as you know, all that is perfectly fine because it's just a lesson so I can do better the next time.

I can't tell you enough how important it is to the overall quality of your life to get control of your ego. You need to get good at resolving these issues as they come up in your life. This isn't something you can put off and say, "Well, maybe another day." Your happiness is directly connected to identifying and resolving these ego-triggers in your life.

STEP 2 – MANAGE YOUR EGO

So how do you resolve these ego conflicts? Let's break the process down step-by-step. The good thing is that resolving them is pretty darn easy.

Remember, as I have said many times, you can't control other people. The only thing you can control is your reaction to other people. Resolving ego-triggers is very much the same.

Step 1: Become Aware of the Ego-trigger in Real Time

Our first guiding principle to resolving ego conflicts is becoming aware. This will require you to get very familiar with the ego-triggers I have outlined above. Once you're aware when an ego-trigger is present, you will begin to react differently in the moment. Remember, by just becoming aware of your ego-trigger, you will automatically weaken it, even if you do nothing else. Also, don't forget your motivation check. Is your ego driving you? I always ask myself, "Does this situation move me closer to God or away from God?"

Anytime you find yourself reacting negatively to a person or situation, this is an indication that you are coming from ego. Likewise, this is true anytime you react negatively to a thought, opinion, or judgment about yourself. You know that monologue that goes on inside your head when you aren't feeling good about yourself? That's an indication that you might be coming from ego.

The next time you feel yourself forming a negative opinion or judgment, try to catch yourself before you deliver it. The first time you try this, you might not see any difference in how you react in that situation, but after a few times, you will either soften up on that opinion or stop yourself before it's fully formed. After you do this a hundred times, it is very possible that those judgments won't even appear in your brain any longer.

Step 2: Detach Emotionally from the Situation

When you are reacting emotionally to a situation, you are probably attached to its outcome. As mentioned before, attachments can wreak havoc in your life, causing anger, sadness, fear, and jealousy. The more you can detach from these emotions, the happier you will be. I am not saying you should be devoid of human emotion. What I am saying is, if you can detach from the negative emotions, you can think much more clearly about the best way to handle a situation. So, once you become aware of an attachment, what should you do?

Attachment comes from the fear of "failure" and the resistance to growth, so remind yourself that regardless of the outcome, failure is impossible. Leave the outcome to the universe (or God) and just focus on the growth, your true reward after any outcome. Assure yourself that you have little control over the outcome. The universe (or God) controls the outcome, regardless of what your ego thinks. As hard as you try to fight it or as much as you might have been attached, your lessons are your lessons. Sure, you might escape a few situations, but I assure you that you will relive that situation again, perhaps in another form, until you learn that lesson (in this life or in the next).

When in doubt, keep returning to the idea of your personal growth, your journey in life. So instead of being sad, fearful, angry, or jealous, be grateful for the situation. While I know this sounds hard to do, all difficult situations are given to us so we can learn. As bad as they may seem, the universe is presenting these to you for you to grow.

> "Attachment comes from the fear of 'failure' and the resistance to growth."

Step 3: Accept Yourself

After you detach, it is very helpful to put something good back into your soul. Remind yourself that you are perfect at this moment in time and that you are growing along your journey through life. Remind yourself that having an ego isn't bad and that you are learning how to better manage it. Each time you make a decision from ego, it can be an opportunity to learn how to move forward in a more positive direction. There is no question that the more you get ego out of your life, the more happiness and fulfillment you will experience. Your ego is blocking you from this and creating much of the negativity you might be swimming in each day of your life.

Step 4: Give Gratitude

If you want to blow away any ego conflict in your life, the best way to do so is just to be grateful. The cool thing is, your ego hates being grateful for anything and is incapable of giving gratitude. The ego would say, "What is there to be grateful for since I am making everything good in my life happen?"

STEP 2 – MANAGE YOUR EGO

Giving gratitude is the easiest and most effective way you can kill your ego on the spot. All you do is say, "Thank you" for the current situation – "Thank you" for whatever your ego is struggling with. When you feel that true sense of gratitude washing over your entire soul, there is no way the ego can live inside that.

You can give thanks for anything in your life, even the bad stuff, because that's where you get your opportunities to learn and grow. And since we are all here to grow, these challenges are actually gifts. Here are a few examples of giving thanks instead of letting your ego take control of the situation:

- You just lost a deal to your competitor. You can give thanks for even being part of the process. Sure, you worked really hard to get the deal, so look at all you learned while you were working on the deal. All those lessons can be used for the next deal.

- You lost your job. Most people would start to blame their employers or maybe coworkers for this. While losing your job creates challenges, be grateful for the time you had there and all the things it gave you. Also, as one opportunity closes, another (possibly better) opportunity opens. This might open the doors to an entirely new career that is more in alignment with your passions. Be thankful for that.

- Your partner breaks up with you. Your greatest growth comes from those people closest to you. They are the ones who teach you your most important lessons. Even if your ego can't handle the rejection, your soul can be thankful for all the valuable lessons your partner taught you. And who knows which amazing person will enter your life next?

I could go on and on with this, but you get the point. In absolutely every situation, you can find a way to give gratitude for it. More on this later.

Exercise: Resolving Your Ego-triggers

For each situation you described in the last exercise, I want you to outline a strategy with specific actions on how you are going to deal with each of these ego-triggers in your life.

Ego-trigger	Strategy with Specific Actions
Judging others	
Gossiping about others	

Criticizing others	
Complaining about others	
Resenting others	
Giving your opinions of others	
Judging yourself	
Doubting self	
Valuing the opinions of others	
Feeling guilty	
Feeling inferior or inadequate	
Competing	
Comparing	
Creating Conflict	

Living with Ego

One of the great things we got from the universe is the choice for how we want to live our lives. You can choose to live from ego or to work constantly to eliminate ego from your life. It is your choice and only yours.

Living with ego is one of the most destructive things you can do to yourself. The side effects of living life from your ego rather than from a place of acceptance and love can make life so much harder than it needs to be. And once you realize this, your life will completely change. Mine did! While I can't say I have eliminated ego from every aspect of my life, I am much more conscious about it and getting better each and every day with managing it. There is no question that I am much happier, much more fulfilled, and more peaceful than ever before. For those of you who are still not quite sure you want to work on giving up your ego, here are a few things to consider.

STEP 2 – MANAGE YOUR EGO

Stagnation vs. Growth

When feeding your ego is your primary motivation, it makes growing and learning your lessons much more difficult. The ego doesn't care about learning lessons. It can't be bothered with this. Your ego already thinks you are right about everything, so you wouldn't even conceive of the need to learn. Changing your motivation from ego to love will bring you tremendous growth.

Alienation vs. Loving Others

It is much harder to carry on loving relationships when you are living from ego. Ego-driven people have a harder time loving themselves, making it really hard to love others. You can't give what you don't have inside you. Also, there is much more conflict with an ego-driven person, so people are less likely to want to be around such a person. Think of some ego-driven people you know. Do they tend to alienate people, or are they in truly loving relationships? The people I know who fit into this category often struggle with external relationships.

Abusing Self vs. Loving Yourself

By now you know it's hard to accept and love yourself if you're living from ego. You are just never good enough, smart enough, strong enough, good-looking enough, and so on. Your ego loves to beat the crap out of you because it is never satisfied. Do you want to live a life of never being happy with who you are? Your ego will battle you every day of your life if you don't resolve your ego challenges.

Unhappiness vs. Happiness

I assure you that living from ego doesn't make for happiness in your life. To the contrary, your ego is what is probably making you miserable. It is the mechanism putting all the pressure on you to "keep up with the Joneses." Your ego is telling you that you aren't good enough. Your ego is blocking you from truly loving yourself and others. Where is the happiness in that? If you decide to choose happiness, then your ego has to go. When you stop living from ego, you will feel a huge weight lifted from your shoulders; instead of life being a struggle, you become grateful for all you have. The struggle to be happy ends.

Striving vs. Arriving

Ego-driven people continually strive for things, usually because they are constantly competing to be the best. While it might sound like a good trait to always be winning and striving, ask yourself, "Where is the fulfillment when my ego says it's not good enough and that I need to do more?" As soon as you win, your ego wants more. If you have $1 million, your ego wants $10 million. If you get a promotion, your ego will say it's not good enough. And when you find that girl or guy of your dreams, your ego finds issues and looks for something better. The search never ends. You never arrive when living from ego.

You Make the Choice

One of the greatest gifts we were given as humans was the right to make choices in our own lives. You can choose to live from ego and struggle through life making things much harder than they need to be, or you can choose to have a life filled with love, happiness, and fulfillment. All you need to do is become aware of the life you are currently living and change your perspective on a new way of living. It will require practice because you have been conditioned your entire life to live from ego. That is okay. Start practicing today. I always say that if you get the choice of whether to live from ego, why not choose the life that makes you happy?

Find an Ego Mentor

Do you know someone in your life who seems to have little to no ego? This person doesn't seem to place judgments on others or on himself or herself. They aren't very competitive, and they don't have to win all the time. Maybe he or she doesn't express jealously. This person just seems to be content in his or her body.

Find those people in your life who match this description and observe them. Watch how they react to all types of situations. Listen to how they speak about themselves. Watch how they treat others and themselves.

I have a friend, and he fits the bill perfectly. I often refer to him as an "old soul" because he seems to have come into life with very little ego inside him. He seems to be so well adjusted. He'll rarely argue with you. He isn't competitive at all. And most importantly, he rarely gives any kind of negative opinion about himself or others. In fact, he really likes himself. And of course, the egocentric person I am is jealous of him (he's an ego-trigger), because he just seems so perfect, and this ego stuff comes so easily for him. Who is this person in your life whom you can observe and model his or her reactions to ego?

Work to resolve as many of these ego-triggers as you can, but be aware that most people won't get rid of all of them. We have all been conditioned since we were babies to react from ego, so it is hard to wipe this completely out of your life. But if you use the tools in this chapter, you'll be able to be in control of your ego rather than the other way around.

Get the latest updates on the book including articles and videos

Visit **KenBurke.com**

STEP 3

Get Clear

CHAPTER 12

Irrefutable Laws of Clarity

Getting clarity in your life is a never-ending process. As you work through one part of your life, you need to continually go back to gain more clarity because your situation keeps changing. And once you achieve a major goal, there's time to go back to the drawing board and get more clarity on what you want to do next. And the process starts over again. It's critical that you master the ability to get clarity in your life anytime you need it, so pay close attention to all the techniques outlined here.

Just when I thought I had clarity on my business life, I went and sold my company. And guess what? I had to start all over again. I went through two years of soul-searching, trying to find what I wanted to do next. And here I thought I had it all figured out, but then I remembered life is always in motion, bringing a new set of opportunities (and challenges).

The control is all yours — but you better know what to do. Fortunately, you can rewrite the script as many times as you would like. You can create amazing relationships in your script; you can create massive riches if you want. You can build a big business or be an expert in whatever you choose to do. You have the power to do all this and more. All you have to do is believe you can do this, take 100 percent responsibility for all your actions, and get really clear on what you want to achieve.

STEP 3 – GET CLEAR

Clarity is the most important tool you can use to live a prosperous life. It is the key to creating an entirely new life of growth for you and to taking transformative action.

The Importance of Clarity

I can't think of anything more important to creating a prosperous life than getting clear about what you want out of it. I assure you that once you get clear with your purpose, your passions, and what you really want to do while you are here on earth, you will be amazed, as I was, on how things start to fall into place.

The universe will literally work with you to bring things like people, money, new ideas, and opportunities into your life. Clarity allows you to see these things appear. Without clarity, your brain doesn't even know where to look or what to focus on. You end up scattering your energies across lots of different endeavors with results usually falling short than where you had imagined. Focusing your energies is like magic. With focus, our imaginations and thoughts will focus a few things that will make our lives prosperous. And with this understanding, you'll be able to take significant actions to transform your life.

Living Life without Clarity

Without clarity, it becomes difficult to know what actions you should be taking daily. If you can't answer the following questions, then I would suggest you don't have the level of clarity in your life that you need. Answers to these questions should roll off your tongue.

- What is your purpose in life?
- What values do you live your life by?
- How are these values impacting you?
- What are the passions in your life that get you really excited?
- Can you state a personal vision for each area of your life (career, finances, relationships and family, physical fitness and health, growth and learning, spiritual life, and philanthropy)?
- Do you know what actions to take to move yourself forward in each of these areas? Do you have a plan?
- What obstacles stop you from achieving?

If these answers seem like a mystery to you, then we might have some work to do on clarity. Since clarity is something that continues to evolve, my guess is that all of us (including me — heck, especially me) need work in this area.

For me, clarity was the key that opened my life to unlimited possibility. I have been clear on what I wanted to do, at least in a general sense, from a very early age. I knew back when I was eight years old that I wanted to be an entrepreneur. My dad loved building things for the house. We worked every weekend on some project, like building furniture or putting up a fence. He found a hardware store in town that was for sale and came very close to purchasing it. While he never did make the leap into entrepreneurship, it planted the idea in my head, and from that point forward, I wanted to own my own business. While growing up, I had paper routes — four of them at once. Back then, having paper routes was very much like running your own little business. I loved it. After graduate school, I could think of nothing else but starting my own business. While I didn't have a handy clarity model (like the one you will learn), I followed many of the steps I outline in this book to start my own internet software company, which I was able to grow into a leading platform for the e-commerce industry.

Today I use this model in every aspect of my life. While I am constantly growing, I'm really clear on what my personal vision is for each area of my life and how I am going to achieve it. This clarity has become the building block for my prosperous life, and I feel very grateful every day to have the privilege of living it.

This is an important choice you must make. Life happening to you simply means that life just comes at you, and you react accordingly. There really is no plan associated with this approach. In many cases, your life controls you rather than you controlling it.

> "Either life happens to you, or you happen to your life— you decide."

When life happens to you, often you feel out of control. You simply respond to things that come at you from your boss, your spouse, your kids, your friends, the government, and so forth. In a sense, you are a victim of life. This is clearly not the way to live a prosperous life.

When you are happening to your life, you are in complete control. You realize you are 100 percent responsible for all your actions. (Oh yes! You are, whether you realize it or not. Because if you aren't responsible for your life, then who is?) It is impossible to be a victim when you are 100 percent responsible for every action and situation in your life. Using this approach, you can be much clearer on what you want out of life and your plan of action to get there. Your belief system becomes completely different. You really do believe you can create absolutely anything you desire. Sure, you might have to work through some growth and learn some lessons along the way, but you can get there. When I think of you approaching your life with this mind-set, I get excited – really excited. I think of people like Steve Jobs, Walt Disney, and Dick Clark, who all created amazing things by living their lives in this fashion. They truly believed (as I do) that you can create anything, and I mean anything, you want. Can you imagine a world filled with people like this? I know I can.

You might see this as a huge burden, but I assure you it is incredibly freeing. No longer is the world happening to you – rather, you are happening to the world. You can make any reality yours. All you have to do is believe it and then build a step-by-step plan on how to get there (and, of course, act on that plan). Clarity will allow you to build that plan. This chapter will allow you to get that clarity.

If you are using the approach of life happening to you, I suggest you make a decision today, right now, on whether this is the way you want to live your life. You can literally make this decision in an instant. Simply change your belief about being a victim. Realize that you control 100 percent of your time. You control the decisions you make. You control your interactions. You control 100 percent of your emotions and your emotional reactions to people and situations.

Exercise: Is Life Happening to You?

Are you ready to change? Let's find out. Ask yourself the following:

- Are you a victim with people or in situations? Do other people control your life or your time?
- Do you believe you aren't 100 percent responsible for everything in your life (both your success and failures)?
- Does life simply happen to you, and you simply respond?
- Do you believe people try to take advantage of you much of the time?
- Are you always doing things for everyone else in your life and never have any time for yourself – and then complain about it or feel bad?
- Do you feel sorry for yourself?

1. If the answer to any of these questions is yes, then life is probably happening to you.

2. Change that belief by telling yourself that you can't live a prosperous life as a victim. Understand that living with a victim mentality is completely unproductive and often leads to unhappy feelings.

3. Create a new belief to replace that. Live as if you are happening to life. You are the one in control, and you have 100 percent responsibility over everything you do. This new belief will lead you to huge success in life and to a path that allows you to create whatever reality you wish. I absolutely guarantee it.

Clarity Is Easier Than It Looks

At this point, you might be thinking this clarity stuff seems complicated or at least a heck of a lot of work. Yes, getting clarity in your life is going to take some serious thought. Remember, this is your life we are talking about. It deserves some serious thought. You might run into roadblocks and obstacles but nothing you can't push through. Also remember, we were given a huge gift from the universe, which is that you get to create your life any way you want it. You are writing the script. You are the artist.

Below is a simple six-step process for getting clear. If you really integrate this thinking into your life, it will soon become second nature. The tools will start working for you "auto magically." When you need a tool, it will literally pop into your mind's space, and you will start using it. You will use some of the tools once a year and other tools each day of your life.

For me, clarity is part of my everyday life. It comes very naturally so that I really don't think about it. I am clear on my purpose, I understand what I am good at (my talents), I check in on my passions regularly to make sure they are still valid, and I go through my personal vision to make sure it is in alignment with me. Then almost daily, I check in on my action plan. Sometimes I review my written plan, and sometimes I just go through the next steps in my mind.

Let me stress one point. Clarity alone won't do it. Clarity doesn't make you happy, rich, or successful. But clarity will provide you with the guidance and direction to make decisions and to take actions to make those decisions happen.

STEP 3 – GET CLEAR

The Irrefutable Laws of Clarity

Before we get to that six-step process, I want to make certain you understand how clarity can work in your life. Below are the irrefutable laws of clarity. Understanding these will help you understand, motivate you to follow the steps, and get you that much closer to your prosperous life.

Clarity Law 1: Clarity Creates Focus and Direction

Focus is a key ingredient in your ability to manifest exactly what you want in your life. Working through this process of clarity will help you to attain the focus you need to achieve.

I run across so many people who are completely scattered in their thinking. Have you ever found yourself with so many things to do that you can't seem to focus on any one of them, leading to massive inefficiencies and poor results? If we could just slow down and really focus on what's important in our lives, just imagine all the things we could manifest.

Getting clear on what you want (and using the exercises outlined in this book) will force you to focus on only those things that are in alignment with your higher purpose, your passions, and your talents. This alignment creates a tremendous amount of energy, which can then be focused on manifesting very specific things.

There are so many things you can do, but it is very hard to take real action toward everything. But when you focus on taking directed action with focus and intent, you are much more likely to achieve a positive outcome. Focus is an extremely powerful tool.

Clarity Law 2: Action and Decisions Lead to Clarity

Clarity for the sake of being clear is nice, but it really doesn't lead you anywhere. It is the decisions you make and the actions you take based on that clarity that will deliver to you the success and happiness you are striving for. Once you have clarity, making decisions becomes so much easier.

Since clarity is an iterative process; the more action you take and the more decisions you make, the more it will provide further clarity. For example, for this book, I had to make many decisions about how I was going to write it, how much research to do, how many hours

I was going to dedicate to it, how much money I would invest to market it, and so forth. I first became clear that writing this book was something I absolutely had to do, and it was part of my life's mission. Then, with each step along the path, I became clearer on what I wanted to communicate. As I wrote parts of the book, I made new decisions that led me to take actions I had never even considered when I first sat down to write.

While writing the book, I learned a huge lesson about clarity and making decisions. About halfway through, I started to doubt my abilities to complete it. I started to doubt whether writing this book was, in fact, my true calling. Was I just wasting my time working on a book no one would read? This was funny coming from a guy who prides himself on being super clear about living an amazing life. I remember sitting in a parking lot at our local grocery store on a Saturday, asking myself whether this was the right thing to do. Then a huge point of clarity came over me. I realized that making the decision to continue and write the book would actually lead me to even more clarity. It was impossible for me to make a bad decision here because the outcome — whether anyone actually reads my book or not — didn't matter. Just by writing the book, I would actually figure out whether this was something I wanted to do for the rest of my life. I would discover whether I really loved writing or whether I should go off and do something else. If I didn't complete the book, I would never get to the next level of clarity. Well, you know the decision I made in that parking lot. That one decision could launch my new career and take my life in an entirely different direction. Now that is clarity.

You don't have to be perfect with your decisions, and your decisions don't have to be "right." In fact, you can't make a wrong decision. The fact that you made a decision or took action provides you with tons of growth, which then provides you with even more clarity in your life. Decisions and actions are critical to clarity.

Clarity Law 3: Get Clear on the "What," and the "How" Will Appear

Many people get so obsessed with how they are going to get something done that they forget to actually get clear on what they want to do. They might have only a vague idea of the "what" when their brains jump right to the "how."

If this happens to you, I applaud you for being so action-oriented, but you should also make sure you are taking actions that are in alignment with your purpose, values, passions, and talents.

STEP 3 – GET CLEAR

Once you truly understand what you want to accomplish, the "how" will take care of itself. In fact, coming up with the "what" is much more challenging than the "how," though most people believe it's the other way around. The real fact is that the clearer you are on what you want, the easier it is to figure out how to accomplish it. If you find yourself struggling with the "how," this is a great indication that you aren't yet clear on what you want to manifest.

As an entrepreneur, I can't tell you how many times I have seen people jump right to the "how." Businesspeople like me are programmed to do this from birth. And can I also tell you how much money I have wasted building software that didn't work right? (Thank goodness, we eventually got it right.) But if we just had focused on exactly what we wanted to build, we could have saved millions of dollars.

Just think about it for a moment. If you had to have brain surgery, wouldn't you want your doctor to be super clear on what he was trying to accomplish before he went in and started? If he just focused on the "how," he might operate on the wrong side of your brain. Yikes! It might be a silly example, but it gets the point across.

Clarity Law 4: Thinking Big Leads to Better Clarity

I have found that people tend to limit their thoughts about what they feel they can achieve. While this is a safe way to live, it isn't the most exciting one, and it isn't likely to lead you to that prosperous life.

I have found that thinking big when you're working with clarity leads to a better outcome. Don't worry — you can always scale back your ideas later. It is much easier to scale down something you are trying to manifest rather than to scale it up.

When I am working on a specific area of my life that needs clarity, I start by dreaming — some call it "dreaming" — about what I want. Remember, they are just thoughts right now, so let your brain go there. If you want to be the world's most famous musical artist, then that is a good thought to put in your head.

The main reason I ask you to think big is twofold. First, if you want to live a prosperous life, then you will have to take risks. It used to drive me crazy when running my business how many of my employees were risk averse. Unless they knew the outcome of a project, they didn't want to do it. I understood that failure really didn't exist, so the worst outcome would be that we would learn something valuable.

This is my first book on self-development, but my dreams – and clarity – go much further than just writing a book. I am very clear that I will be taking my ideas to millions of people through the book, giving speeches worldwide, and being on TV and radio.

Second, I absolutely assure you that if you don't think big, you will never achieve big. If you don't conceptualize what you really want, you will never get it. Let's say you want to start a deli shop. If your idea of the business is one deli on the corner, then that is what you will get. However, another entrepreneur's idea of a deli business is to open five hundred deli shops across the country. My brain goes one step further. I would want thousands of delis all around the world, something the franchise sandwich shops call "Subway."

When I started my company, I suffered from not thinking big enough. I know I wanted to start a company, but I really didn't think about how big or successful it would become. I just wanted to run a company. About four years into the business, I got much more clarity on what this business could really be. I rented out a conference room at a local hotel and spent days creating my big vision for the company. And guess what? That was when the business really took off. The result was that MarketLive became a top e-commerce software platform, generating over $2 billion in commerce transactions per year.

Clarity Law 5: The More Specific You Are, the Clearer You Will Become

While a big part of getting clear is dreaming and thinking big, I have always found that in every case, you need to add lots of specifics to that dream to make it real. At some point, the specifics of what you want to manifest become important points of clarity for you. So really push yourself to take your ideas to the next level with details. And then push yourself again to take your ideas to even greater detail.

The specifics are important. If you want to create a business, for example, you really need a business plan. The main reason for a business plan is not to get investors interested in giving you money, which is what most people think, but to allow the entrepreneur to get clear on what the business will be, including whether it will be financially viable. This is a good thing to know before you invest your life savings in the business.

STEP 3 – GET CLEAR

As we go through the steps of creating clarity in your life, I will force you to get to the specifics of what you want to manifest. Trust me, the more specifics you have, the greater will be your ability to actually realize them.

Clarity Law 6: Breaking It Down Makes Clarity Easier to Obtain

All this clarity stuff can be overwhelming at times. It can help to start breaking down what you want to manifest into little, bite-size pieces. You will be amazed that as you do this, your fear will dissipate, and your sense of being overwhelmed will go away.

As soon as you start to break down your idea, it will become more real to you. It becomes something you can achieve, and your brain won't block it. For instance, let's say that you need to lose some weight – a hundred pounds or more. It seems like an impossible feat to you. But you can begin by breaking it down to weekly goals. Determine what you will eat each week, each day, and at each meal. Figure out your exercise routine. Break it down to what exercises you are going to do each day.

Writing this book was a huge project. I knew I wanted to share what I have learned about living a prosperous life with millions, but writing a book was something I had never done. Where the heck would I start? Just the idea of staring at a blank computer screen and having to fill it up with three-hundred-plus pages of brilliant prose is a pretty overwhelming thought, even though I had been researching this book for twenty years, and intensely so for five.

To allow my brain to process this project, I pulled out a program called MindManager. It allowed me to graphically outline the book by connecting my ideas together. I started with an overview of each chapter. After that, I felt I was ready to sit down and start writing, so I did. I quickly realized that I didn't have nearly enough detail to put my thoughts together, so I took my MindManager program and spent days (and weeks in some cases) outlining each chapter in detail. I took topics and broke them down into subtopics and subtopics to individual ideas. Once I did that, I was amazed by how easy this book was to write. I seriously doubt I would have ever finished the book had I not used this tool.

I assure you that anyone who has created anything big in his or her life started by breaking what he or she wanted to manifest into small pieces.

Clarity Law 7: Clarity Is a Continuous Process

The gift of clarity may be short lived, because the great thing about growth is that the more you grow, the more things change, both inside you and around you. You will need to make obtaining clarity a part of your normal growth plan. As soon as you start to feel out of sync with your purpose or passions, then it's time to check in with that plan and make adjustments to get yourself back on track. I am constantly checking in with myself to make certain I'm still on track with my life purpose. This chapter will provide you with several tools to help you do just that.

Your life journal is a great tool. Typically once a week, I just start writing about things happening in my life and the lessons I am learning. Then, about once a month, I generally restate my passions, my life purpose, and the things I am going to do in each area of my life to continue my growth path.

And then once a year, I reassess everything to make certain I am still in sync with my life purpose and passions. I use the exercises I am writing about in this book to ensure I understand my current values, my passions, my vision statement for each area of my life, and my growth plan going forward. I also jot down any obstacles I need to be aware of, including any fears or challenges that might present themselves. Then I continue my visualization exercises, believing fully that I have already achieved what I want to achieve in the coming year. I typically do this during the first week of the New Year since it works as a good marker for me. Pick a time, such as a birthday or special anniversary, that works for you.

Clarity Law 8: Clarity Leads to Attraction

You get what you put your attention on. There is absolutely no question in my mind that this is true. The clearer you are on what you want, the more you will ignite the law of attraction, and you will find that what you are focused on will start to appear in your life. Here is the cool thing about the law of attraction – it builds on itself. This means as you start to attract things into your life, it helps you get even clearer, which in turn helps you to attract even more. Being clear on what you want is such a powerful tool that it can have a multiplying effect on all you are trying to manifest.

STEP 3 – GET CLEAR

Think about a time in your life when you were really clear about something you wanted to manifest. Let's say it was getting into the school of your choice, or maybe it was buying your dream car or house. Perhaps you got clear about starting a new business or changing jobs. Think about what happened. Did it seem like things just fell into place? Maybe the situation wasn't quite that easy, but I'll bet things started to happen to move you just a little closer to that goal. If it was that new business you wanted to start, maybe you started to research the business and write a business plan. As you began working on this, you started to meet people who provided you with input on this new business. That input led you to make new distinctions about the business, and your knowledge, confidence, and excitement about the business began to build. This pushed you forward to take the next step and maybe even break through some fear you had about your own success. Then you got more comfortable and took the next step to make some sample products. Fast-forward a few years; those sample products turned into a full production line of products for retailers all across the country.

Each step you take gets you clearer about the next step you need to take to manifest what you want. This is how the law of attraction actually works. Others portray this as some mystical or spiritual thing. Somehow, they say, if you think of something, the universe will suddenly drop it into your lap. Unfortunately, this isn't the way it works. There is a process to the law of attraction. It starts with a little clarity around what you want, which allows you to move in the direction of that clarity. As you move in that direction, things naturally start to come in because you are putting energy toward what you want to manifest. You are taking action, which in turn creates more clarity, which in turn allows more things to come in. And the process goes on.

I do believe there is something about the law of attraction we can't see. It is called "energy." Once you start to put energy toward what you want, then that energy attracts like energy. And the more energy you have going toward something, the more likely you are going make it happen. I can't fully explain this law of the universe, but I have experienced it in my life many times.

This is exactly how I built my business. It started with one server and a few dollars in e-commerce sales, and after twenty years, we had thousands of servers running our software, generating over $2 billion in sales for our clients.

CHAPTER 13
Roadblocks to Getting Clear

As you work with getting clear, I have found it's really helpful to understand the potential roadblocks you might encounter on your journey. Just being aware of these roadblocks can help you push through them and see your life through a different lens. Getting clear — and I mean really clear — isn't necessarily an easy thing. I run into people every day who struggle with this and think if they could only see their lives through a different lens, what a wonderful life it would be. Clarity in your life can be so freeing and refreshing. I ask myself why so many people struggle with this thing we call clarity. I have found that it's because of one of the roadblocks below. Spend some time really understanding these and ask yourself whether these roadblocks apply to you and to what degree. I think all of us have a bit of each of these in us. The questions are, to what degree are these roadblocks present in your life, and are they stopping you from the success you want to manifest in life?

Roadblock 1: Your Limiting Beliefs

This isn't just your average roadblock; this is a massive one for most people. It took me years of reading hundreds of self-help books to really understand this one. Simply put, limiting beliefs are those thoughts (or beliefs) you have in your head that stop you from manifesting exactly what you want in life. Period.

STEP 3 – GET CLEAR

Here is the problem. Your limiting beliefs also stop you from even allowing yourself to dream and fantasize about what you want to create. Furthermore, if you do allow yourself to fantasize about something you want to manifest, your limiting beliefs will be right there to knock you down and stop you from moving forward with your dreams. This is bad stuff. Now, the concept is quite simple, but recognizing these beliefs inside you isn't as easy.

The reality is that you can manifest absolutely anything you want in this world – anything that limits you from this overriding belief you might want to take a look at. If you don't yet strongly believe you can manifest anything you want in your life, then you might need to look at owning this belief in your brain. Anytime you think you can't manifest something, just replace that thought with the thought that you can literally manifest anything you want. Anytime you think you don't deserve something, just replace that thought with the thought that you deserve everything life has to offer you. I will walk you through an exercise in a bit that will help to remove these limiting beliefs, so hang tight.

Your beliefs are yours and no one else's. If you can believe anything you want, then why, oh why, wouldn't you choose to believe something that would support your ability to manifest rather than something that would limit your ability to manifest? It's actually as simple as making a choice to believe thoughts that support you. At least give it a try.

Where do limiting beliefs come from? It's helpful to know where these nasty things come from so you can better identify them in your life. While I'm sure your parents (or the people who raised you) were wonderful people and gave you lots of great things, they also gave you these little gems. Most likely this step was to protect you from getting hurt. But in the process of doing well, these beliefs were introduced into your thoughts. Don't blame only your parents; you actually collect limiting beliefs throughout your life. When you were younger, you got these beliefs from your other relatives, friends, and teachers; when you got older, you could have possibly gotten them from your significant other or a boss. You are quite possibly still collecting and storing these limiting beliefs in your thoughts.

So why do we have these limiting beliefs? I have found that many of our limiting beliefs were created to protect us, as I stated earlier. We are programmed to avoid pain both physically and emotionally, so we create these beliefs to avoid this pain. Similarly, limiting beliefs can come from a fear we have. I might create a belief that I'm not smart enough to start a business. Having this belief will not only stop me from even thinking about starting a business but also not allow me to experience the fear associated with that. I am avoiding the fear. A fear is just another form of protection for us.

We cannot forget your egos. Our egos also need to be protected so we will create limiting beliefs to protect them. For example, if you believe people shouldn't be rich (which by the way is a popular limiting belief), then your ego won't be compromised when someone who has more money than you walks into the room. Silly, I know, but this is where this stuff comes from.

Examples of Limiting Beliefs

The funny thing about limiting beliefs is that if you don't have a particular one someone else does, the belief sounds completely ridiculous. Here are some limiting beliefs. See if you hold any of them (and if they sound ridiculous to you, then you probably don't have them).

- I am not good enough (scary, but this is the most common one; people really believe they have something horribly wrong with them).

- I am not worthy of love, wealth, or happiness.

- I am not in shape, so I can never be a . . . (tennis player).

- I am not smart enough to . . . (go to college).

- I am too lazy and uninspired to . . . (get into shape).

- I don't have enough money to . . . (start a business).

- I am not attractive enough to . . . (find a date).

- And the list goes on . . .

If you are like me, can you see how crazy it is to actually believe these ideas?

I have experienced limiting beliefs in my own life. When I was growing up during those formative years, I was a bit chubby. My weight made me feel ugly and undesirable all through school and well into my adult life. This feeling was reinforced by some of the mean-spirited boys who made fun of me throughout school. In high school, I became a loner and avoided interaction with practically everyone except my teachers. You can imagine my high school days weren't my favorite. I never had a date and didn't partake in any parties normal kids enjoyed. This trend continued through my undergraduate and graduate years. I always told myself that maybe after I lost weight, I would be desirable and could date. Here is the interesting thing. I lost the weight several years later but still believed I was fat. So even when I was thin, I had a belief that I was fat. This is strange, but lots of people go through this.

Then about six years ago, I was able to change the limiting belief. Suddenly, I had dates. And I was surprised and stunned that people actually thought I wasn't chubby anymore. Suddenly, I was desirable. So was it losing the weight that made me desirable or was it ridding my mind of the limiting belief? Given I had lost the weight many years prior, I am pretty sure it was changing my limiting belief. And since then, I have had more fun in my life than all the years combined. To be perfectly honest, I still struggle a bit with this belief. It creeps up now and again, but I quickly squash it. This was a big one for me. What is the big one for you? Let's figure that out next.

It can be a bit tricky to identify limiting beliefs within you. Much of the time we don't even know we have limiting beliefs. Have you ever had someone point out a personality trait in you that you never knew you had? And when they do this, you are shocked and maybe even deny it. Well, limiting beliefs are just like this. But unfortunately, your friends and family don't always point these out to you because they are less obvious, making it harder for others to spot them in you. The good news is that each limiting belief inside you has clear indicators to the outside world (meaning outside your brain). See, your thoughts drive your actions, so by analyzing your actions, we can identify these limiting beliefs and ultimately get rid of them once and for all. Just like with other things about you, it is difficult to recognize limiting beliefs. So let me give you a few key indicators to look for to help identify your limiting beliefs.

In almost every case, when you find yourself stuck with something you want to manifest, there is a limiting belief standing in your way. This conflict is your signpost for identifying and ultimately removing this limiting belief. When you get frustrated or angry with yourself, use this to help you identify what is behind the frustration. Usually it's a limiting belief.

Sometimes limiting beliefs really limit your ability to even dream at all (or dream bigger). If you are having a problem even getting a vision of the future and dreaming about a prosperous life, then it's quite possible there is a limiting belief behind that. If you know there might be something more for you out there, but you just can't quite grab it, then ask yourself what limiting belief is holding you back.

Exercise: Identifying and Removing Limiting Beliefs

If you are still struggling to come up with some limiting beliefs in your life, then you might want to turn to a trusted friend and ask him or her what he or she thinks is holding you back from manifesting a particular thing. Try to be specific with your friend. The more specific you are, the better the answer will be.

Remember, the quality of your life can often be attributed to the types of questions you ask yourself or others.

Identifying some of your big limiting beliefs in advance can really help you become aware of when you are in a situation when they come up.

It's hard to get true clarity in your life if you first don't identify your limiting belief.

Roadblock 2: Can't Get "There" from "Here" Syndrome

So many people (including myself sometimes) think about what they want to manifest in life, and before they even get started, they say, "There is no way I can get there from where I am today." They can't see a clear pathway forward, so instead of working on getting clarity, they simply don't even allow their brains to think about ways of figuring out how to get there. This way of thinking stops them from dreaming, But dreaming is critical to filling in those details and to showing them how to get what they want to manifest.

As you get clearer with things, you will find that this roadblock starts to melt away. Clarity, in fact, will provide you with the points that connect where you are with what you want to manifest. Instead of just giving up on your dreams and on what you want to manifest, all you need to do is to connect the dots in your mind on the steps you would take to move yourself forward. Trust me, the picture will become clearer as you fill in the details.

Roadblock 3: Living from Ego

That dreaded ego comes up again (and again). It comes up all the time because it is a huge roadblock to living a prosperous life. It comes up again because people who live from this place find it very difficult to be happy and joyful. Since we have an entire section of this book dedicated to managing your ego, I will just say a few words about how clarity is impacted by your ego.

The biggest problem with ego and clarity is that your ego has an agenda that is different from what your true self wants. Your ego is brilliant at distorting the truth. Its job is to serve and protect itself from any harm, but it doesn't necessarily allow you to live the best life possible. The ego promotes judgments, competition, fear, doubt, status, and many other things. These negative attributes actually work against all those things you want to manifest.

If your motivation for what you want to manifest is coming from ego, then it could very easily lead you in the wrong direction. Be very careful because the ego can be very deceptive to your true self. As inputs come into our life, your ego interrupts them based on its beliefs of how things should be. The more pronounced your ego is, the stronger the filter and the less truth that gets through to your true self.

To work around this problem, anytime I am working on my clarity, I always ask myself, "Is my motivation for what I want to manifest coming from ego or from my true self?" If my reason for wanting to manifest something is coming to help my ego get bigger (in other words, to compete and win, increase my status, associate with important people, make more money just for the sake of being better than others, lose weight to improve what others think of me, and so forth), then I would suggest that you have some issues with your clarity, and it needs some work. Your ego might be tricking you into thinking you are clear, but if what you are trying to manifest isn't in alignment with your true self, then what is the point of manifesting it? It is pretty much guaranteed that once you manifest it, you won't feel that joy and happiness you are seeking.

If the answer to the question above is that you aren't coming from ego, then that is an indication you are on the road to getting clear about what you want to manifest in life. It's just one of a number of data points you want to look at when you're working on getting clear. There is much more on managing your ego in an upcoming section.

Roadblock 4: Being Fearful

Nothing will muddy the clarity waters like fear. Similar to limiting beliefs, fear can stop you in your tracks. Fear inhibits your ability to dream and to fantasize because as soon as you even start to think about manifesting something new, your brain will go into protection mode and find lots of reasons why you should take action. These are thoughts like, "I can't do that," "I will fail," "I will hurt myself physically or emotionally," or, "Someone will hurt me physically or emotionally." With these kinds of thoughts, how it is possible to get clear? Your brain will shut those thoughts right down.

For many people, the avoidance of fear puts them right back into this very nice place called their "comfort zone." While it is a comfortable place to be (as the name suggests), it will also lead to an ordinary life, not a prosperous one. You will find that you aren't living your dreams because you won't take the risk. Your objective to continually avoid risk is just your fear of failure raising its ugly head.

Once you realize the fear of failure is just an illusion, as I have stated earlier, it is impossible to fail. Once you realize any so-called failure is just an opportunity to learn and grow, your fear will vanish. Starting that new business, entering college, taking on a new job, or starting a new relationship can now be seen as an opportunity to learn and grow. If you learn something from it, how is it possible to fail? Can you imagine a life without fear? Change the lens by which you look at fear, and it can be eliminated in a second.

I experience much less fear in my life now than I did ten years ago, but time and again it does pop back up. One of my greatest fears is wasting the time I have on this earth. I have so much to do with the limited time I have; when I think I am doing something (like running a business, writing a book, or staying in an unproductive relationship), I get fearful that I am wasting time, and to me, wasting time is another form of failure (I know, call me crazy 😊). One fear that has held me back as a serial entrepreneur is starting a venture. I will spend months, if not years, going back and forth with a business idea. Is this the right idea? Am I qualified to do this venture? Can I make a successful business out of this? If you are an entrepreneur, you might have had some of the same fears around your own idea.

You see, doing something (taking action) always leads to growth. It is so much better to take action, even if it ends up being the wrong one. It is so much better than doing nothing at all. Doing nothing leads to an ordinary life, and doing something leads to a prosperous life, because you are learning and growing.

Roadblock 5: Analyzing Everything

I am sure you have heard this phrase before: *paralysis through analysis.* Well, this can be a major roadblock to clarity. Do you find yourself thinking about something and analyzing every aspect of it over and over again? Do you find yourself collecting more and more data about something you want to manifest but never actually getting to the manifesting? I will say that spending some time analyzing what it is you want to manifest is a good thing. But when you keep doing so, your head begins to spin and becomes so filled up with data that it distracts from getting clear. Information begets more information, and it never stops. Remember, there is an element of clarity in your gut and not in continual analysis. So watch for this. Remember, part of clarity is taking action on something so you can get more information to move to a higher level of clarity. With paralysis through analysis, you never take action; you just keep thinking about the same thing. There are lots of people who are afflicted with this challenge.

Roadblock 6: Being a Perfectionist

This is the game you can't win. If you are working on getting clarity in your life and if you have perfectionistic tendencies, please pay attention. The perfectionists generally have a hard time obtaining clarity because, just like with everything else, they are so caught up with making things perfect that working on clarity is a never-ending project. Since their basic premise in life is to perfect things, you actually never get clear because the goal itself is impossible to achieve. One hundred percent clarity on anything just isn't possible. Clarity is much more fluid than that. To get clarity, you have a thought that leads to another thought, which leads to an action that leads to new distinctions, which lead to new thoughts. This blows the circuits for a perfectionist. A perfectionist wants things perfect before taking action. Now I don't mean to say that perfectionists never take action, but they are less inclined to reach a high state of clarity because they find it difficult to go through this iterative process required to obtain clarity.

Also, perfectionists don't like to fail, and failure can be a big part of obtaining clarity. This goes against everything that is a perfectionist thing. These barriers can then stop the process of getting clear for a perfectionist.

If you fall into this category, first become aware that you have these tendencies and watch for things that will derail you from getting clear. Embrace the fact that you don't need to be perfect.

There is an old saying in business that was drilled into my head early in my career. "Do the right things, don't just do things right." There is a lot of wisdom in this statement. The perfectionist is much more about doing things right rather than focusing on first doing the right things. You might spend a bunch of time perfecting a certain project and come to realize it might not have been the right project to work on. You could have done work on something that was in alignment and purpose instead of just trying to perfect whatever you were doing. Perfectionists need to step back and spend their time getting clear so they are in fact doing the right things, not just doing things right.

Roadblock 7: Being a Worry Wart

Are you the type of person who is so worried about making the wrong decision so you simply never make a decision (or very few)? Well, a big part of clarity is making decisions that in some cases will change your life. As you go through the clarity process, you will see that it's all about figuring out what is important to you, what is in alignment with you, and deciding on what action steps you will take to manifest what you want. It is both the person who is analyzing everything and the perfectionist who suffer from this challenge. The fear of making the wrong decision is a key driver here. We already know what I think about fear. There is no wrong decision. The only wrong decision is the one you don't make. When you find yourself in this situation, opt to make a decision. Work to get the data you need to make an informed decision but also balance that with the need to make a decision. Those decisions you make will lead you to other points of enlightenment, which will move you forward.

Roadblock 9: Being Overwhelmed

How can I possibly think about doing more when I am already overwhelmed? "Who has time for clarity? I am just trying to get by." The problem with being overwhelmed with life is that you are unable to raise your head long enough to stop the insanity. Realize you are the one choosing to be overwhelmed. This is a complete choice by you and no one else. Please make certain you take responsibility for this so you can also not live a life of constantly being overwhelmed.

Let's look at this through a different lens. If you had more clarity in your life, you might not be so overwhelmed. Clarity will actually lead you to being more in alignment with your purpose and will reduce or eliminate other things in your life that aren't necessary. In fact, you will find there are many things you do and obsess over that aren't necessary.

One other recommendation I have for you is to find those things that really drain you of your energy. Anything that sucks your energy might not be productive in your life. Become aware of those things that suck your energy (write them down). Then analyze whether these energy sucks are valuable in your life. If they are, then you might look at a different approach that doesn't make the situation so taxing on you. If they aren't productive in your life, then find a way to eliminate them from your life. Again, remember you are the artist of your life, painting your own masterpiece.

CHAPTER 14

Getting Ready for Clarity in Your Life

5 Steps to Getting Clear

Now that we have explored many of the things that will hinder your journey to become clearer, you are ready to begin your road to clarity.

I am sorry to say that getting clear is a lifelong journey. As you grow, new beliefs and circumstances enter your life and change your thinking. As your thinking changes, so does your clarity. Clarity is an iterative process you can be working on all your life. If you are growing, you are following in and out of clarity along the way.

The clarity framework I am going to take you through looks at clarity from a big-picture perspective. It looks at all aspects of your life and works to answer the question, "What am I doing to create a prosperous life?" But the same framework works anytime you find yourself stuck and needing to get clear on a particular situation or circumstance in your life. The same principles apply.

STEP 3 – GET CLEAR

Here are the five key steps to getting clear with anything in your life:

- Step 1: Discover Your Values, Passions, and Talents

- Step 2: Determine Your Purpose

- Step 3: Dream about What You Really Want

- Step 4: Create a Personal Vision

- Step 5: Develop a Growth Plan

I assure you that if you follow these proven steps, you will get clearer on whatever you are working on. The process will take a little dedication the first time you go through it, but it gets easier as you get clearer. Soon, you will be so clear that you will be able to do these exercises superfast anytime you need a clarity tune-up.

Getting Warmed Up (Start, Stop, and Continue Tool)

Before we get started with the clarity framework, I want to get your brain thinking about your current life and help it get focused on what is important to you at this moment in time. This is one of my favorite tools.

I highly recommend that you use this tool on an ongoing basis. At a minimum, please do this exercise once a year. It can help remove the clutter in your thinking and get you focused.

It is called the Start, Stop, and Continue Tool. It is really simple, but I assure you that it will get your brain turning. The main purpose of it is to get you focused on what is working and not working so well in your life. We'll figure out what you should start, what you should stop, and what you should continue to do in each area of your life. Let's break it down.

Start

All you are going to do here is take a current look at your life and determine what things you would like to start doing that will change your life for the better. Select a thing or two to start in each of the following categories:

- Relationships and family

- Career

- Money

- Physical life and health

- Growth and learning

- Spiritual life

- Giving back

Please note that you don't need to use these categories. Put anything on your start list that you want. What are those things you want to start doing while going forward?

What are some things that might be on a start list? Here are some examples:

- Relationships and family: I want to start giving more time to my partner so we can foster our relationship and grow closer.

- Career: I want to start working on a plan for that business I have been itching to start.

- Money: I want to start saving one hundred dollars a week toward my retirement.

- Physical life and health: I want to start running or working out three times a week to start getting the body I have always wanted.

- Growth and learning: I want to start to learn how to speak Italian.

- Spiritual life: I want to start reading one spiritual book a month to keep me grounded.

- Giving back: I want to start volunteering for the local food bank once a month.

Once you've created your list, take a moment to prioritize it. Force yourself to give each entry a different number or priority. This is called a "serial rank order." It really forces you to focus on what is important.

STEP 3 – GET CLEAR

Here is a handy worksheet for you to fill out to complete this part of the exercise. Ignore the priority column for just a moment. Please feel free to have more than one for each area of life.

Area of Life	Start: What Do You Want to Start?	Priority

Stop

Now let's take a look at things you want to stop doing. Ask yourself, "What am I doing to prevent myself from creating my prosperous life?" We all have things we need to stop doing because they distract us from manifesting what we want in life. At some point, these things may have served valuable purposes, but they're no longer useful. Get rid of them. Don't feel bad about this list; embrace it.

This exercise works exactly the same way as the start exercise. Here are some examples of things from the stop list:

- Relationships and family: I want to stop working so much so I can spend more time nurturing my partner and children.

- Career: I want to stop my frustrations with my boss since they are completely unproductive and negative in my life.

- Money: I want to stop spending money and not paying my bills on time.

- Physical life and health: I want to reduce my carb and sugar intake and lose weight.

- Growth and learning: I want to stop watching TV four hours a day, and I'll use the time to learn a new skill.

- Spiritual life: I want to stop doing activities that move me away from God.

- Giving back: I want to stop being so selfish with my time so I can better serve others.

As before, prioritize this list using the serial rank order method. This is a very important step.

Area of Life	Stop: What Do You Want to Stop?	Priority

STEP 3 – GET CLEAR

Continue

Finally, we get to the things you don't need to change. It is really important that you acknowledge what you're doing right. This awareness is critical to helping you "continue" to do them. Guess what? This exercise is exactly the same as the last two. Make a list by area and then prioritize. Here are some examples of things to continue:

- Relationships and family: I want to continue to be there for my family by loving and supporting them in good times and bad.

- Career: I want to continue to have balance between my personal life and my work life.

- Money: I want to continue to be mindful of the money I spend each month and to spend only to the limit of my budget.

- Physical life and health: I want to continue working out at least five times a week.

- Growth and learning: I want to continue to travel the world so I can learn about other people and cultures.

- Spiritual life: I want to continue to go to church each Sunday since it fills me up with hope for my life.

- Giving back: I want to make certain I continue my small contributions to the local food bank each month.

All the things on this list were already in your brain, but this exercise forces you to organize your thoughts, which make them more actionable – and that's the next step in the warm-up.

Area of Life	Continue: What Do You Want to Continue?	Priority

Check out **KenBurke.com** for the Companion Guide that
contains useful worksheets for this exercise.

Make It Actionable

Take the top three things in each of the start, stop, and continue lists (nine in total) and focus on them. Start the top three things on your start list, stop the top three things on your stop list, and commit to continuing the top three things on your continue list. If you try to take action on the entire list, it will be quite challenging, but even taking action on one thing can start to make a big difference.

Everything you manifest starts from one small action and builds. For example, people ask me all the time, "How did you build such a big and successful software company?" I started by building a few web pages — this was back when the web had just started in 1995 — and then I built a few more, and then I hired an employee to build them so I could go and sell more. Then we started building small e-commerce sites. A few led to hundreds, and hundreds led to literally thousands of small websites. Then we started building larger websites using our custom software platform. Our software handled a million, then two million, and then a hundred million; now it does over $2 billion of commerce each year for some of the biggest companies in the United States. That's it. It all started with an idea and an action.

Do you see why getting clear is so important? This works for just about everything you want to manifest, whether it is a business, money, a relationship, a new career, or learning something, like how to cook.

Remember to break everything down into small, bite-size pieces. This is the key to clarity and to manifesting what you want out of life. Otherwise, your brain will get overloaded and shut down.

I hope you found this tool valuable. Please remember to use it on a regular basis. This alone can make a huge difference in staying focused on what is truly most important to you.

CHAPTER 15

Step 1: Discover Your Values, Passions, and Talents

Now that you're warmed up and are on the road to clarity, let's build a solid foundation for your next steps toward your prosperous life. To move forward with complete clarity, it's important to start with what's already inside you, and by this, I mean your values, talents, and passions. In this next step, we'll identify these and make them explicit by not only writing them down but also ranking them.

As you start exploring your God-given tools, be on the lookout for a burning desire — something inside you that just might be propelling you in one direction or another. Maybe it's something that's already formed deep within you, something you haven't been able to connect with because of fear. Maybe it's something you haven't quite figured out yet, because you've never done such a methodical job of figuring out what really makes you tick. As people start to uncover their deeper truths, it isn't uncommon for such a desire to surface. If this happens, great. You'll be well on your way to the next steps.

Once you've determined and fully embraced your values, passions, and talents, you'll be ready to take all you've learned about yourself and craft your purpose, which is the next step toward the life-changing actions that will transform your life from ordinary to extraordinary. But first your God-given ingredients — let's start with values.

STEP 3 – GET CLEAR

Your Core Values

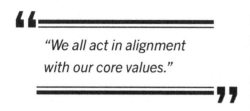

"We all act in alignment with our core values."

Values are what really make you tick. Do you really know what drives you? Do you know why you make the decisions you make? Do you understand why you take certain actions while other people take others? Do you know why you pick your friends or your partner? If you understand your core values, then you will be able to answer these questions and lots more.

What are core values anyway? I think of core values as those things you feel are most important. What do you value most? Relationships, friends, health, money, career, success, happiness, fame? These are easy to figure out, but the harder part is putting them in rank order. I am going to force you into some upcoming experiences to clarify that ranking.

In fact, you already know your core values in your subconscious mind, because they guide all your decision-making. However, it's important to know them consciously. When they sit in your conscious mind, you have more control over your actions, and you can modify them while you grow instead of just leaving them up to your emotional responses. There are many benefits to this, including the following:

Building Blocks to Purpose and Passions

At the most fundamental level, it is critical that you really understand your core values, which are ultimately what drive you to figure out your purpose and passions. Once you understand what is important to you, then your purpose can become clearer to you. When contemplating your purpose, it is much the same thing. You are trying to figure out what is the most important things to you and dedicating your life to that mission, that purpose. Your core values play a huge role in that process. This is like figuring out your passions. Typically, what is most important to you will drive those things you are most interested in doing and most passionate about.

- Provide guidance. Once you know your core values, you can use them in your daily life to guide your decision-making. This gives you a framework to evaluate the things you are doing in your life. Those are small decisions you make, like "Should I go on vacation this year or work?" or those bigger ones such as "Should I buy that big house, or would I be safer renting a nice apartment?"

- Predict current and future behavior. Much of your current and future behavior comes from your subconscious mind. You really don't think about your behavior in many cases; you simply react based on your instincts or past patterns derived from your subconscious mind. Wouldn't it be much better if you had some control over this instead of reacting without even knowing why? Core values can be a great predictor of your current and future behavior. Once you consciously understand what drives you, it provides a framework for thinking about the future. When you have control over your behavior, you can more effectively control the outcome. If one of your core values is valuing relationships over advancing in your career, you are probably more likely to forego getting a promotion or even making more money rather than hurting someone just to get ahead. Trust me, there are plenty of people who value money over relationships and will do whatever it takes to get ahead.

- Help in your decision-making. When making decisions, you can use core values to measure that decision against your list of core values ranked in order of importance. Look at the decision you are trying to make and take measure that the decision is based on your highest ranked core value. Are they in sync with one another, or are they in conflict? Let's say you are trying to make a decision on whether to have another child (a pretty big decision). Review your core values and see how important family is to you as it relates to other things you might value, such as freedom or even money (more kids cost more money). As you can see, knowing your core values can be a very handy tool for you to use.

- Enhances your relationships. Core values are beginning to sound like the cure for just about everything in your life. Well, maybe they are. In fact, core values are the basis for most relationships, including your love relationship. If you want the secret to creating a successful and fulfilling relationship, understanding core values is the key. First, start off with understanding your own core values. The first step is to know your own core values and effectively communicate them to your partner. The next step is to get your partner to do the same thing. Have him or her go through the core value exercises in this book and figure out explicitly what is important and what drives them in his or her life. This knowledge is invaluable to better understanding your partner. While your core values don't need to be exactly the same to have a successful relationship, you can do a much better job at communicating with them and working with them as a life partner when you know this information. There is a lot more you will discover once you start understanding the core values of your partner (or even a friend or business associate).

STEP 3 – GET CLEAR

Consider this: there are no wrongs or rights with your core values. They are your core values, so they can't be wrong. While you might feel that society or your friends or family might rank things differently, you don't need to subscribe to what society might believe. For example, let's say you value money over having a loving relationship, and you marry someone for money and not love. Well, society (and your friends and family) might say that is horrible. How could you value money over love? Who does that? Well, you might do that. It doesn't make you a bad person because someone else may value things differently. In fact, many people value different things. That is what makes us all unique. And you can't judge someone else's values and not allow someone else to judge how you rank your core values. If other people or society overly influences you, then your core values won't be in alignment with who you really are. It will be very difficult to live using someone else's core values.

Core Values Workshop

The core values workshop is going to walk you step-by-step in determining your specific core values. They are actually pretty easy to come up with, and I will guide you through the process. It will be painless, I promise.

First, I want to get you thinking about what is most important in your life. What do you really value in life? Where do your focus and attention go when in a certain situation? These ultimately determine how you might act. What decisions will you instinctively make based on your values?

Second, we will create what I call "guiding principles" for your life. These are your most important core values put into a rank order. This is critical when using core values to obtain clarity, take action, and make decisions about your life. Let's get started.

Step 1: Brainstorm What Is Important to You

Answer the following questions. I suggest you provide no more than five answers for each one, even if this forces you to be a bit selective. Please note that some of these questions might sound a bit redundant. We are looking for patterns, so it is fine to use similar answers. At the end, we will discover these patterns, and they will lead us to your core values.

1. What do you get most excited about?

2. What things give you lots of energy?

3. What things do you really enjoy doing? What gets you out of bed in the morning, excited for the day ahead?

4. What do you spend your time on?

5. What do you spend your money on?

6. What do you love talking to people about? What topics of conversation keep coming up for you when talking with friends and family?

7. What things grab your attention?

8. What part of your life seems to be the most aligned to you? In other words, what part of your life seems to be working the best?

9. What do you fantasize or dream about?

To get you started thinking about your own answers, here are my own:

1. What do I get most excited about?

    a. Helping people live their dreams

    b. Running businesses that help make the world a better place

    c. Speaking in front of large groups of people to educate them in some way

    d. Traveling the world and exploring new places

2. What things in my life give me lots of energy?

    a. Speaking to large groups

    b. Talking to people about living a prosperous life

    c. Helping people achieve something

3. What things do you really enjoy doing? What gets you out of bed in the morning, excited for the day ahead?

    a. Growing businesses

    b. Learning new things

    c. Nurturing loving relationships

     d. Playing with my godchildren

     e. Spending time with my friends

4. What do you spend your time on?

     a. Running my business and creating new ones

     b. Working out

     c. Traveling

     d. Writing

     e. Studying and learning new things

5. What do you spend your money on?

     a. Travel

     b. Friends

     c. Relaxation and comfort

     d. Educating myself

6. What do you love talking to people about? What topics of conversation keep coming up for you when talking with friends and family?

     a. How people can live better (and more prosperous) lives

     b. My travels

     c. My business and new business ideas or helping people with their businesses

     d. Other people's relationships

7. What things grab your attention?

     a. Beautiful things (art, glass, people, architecture, and so forth)

     b. Exploring new places

     c. Nature

     d. Successful people and businesses

8. What part of your life seems to be the most aligned to you?

     a. My friends and closely held relationships

     b. My business and wealth

    c. My travels

    d. My possessions (I have most everything I want)

9. What do you fantasize or dream about?

    a. A family with kids

    b. Even more travel or living in another country

    c. A loving relationship

    d. A beautiful house with spectacular views

    e. Writing a book and speaking on things that help people live prosperous lives

Step 2: Ego Check

Review the list of questions you just came up with and see whether any of your answers are coming from your ego rather than from the essence of who you really are. Which of your answers involves acquiring more things just to boost your ego or gaining more power just for the sake of having power over others? The important thing here is to look at where your motivation is coming from. Why do you want what you want? The fact you want to make a lot of money doesn't necessarily mean you are coming from ego. Look at why you want to make a lot of money. Do you want lots of possessions so you can be "better" than other people, or do you want to make lots of money so you can help people with it? It's all about your motivation.

Go back through your list and highlight all the ones you think are coming from your ego. That means the items on your brainstorming list where your motivation is to show the world what you have or that you are better than someone else. This will tell you what is driving you: your ego or your heart. We want to focus on the items that are coming from your heart.

Step 3: Create Your List of Values

Here's the best way to create your list of values. Review the brainstorm we did in step one and look for patterns and themes that keep coming up for you. What should emerge from these patterns is a strong indication as to what you value in life. Here is a list of my values:

- I value travel.
- I value helping people.

- I value the thrill of creating new businesses.
- I value my relationships with my friends.
- I value travel and adventure.
- I value success (mine and others).
- I value looking and feeling good physically.
- I value learning new things in life.
- I value wealth and creature comforts.

With this list of values, you're that much closer to an understanding of yourself and the clarity you need to continue to the next step in your journey.

Step 4: Create Your Hierarchy of Values

This is the most critical step in this exercise: prioritizing your values in order of importance to you (or what I call serial ranking your values). Based on the list you created above, ask yourself, "Which of these values are most important to me at this moment in time?"

You will always act in alignment to your highest value, which is relevant to the situation or circumstance you find yourself facing. These values guide you through your entire life. This explains a lot about who you are and why you do what you do.

Rewrite your list of values in hierarchical order. I suggest you go one step further and memorize this list of values by writing it on a card or printing it out and placing it somewhere you look at frequently.

Discovering Your Passions

How many times have you asked yourself, "What am I really passionate about?" I have asked myself this question many times throughout my life. I still ask it because passions can change. As you grow and learn new things, your perspective on life also

Would you like to better understand the people in your life? All you have to do is understand their hierarchy of values. Strangely enough, they also act exactly in alignment to their hierarchy of values. All you have to do is run through this exercise, but instead of writing down your values, write down theirs. People show what they value to you by their actions, so it's really easy to figure this out.

Want to take it one step further? Once you know the hierarchy of values for anyone in your life, you now have the key to relating better to him or her. If you can act, speak, or both in accordance to their most important values, you will see them completely change when they relate to you because you are now speaking.

changes. New lessons you learn might open new possibilities for you that take your passions and your life into a whole new direction. In my opinion, this is the exciting thing about life. It is always changing and very unpredictable — well, unpredictable if you are working on living a prosperous life, that is.

Can you imagine a life where each day you wake up living whatever you are truly passionate about? Maybe it is your career, your family, helping others, or something else. Maybe you are already living your passions every day. What new passions can you develop to allow yourself to grow even more? The great thing about passions is they keep going and going, just like growth. This happens throughout your life, so uncover and embrace them.

God or your higher source gave you your passions. They are tightly connected to your purpose here on earth. I also believe you have a responsibility — even an obligation — to your higher source to live out these passions in this lifetime. You were given these gifts so you could share them with the world in a very special way. Why else would you have them?

Your passions are very closely tied to your core values. All the work we did in the last section will pay off here. With most people, the things that are most important to you are also the things you are most passionate about.

I can tell you today that I am living my passions, so I assure you that it is possible. This isn't to say that I don't have lots of new things I want to do, but each day, I wake up with passion, excited for the day and the things I get to do. Whether it is traveling to new lands and exploring new things, running my own business, or meeting new people, I can't wait to see what life has in store for me each day.

Unfortunately, there are many people out there who don't know whether they are living their passions because they are unclear about what they are. Maybe you have never gone through a formal process of figuring out exactly what you are passionate about. Or maybe you knew your passions when you were younger but have since lost them. Or maybe you have realized some passions, then stopped and didn't uncover any new ones. That is okay — we're going to fix that right now.

A Burning Desire

You know that feeling deep inside you. When you start thinking about your life's purpose and your passions, there is an almost indescribable feeling that says to your soul that you need to execute a specific passion. It is almost like you have no choice in the matter. It is something you were put on this earth to do.

While it is hard to describe a burning desire, that is my attempt at it. Have you felt it before? Do you have a burning desire for something? That is a passion that is waiting to burst out of you. I have had that feeling before. I have known since my early twenties that I wanted to teach people about living a better and more fulfilled life. I have no idea where it even came from. It was just something that felt right for me. It took over twenty years and lots of life experiences to begin to even realize this passion with the writing of this book. But that burning desire has been burning for that many years.

Having a burning desire for something is a critical ingredient to living your passions. It provides the essential motivation to propel you forward. As you are living your passions and experiencing new things, I assure you that some self-doubt will creep into your mind space. This burning desire provides lots of the energy to break through that self-doubt and to know you are doing exactly what you are supposed to be doing. I would suggest to you that if you have a passion for something, then you are already on the right track merely by having the passion to begin with. So get rid of the self-doubt and focus all your energies on living your passions.

Discovering Your Passions

Below is a procedure to help you get clear on your passions. But first, here are some guidelines to help you think about them.

Don't Censor Yourself

Remember, your passions come from your heart, so don't let your brain censor you. Just focus on getting your passions down on paper. Open your heart and just dream about what could be. There is no need to worry about the "how"; focus on the "what." We will get to the "how" later. If you start thinking too much about your passions, it will be quite difficult to really get them out of you. Don't think them — feel them.

Be Unrealistic

It might take years to develop the skills to really execute your passions, so don't worry if they seem unrealistic now. As you start to set a course toward those passions, they will become less unrealistic as you get closer to them. Growth is an amazing thing, isn't it?

When I was studying to get my MBA, I always knew I wanted to be an entrepreneur, but I never thought I would create one of the leading e-commerce software companies in the world. When I look at it today, it doesn't seem like a huge achievement, but if someone had told me I would create this while in school, I would have thought they were crazy. How the heck would I do that? I had no idea how to run a big business like that. Hmm ... now I am doing it. So be unrealistic.

Your Passions Exist in the Present

Don't look in the past or the future for your passions. They are right in front of you, here and now. You might have new passions that arise in the future, so let's leave those for the future.

You are never too old to discover and live your passions. Sure, there might be some physical limitations if your passion is to play in the NFL and you are sixty years old. But you might have heard the story of the lady who was eighty-five and graduated from college. Why not?

Passions Aren't Goals

I don't want you to get passions confused with goals. Passions are much more emotional and come from the heart. Your passions may not be about achieving something; they just might be a way of life. I think of passions as being much bigger than goals. They might transcend many of the goals in your life.

Don't Underestimate Yourself

Please don't underestimate your abilities. Your abilities will come if you have a burning desire to realize your passions. Remember, that passion wouldn't have been put there by your higher source if you didn't have the talents and abilities to actually manifest it.

Exercise: Uncovering Your Passions

All right, let's get to work and start uncovering those passions, keeping the above guidelines in mind. Even if you think you already know your passions, work through this exercise. You might be surprised, since passions have a way of changing as you grow. And if you are already

STEP 3 – GET CLEAR

living passions in certain areas of your life, it's now time to consider passions you might have in other areas of your life.

Step 1: Answer These Questions

Below is a series of questions about what excites and motivates you. Remember to keep an open mind, think big, and don't edit anything. For each question, feel free to list as many answers as you would like. Try to produce at least three answers per question. Push yourself if you have to. Let's start off by closing your eyes again, taking ten deep breaths to relax you, and getting your mind energy flowing. Then answer the following:

Question	Passions
What gets you really excited?	
What inspires you?	
What do you tend to focus on?	
What do you do in your free time?	
What hobbies do you enjoy doing?	
Whose life would you love to live and why?	
What are you drawn to and grabs your attention?	
What magazines, newspapers, and books do you read?	
If you had a million dollars, what would you spend the money on?	
What things do you love talking to your friends about?	

You will find that this exercise and the exercise you did for core values are quite similar. As you know, core values and passions are very closely linked.

Step 2: Look for Common Themes

Now we have a big list of things you are interested in, excited about, and motivated for. Read through the list and pick out themes that seem to repeat themselves. What are those things you love to do? What are those things you love to think about and talk to others about? Maybe it's playing with your kids, running your business, playing sports and competing, learning something, making money, taking international vacations, and so forth. I suggest coming up with at least ten themes. Here are some of mine:

- I love anything that helps people live a great life.

- I love running a business.

- I love working out and staying fit.

- I love being with my friends and family.

- I enjoy nature and activity.

- I love to travel a lot and explore.

- I love animals.

- I love relaxation.

- I love luxury.

- I love to learn new things.

Step 3: The Ultimate Question

Now it's time for the ultimate question. By answering this question, you will be able to focus on your passions. Write down ten answers. It is important that you give ten answers so you can really flush these passions out of your brain. I would also suggest no more than ten, because

STEP 3 – GET CLEAR

it might become overwhelming. Don't worry about the order currently. We will get to that in a moment. All right, here's the question in a fill-in-the-blank form:

I am living my prosperous life when I am _____.

This ultimate question really gets you to focus on those things you are passionate about and the things you want to manifest. Here is my top-ten list of things I am passionate about:

Learning something new every day to develop myself and grow as a person
Helping people around the world to live a better life
Sharing my experiences and lessons with other people
Feeling great physically, and being active every day
Running my successful businesses, which people enjoy, and making the world a better place
Raising my child to become an amazing person
Having a close group of friends and family and the time to spend with them
Traveling and exploring the world, and learning new things about places, people, and things
Sharing my life and experiences with an amazing life partner, whom I can grow with
Helping people through my philanthropic activities

Step 4: Rank Order Your Top-Ten Passions

Take your list of passions and determine which is the most important, most meaningful one to you. This exercise isn't an easy one, so take your time. If you are having challenges prioritizing these passions, go through your list, take the first passion on your list, compare it to each of the other passions, and ask, "Which one is more important to me?" When you compare each passion against the other, one will emerge stronger. If you do this for each one, your rank-ordered list will be created.

STEP 3 – GET CLEAR

1.	
2.	
3.	
4.	
5.	
6.	
7.	
8.	
9.	
10.	

Here is my rank-ordered list, just in case you were curious. I assure you it wasn't easy for me to come up with this list either, so I can appreciate the challenge.

1.	Helping people around the world to live a better life
2.	Learning something new every day to develop myself and grow as a person
3.	Running my successful businesses, which people enjoy, and making the world a better place
4.	Raising my child to become an amazing person
5.	Traveling, exploring the world, and learning new things about places, people, and things

6.	Sharing my life and experiences with an amazing life partner, whom I can grow with
7.	Feeling great physically and being very active every day
8.	Helping people through my philanthropic activities
9.	Having a close group of friends and family, and the time to spend with them
10.	Sharing my experiences and lessons with other people

Check out **KenBurke.com** for the Companion Guide that
contains useful worksheets for this exercise.

Wow. Every time I do this exercise, I learn something new about myself. I am the kind of person who wants to do everything in life and go for it, so it's hard to put things in the lower slots on the list. These are my passions, and they are all important, so how can I even think of prioritizing things so low? Then I remind myself that out of all the things that can be done in the world, this is my top-ten list, so yes, they are all important, regardless of where they sit on my list. I hope you learn something new about yourself as well.

Step 5: The Passion Matrix

Now that you've got your list of top passions ranked in order, we're going to add a couple more pieces of information to create what I call the "passion matrix," which will bring all you need to know about your passions into a single place. I highly recommend that, after you complete this, you refer back to it regularly. Put it on your refrigerator door or tape it to a mirror. I have mine on a note card in my journal, which I carry with me everywhere. For each passion in your list, do the following:

Identify Which Area of Life Your Passion Impacts

This helps you see whether there is an area of your life you want to focus on more specifically.

STEP 3 – GET CLEAR

Determine Why Each Passion Is Important to You

Does it give you energy? Does it make you happy? Does it provide a sense of fulfillment? Does it make you a better person or help you grow and learn new things? Understanding why these passions are important to you provides additional emotional connections to your heart, which will help you to act on these passions.

Finally, Match Your Passions to Your Core Values

Do a gut check against your core values. Make certain each of your passions is aligned with them.

	Passion	Area of Life	Why Important?	Core Values
1.				
2.				
3.				
4.				
5.				
6.				
7.				
8.				
9.				
10.				

For those of you following my journey, here is my completed passion matrix:

Passion	Area of Life	Why Important?	Core Values
Helping people around the world to live better lives	Career	Fulfilling my life's purpose	Yes
Learning something new every day to develop and grow as a person	Growth and Learning	It makes me feel a sense of fulfillment and growth when I learn new things.	Yes
Running my successful businesses, which people enjoy, and making the world a better place	Career	It is extremely exhilarating to create something out of nothing and watch it grow.	Yes
Raising my child to become an amazing person	Relationships and Family	This would be the ultimate growth experience for me.	Yes
Traveling, exploring the world, and learning new things about places, people, and things	Growth and Learning	It is extremely stimulating to learn about the world firsthand, and it makes me very happy.	Yes
Sharing my life and experiences with an amazing life partner, with whom I can grow	Relationships and Family	I learn so much about myself by loving someone else. Giving love and support to that person fulfills me.	Yes
Feeling great physically and being active every day	Physical Life and Health	It makes me feel great about myself to look and feel good physically.	Yes
Helping people through my philanthropic activities	Giving Back	There is complete fulfillment when giving to others you don't even know to make their lives better.	Yes

| Having a close group of friends and family and the time to spend with them | Relationships and Family | It makes me feel warm and happy inside. | Yes |
| Sharing my experiences and lessons with other people | Growth and Learning | It gives me incredible positive energy. | Yes |

Check out **KenBurke.com** for the Companion Guide that contains useful worksheets for this exercise.

The Power of Your Passions

Now you've got a complete understanding of your passions. Why the heck is this so important? Getting crystal clear on your passions will allow you to focus on the things that really matter to you. This attention and focus will allow you to manifest these passions. It really is that simple.

Discovering Your Talents

Now that you've identified your values and passions, it's time to move to the final component of this trio: your God-given talents. Passions and talents are closely related. Just like passions, your talents come from your higher source. They are given to you at birth and are brought out as you live your life. Just like with passions, I strongly believe you have an obligation to use your talents. It is an obligation you should take very seriously because it is something God or the universe bestowed.

My thinking on this topic goes a bit further. You are doing the universe a disservice by not using your talents to the fullest. The point isn't about you or your ego; it is about your obligation to make the world a better place. You were given your talents for a reason, and that reason is clear: to use them! The answer really is that simple.

Talents and Your Ego

Before we get into our work to uncover your talents, a word of warning. Your talents don't come from you. They are given to you. It is important that you understand this. If you don't instill this belief into your mind-set, your ego will have a field day, taking credit for all your talents. Maybe you are super smart, great looking, a great athlete, or even a wonderful singer. While you have 100 percent responsibility and control over how you develop those talents, they aren't solely your creation, so don't let your ego get ahold of them.

People have a really hard time with this one because we all want to think our achievements, brilliance, or successes are all about us and something we create. Instead of having your ego take credit for all you have and achieve, replace that feeling with gratitude for all you have and give thanks for these incredible gifts and what you have been able to do with them. I assure you that the feeling of gratitude for what you have and the thanks you have for the universe is a much more powerful and long-lasting feeling than simply taking credit for your success.

Exercise: Uncovering Your Talents

Step 1: Inventory Your Talents

Start off by closing your eyes and taking ten deep breaths to relax yourself and to get your mind's energy flowing. Once you are relaxed, open your eyes and answer the questions below. List as many talents as you'd like for each question.

Question	Talents
What are you naturally good or great at?	
What subjects in school were you good at or came naturally to you?	
On what do people compliment you?	
What do you love to do?	
What do you do better than most people?	
What unique skills do you possess?	

STEP 3 – GET CLEAR

I also went through this exercise, and here is what I came up with. It might help you a bit to see how I answered these questions.

Question	Talents
What are you naturally good or great at?	Public speaking Leading and managing people Starting businesses Giving advice to people Being a caring and loving person Creating new ideas and working to manifest them
What subjects in school were you good at or came naturally to you?	Business Computers Math Strategy Psychology
What do people compliment you on?	Speaking abilities Being caring and empathetic Being a good boss Dressing with style
What do you love to do?	Creating and building businesses Public speaking Being creative Advising others Talking about my beliefs
What do you do better than most people?	Creating businesses Understanding people Communicating my ideas and thoughts
What unique skills do you possess?	Speaking

Step 2: Ask your Friends, Family, and Colleagues

This part might be a bit more difficult, but it's equally, if not more, important. I want you to ask five people who are close to you and know you pretty well. Try to ask at least one family member, one friend, and one colleague. This step will give you a bit more insight than just asking all friends or family members.

Their answers may surprise you. It is funny how other people's perspectives about us can be very different from our own. You just might find you are much more talented than you think. After people do this exercise, this is usually the case. I don't know why we don't give ourselves as much credit as other people do. One piece of advice: please make sure to remove any judgments from the answers you receive. Use this as input to make your life better. You are asking for their opinion, so welcome it and don't judge it.

We are going to keep this one pretty simple. Ask them, "What do you think my talents and special gifts are?" Ask each person to list a minimum of five talents and ask him or her which of these stands out above the rest.

Name of Person:

Question	Talents
What do you think my talents and special gifts are?	

Name of Person:

Question	Talents
What do you think my talents and special gifts are?	

Step 3: Summarize and Rank Order

Look for themes across your answers and the answers from the people you asked. What talents keep coming up over and over in your answers? Did you see those repeated in your friends' answers? Create a list of the top five to ten talents. Then rank the list so the most dominant talents have the highest rank.

STEP 3 – GET CLEAR

Rank Order List of Your Talents

1.	
2.	
3.	
4.	
5.	

You now have a clear, comprehensive understanding of your values, passions, and talents. You'll use these for the next big step on your way to clarity while figuring out your purpose.

Look over your answers for all three sheets and see what patterns and similarities you can spot. Reflect on what you see. Make a few notes about your insights. Use all this information to remind yourself of what matters most. What matters to you is clear; you just need to remember what it is.

To enhance your experience with this book, make sure to get the Companion Guide which contains valuable worksheets and other helpful resources.

Visit KenBurke.com

CHAPTER 16

Step 2: Determine Your Purpose

For everything else to work, you need to understand the idea of purpose and how it plays a role in your life. I know some of you avoid this question just like you avoid going to the dentist, but it is the fundamental question of your life. We are going to tackle it head on. But first, here is a little about myself as an example.

Long before I ever wanted to write a self-help book, I was clear in my purpose and have been stating it openly for many years to anyone who asked. (Of course, not that many people ever ask me about my purpose in my daily life.) Here it is: My purpose is to grow and develop as a human, making myself better each day so I can serve others to the best of my abilities.

This is simple but also very powerful. The cornerstone of my purpose is to serve others. Notice my purpose isn't about myself, and I certainly hope it's not ego driven but rather about being a better person so I can serve others more effectively. This is what drives my desire to grow, develop, and learn new things. This growth allows me to share my growth with others.

Once I understood my purpose, everything started to fall into place. The world opened up. Now I have the insatiable desire to learn as much as I can about pretty much everything: from how the world works to understanding other cultures, to understanding how to run a business, to learning to cook, to learning Italian, to playing the piano ... The list goes on and on. My desire to learn is driven by my greater desire to share my knowledge and insights with others. This really becomes clear for me when I fantasize about helping people live prosperous lives. Nothing excites me more. That is why I have read hundreds upon hundreds of books over the last twenty years, and it is why I work on living what I have learned every day. Every day is like being in school for me as I learn, grow, and make new distinctions in my life.

Why is your purpose important to understand? You have a choice. You can choose to ignore your purpose and live without knowing if you are living for the reason you were put on this earth. Or you can choose to embrace your purpose and experience a deeper meaning as to why you are here and what you are supposed to do. You aren't just here to breathe the oxygen and take up space. You really are here for a reason, so let's figure out what that is. And if you have already done so, let's just check in to make sure you are still on point.

Understanding your purpose will provide you with tremendous guidance throughout your life. You have so many things you can do with your life that it is mind-blowing. I know so many people who get completely overwhelmed with even the thought of having to make choices. In fact, I am one of those people. I am the kind of person who wants to do everything. I have a hundred lifetimes of stuff to cram into this one little life. I don't want to miss anything.

You can be a father or mother, writer or surfer, singer or farmer. How does one decide? That's where purpose comes in. Once you begin to get clear on your purpose, you will discover a framework for making decisions. When you're wondering what you should do, you can go back to your purpose and evaluate your choices against it and make a decision that will be in alignment with your purpose.

Keep in mind that none of this is set in stone. *Your purpose can be anything you want it to be, and it can change anytime you want it to.* It is all up to you. Remember, it's your life, not someone else's.

> *"Your purpose can be anything you want it to be, and it can change anytime you want it to."*

Components of Purpose

Understanding your mission in life is a foundational piece of the puzzle for the continual process of obtaining and retaining clarity in your life. It is interesting because it is both the starting point and the ending point. There are a host of other components to clarity that you also need to figure out to refine your purpose. These pieces actually work together to create your story.

To determine your purpose, I have found it important to understand your values, passions, talents, and burning desire. We will go through a bunch of exercises to help figure all these things out, and then we will come back to purpose to see whether we need to make any adjustments. But I also want you to start working on your purpose statement in this step as well.

Let's take a look at each component of purpose to help connect the dots.

Values

Understanding your values is probably the most important part of truly getting clarity in your life. Values are simply those you hold near and dear to your heart. It is funny because everyone has values, but few people actually explicitly know them. Well, in this book, we are going to explicitly know them because they are at the very core of what drives you and makes you tick. You will be amazed by how much you can learn from understanding your values.

To get to your core values, you really need to ask yourself some really good questions, and they will just pop right out of you. The basic questions to ask are, what do you value in life? What are those beliefs that are really important to you?

Understand that values deal more with your belief system than actually with what you do. What you believe and what you do can actually be two different things. Also, your belief system can trick you, so we have to be careful. As we learned earlier, you can have a lot of limiting beliefs that serve little to no purpose in your life.

To really understand your purpose, you must understand what drives you, and that comes from your core values.

Passions

While values can be a bit tricky to come up with, discovering what you are passionate about should be much easier. Passions are key indicators to why you are here on earth; that's your purpose. I like to think that passions come from something outside us (and our egos). I think they are more God inspired than anything else. Hence, this is why purpose (which is also God inspired) and passions are so closely linked.

STEP 3 – GET CLEAR

The primary tool to finding your passions is to ask really good questions. I have a bunch of them coming up, but for now, just ask yourself, what am I really passionate about? What gets me super jazzed when I think about it? What gets me up in the morning, energized to face the day?

Talents

Just like purpose and passions, I believe your talents are also God inspired. Why are you good at what you are good at? How did you get that way? I am not asking you to answer these questions but rather to consider the possibility that something outside you created these talents. Could it actually be possible that you aren't responsible for your talents? Is it possible that your ego can't claim ownership to all the things you are really good at? I would suggest that it's possible. Not only possible, but, in fact, this is how it all works. You didn't create your talents as you would like to think.

Yet another key indicator of your purpose is what your God-inspired talents are. Ask yourself, what am I really good at? We will run through a number of exercises a bit later, but for now, just think about that. And ask yourself how you think that answer relates to your overall purpose.

Burning Desire

This is the magical ingredient to living on purpose. A burning desire provides you with that fire in your belly, that motivation that gets you up every morning, so excited you can't wait for the day to begin and never want it to end. Does this sound crazy to you? Well, I have to say I wake up (almost) every morning with this belief.

You can't fake a burning desire. It's something deep inside you that has so much energy surrounding it that you almost can't control it. That desire comes from living on purpose. Once you really understand your purpose, you will see each day how you are aligned with it. That alignment is energizing and creates this burning desire I am talking about it.

You will know when you feel it. It's a bit like falling in love. Love is hard to describe, but you know it when you feel it. That is exactly how a burning desire works (well, at least for me). Here are some characteristics of a burning desire so you will know when it happens to you:

1. Your brain might start racing, with new ideas constantly flowing through you.

2. You might have a hard time focusing because you are so damn excited about what is.

3. You might feel butterflies in your stomach because of the extra excitement in your system (and possibly even a bit of nerves when you're trying new things aligned with your purpose).

4. You might find it hard to control talking to people about what you are doing.

A burning desire is truly magical; it is better than any drug or alcoholic drink. It's life's ultimate high.

Each of these is a pointer to your purpose. Once you start understanding your core values, passions, talents, and burning desire, you will start to understand your purpose. You can now see that discovering your purpose isn't such an overwhelming task but something each of us has the power to discover.

Guidelines to Discovering Your Purpose

If you are having trouble taking the last step to make it completely clear, here are a few tips to make it easier. These are a few things people get hung up on. I have seen these come up as I have worked with people on discovering their purpose.

Relax

Trying to define your purpose sounds like such a big deal that people get very tense. I suggest you just sit back and relax when contemplating this. Spend some quiet time either meditating or just sitting and breathing for fifteen minutes or half an hour. It's important that you still your brain a bit and let the energy flow through you.

Don't Overthink It

This is such a big topic that you really want to get it right, so this might sound strange. But if you overthink this, you will block your brain, and you'll have trouble coming up with what is really inside you. Trust your gut; you want to come up with the things that are true to you, not things your analytical brain creates. You can't get analytical when defining purpose, so if you have a tendency to do so, just watch for it. Your purpose is already inside you, so all you need to do is bring it out and make it visible to your consciousness.

Disregard the Opinions of Others

Your purpose is your purpose, not someone else's. You have many influences in your life, including your family, friends, lovers, children, bosses, and so forth. I am sure they all have opinions about your life and what or who you should be. But they aren't living your life; you are. I am a big fan of listening to feedback and adjusting my behavior if I feel it is in alignment with me, but when it comes to discovering purpose, it has to come from within.

Be Specific

To make your purpose actionable, it needs to be specific. Otherwise, it won't provide you with much guidance. For example, some people might say the purpose of life is to be happy. That's a good goal, but saying a bit more about what it means to be happy might give you more guidance. For example, I feel happiness and gratitude each day for my family, my career, and my service to others. Specifics give you more to focus on.

Decide

I think this is the most important tip I can give you about purpose: just decide. After you have done some good thinking and reflection, decide what it is and put your energy into motion around that purpose. Remember, there are no wrong decisions in life. There are no mistakes, because you will learn from whatever direction you set for yourself. If you realize your initial purpose isn't in alignment with you, you can always adjust it. You can also adjust your passions, talents, and even core values if needed. Then you can refocus and commit to your new direction. Any action you take will give you useful information to help you revise your purpose or take a new direction if needed. So please, I beg you, just decide. This is one of the most important ingredients to clarity.

Living in Alignment with Your Purpose

Once you understand your purpose, it's very important that you do regular check-ins to make certain you are living in alignment with it. In fact, every decision you make should be evaluated against your purpose, values, passions, and talents. I suggest doing these check-ins twice a year. I have gotten into the habit of checking in at the beginning of the year and then again over the summer. Another good time for a check-in would be right around your birthday, because it is a key time when you might become more introspective.

If you are in alignment, you will know it. Things just seem to fall into place. Life becomes a bit easier, and you feel happier. When you're living in alignment with your purpose, this will give you energy. I think of it as an extra boost from the universe. I believe energy builds on itself. When you have positive energy pushing you forward, it makes everything that much easier.

You might have also experienced the opposite effect. Have there been times when you felt out of alignment with your purpose? Maybe a time when things weren't going so well, and it seemed like everyone was out to get you? Do you remember how that felt? You know when you are out of alignment with your purpose; you just don't always know how to identify it as such. Once you identify it, you can control it and act upon it. Here are some indicators to watch for. When you recognize these in your life, this is probably a sign you're not living in alignment with your purpose.

You Are Uncomfortable or Anxious

If you are regularly feeling anxious or uncomfortable, it's time to check in to see why that is the case. I would suggest it's a lack of clarity. Typically, when you feel anxious, it's about something that might happen in the future or something you are doing now that will impact the future. Once you fully understand that everything you do leads to your purpose, then this anxiety goes away. When you are aligned with purpose, you don't experience anxiety regularly.

You Feel Stuck

This is a big one for a lot of people, whether it's in regard to a relationship or your career. But once you put everything in perspective with your purpose, your path on how to get unstuck will start to emerge.

STEP 3 – GET CLEAR

You Easily Get Frustrated or Angry

Clarity of purpose can help reduce or eliminate these frustrations. Believe it or not, there are people in this world who don't experience these negative emotions very often, if at all. Why not? I would say it's because they understand who they are and where they are going. In other words, they have clarity.

You Easily Get Tired or Stressed

When things are flowing and you are aligned with your purpose and where you want to go in life, your stress levels will be reduced. I can honestly tell you that I experience very little stress in my life, and the stress I do experience is when I am not aligned with my purpose and not doing the things that help me grow.

You Aren't Loving Yourself

Not feeling love for yourself is a key indicator that something is out of alignment. Your activities and behaviors are moving you away from your purpose. You will be much happier if you know your purpose and realize you are growing in that direction. It is much easier to love yourself when your life is flowing in the direction you want it to. And there's no question you will experience more happiness when you are living on purpose.

Exercise: Discover Your Alignment with Your Purpose

Determining whether you are aligned with purpose is really a simple process of comparing your stated purpose with where you think you are in life. I like to evaluate each area or activity of my life as it relates to my purpose a couple of times a year. Next, I determine for each area or activity whether I am moving closer or further away from my purpose. This helps me figure out the areas I need to focus on. Finally, I look at what actions I might need to make either to change my direction, if I am moving away, or to accelerate.

Area of Life	Movement	Actions to Correct or Support Alignment
Relationships and Family		
Career		
Money		
Physical Life and Health		
Growth and Learning		
Spiritual Life		
Giving Back		

Roadblocks to Your Purpose

Finally, if you're still having trouble determining your purpose or figuring out how to live in alignment with it, you might be struggling with one of the following roadblocks. Just recognizing one of these in your life can help you start to reverse it.

Roadblock 1: Avoidance

Plain and simple, some people just don't want to think about purpose. For many of us, the idea is so massive that we would rather just not deal with it. But if you break it down, you can learn about yourself a bit at a time and arrive at your purpose. The key is just beginning.

Roadblock 2: Ego

Your ego can block your ability to get clear about your purpose, so watch out. Your purpose doesn't come from your ego; it comes from your spirit. Just do a gut check to make certain your purpose isn't ego-driven, like riches, fame, or power. These won't motivate you to achieve anything of meaning.

Roadblock 3: Fear of the Future

The future is not something to be feared but embraced. Once you put your life in a growth perspective, the fear can cease, and the future becomes quite exciting. As long as you are growing, it is impossible to fail, so fear, which is almost always the fear of failure, simply goes away.

Roadblock 4: Limiting Yourself

When you are living from ego, you will limit yourself to avoid getting hurt or damaged. Your ego thinks it's protecting you. When working with purpose, you have to be careful not to limit yourself or what you can achieve. It is my strong belief that you can achieve almost anything you want. (I say "almost" because there are some things that are physically impossible.) Don't put limits on your purpose in life. Your life is a magical gift you have been given, so use it to its fullest.

Roadblock 5: Living Someone Else's Purpose

Have you ever done something big mainly because someone else, like your parents or partner, wanted you to? Maybe it was attending a certain college or taking that job you really didn't want. And you knew in your heart it was a bad decision, but you did it anyway. Don't be overly influenced by someone else's opinion of what you should do or be. Your purpose comes from deep inside you, not from someone else. If you are being overly influenced, then acknowledge it and use it as input to your decision-making if you think the opinion is valuable.

Now that you know your purpose, it's time to take the next step toward your prosperous life by unleashing your creativity and dreaming about the endless possibilities awaiting the new you. But first, let's check in on that burning desire again. Did something surface for you as you were doing the exercises in this step? Did your work with your values, talents, or passions bring something to light that maybe you'd repressed or were too scared to embrace? If so, you're well on your way toward a purpose and taking action. If not, don't worry; you're going to expand your mind in the next step. Remain watchful and honest, and you'll feel that momentum building.

Living on Purpose

Now that we have some direction on understanding your purpose, it's very important that you do regular checking in to make certain you are living in alignment with your purpose. In fact, each decision you make in your life should be evaluated against these key ingredients to clarity.

CHAPTER 17

Step 3: Dream about What You Really Want

Get ready to have some fun! While coming up with your purpose can be lots to think about and can weigh heavily on your thoughts, this next step is nothing but pure fun and excitement. Dreaming about what you want out of life is really the starting point for exploring your dreams and making them come true. This is where it all begins, so hold on tight, because here we go.

Your imagination is an extremely powerful tool for you to use in living a prosperous life. It's like gold. In fact, I would suggest it's more valuable to you than anything you possess, including your relationships or any successes you might have achieved. Your imagination is what creates your future.

Your imagination is limitless; anything (and I mean *anything*) you want to create starts first in your imagination. Many of you have heard the expression "thoughts are things." Everything you create comes first from a thought generated in your imagination. Just like with anything else, you can learn to tap into your imagination more effectively. The more you do it, the better you get. In this section, we are going to explore ways to tap into your imagination and to draw out those things you want to manifest more specifically. When you get clear on what is in your imagination, you have a much higher chance of manifesting it.

STEP 3 – GET CLEAR

Understand that your imagination isn't just filled with random stuff but rather thoughts that are based on your core values. Your fantasies manifest from things you feel are important to do or to have. They develop from vague ideas to tangible, actionable tasks that lead you on your way toward manifesting what you desire. There is no magic to this stuff. Thoughts grow in your imagination like a plant grows when it is watered. The more you think about something, the more you are watering your thoughts. These thoughts turn into things via your actions. It's that simple.

I have a belief I feel is very important, and I really want you to understand it. I believe you have these thoughts because you are supposed to follow them, that you are supposed to grow and manifest these new things. I'm not saying to act on every thought in your head, but those thoughts that really resonate with you are there to help you learn and grow. So you should follow your instincts and act on them. You won't always know why at the beginning, but some of the greatest growth comes from this drive.

Roadblocks to Dreaming

As you start the dreaming exercises, please watch for some of these roadblocks that will inevitably pop up as you work through your dreams. Just be aware of them, so when they do come up, you can acknowledge them. That is all you have to do to start removing the roadblock.

Roadblock 1: Limiting Beliefs

By now, you know all about limiting beliefs. Any belief that stops you from growing and moving your life forward is a potential limiting belief. When you fantasize, these beliefs will creep into your mind space for sure. Watch for them. When you start saying things like, "I can't," "I don't have," or "I am not," that is a good indication that you are introducing a limiting belief into your thinking. Don't go there.

Roadblock 2: Fears

Nothing will block your ability to fantasize more than fear. The fear of failure, rejection, or embarrassment brings pretty powerful emotions that will limit your ability to dream and to fantasize. Fear can stop you from even allowing your imagination to think those thoughts. It will shut that creative part of you down so fast that your end will spin.

Roadblock 3: Self-Doubt

Continual questioning of yourself and your abilities doesn't help when you are at the early stages of manifesting. As I said earlier, you can do absolutely anything you want. This self-doubt is only in your mind. When you find yourself questioning your dream over and over again, that is a good indication that self-doubt may be part of the equation. Asking questions to figure out whether a dream is in alignment with your core values is a good thing. Questioning whether you have the talent, money, or skill to do something might not be so good. If you have a burning desire about the things you are dreaming about, that might be all you need.

You have 100 percent control to eliminate it from your thinking. All you have to do is change the belief the self-doubt is coming from. Ask yourself why you hold that particular belief ("I am not smart enough," "I am too ugly or too fat," and so forth) and where it came from. Is this belief still serving a purpose in our life? Most likely it isn't, so decide to change it and replace it with a new belief, one that is more positive and supports your growth.

Roadblock 4: Obstacles

Remember, you are just dreaming. Right now, all this dreaming leads only to thoughts, so why would you have any obstacles at all? They are just ideas you might (and let me stress *might*) manifest someday. If you start thinking of all the obstacles that might be in your way (no money, no time, no support, and so forth), then you will block your dreams from even coming to the surface. You will immediately squash any thoughts.

Here is the interesting thing about obstacles: as you develop your dreams and start to make those thoughts turn into real successes, you will find that many of the obstacles you thought you might have don't actually materialize. They were just in your mind. Once you start working on this, things will appear in your life as you are working on manifesting your dreams. One of the biggest ones I hear is, "I don't have enough money to do that." Well, there are many ways to start small and break your dream down into small, bite-size pieces. Also, you might not have the money today, but if you can create one dollar, you can create two dollars, and so on. Money begets money. There are literally millions of ways to create money (legally 😊). You create money in your life for things you want to do one dollar at a time. Obstacles are absolutely no excuse for not dreaming and manifesting your future.

Roadblock 5: Getting Caught Up in the "How"

While you are dreaming, if you keep trying to figure out how something is going to happen, you will be stopped right in your tracks. This is a really hard one for people because many of us are quite practical. "I don't want to waste my time on dreaming about something unless I know how I am actually going to manifest it." Here is the good part about the dreaming process: you don't have to figure out how to manifest something. All you are trying to figure out at this point is what you want to manifest, not how you are going to manifest it. Trust me, we are going to get into the "how" a bit later in the clarity process. It is imperative that we separate the "what" from the "how."

Before you start putting up all these roadblocks, I want you to remember something. It isn't just that your imagination is limitless; *you* are also limitless. You can absolutely and unquestionably manifest anything you want to manifest. In one of my favorite books, *Outliers*, Malcolm Gladwell researched and surmised that if you want to master anything, you can do it in about ten thousand hours of work. This works with anything you want to master. That information really stuck with me. Some people might have more of a talent for certain things, but you can master what you want to master with ten thousand hours of practice. It is a powerful thought that says if you want it bad enough, you can have it.

Guidelines for Dreaming

Let's get started! Here are some guidelines to help you, because this stuff doesn't necessarily come easily for everyone.

Be Open to Everything

There is nothing you can't do, so don't start out by putting limits on yourself. Just be open to any possibilities. Give yourself permission to dream big. Don't think about how you are going to get things done. Focus on the "what," not the "how."

Make Sure It Is Your Dream

Check to make sure you are dreaming about things you want, not things someone else wants for you. This is your life, and these are your dreams. Check to ensure that whatever you are dreaming about is in alignment with your purpose, passions, and core values. If it isn't, then it might be someone else's dream.

Ignore Your Current Situation

So many people get wrapped up in their current lives that they find it hard to dream about anything. You aren't dreaming about your very next step but rather where you ultimately want to go and what you want to create. If you let your current situation come into your mind, you will limit your dreams. But this should be about what you can create, not about what you have already created.

Think Big

Don't limit yourself to "realistic" or "practical" dreams. Give yourself permission to dream big. If you don't dream big, you will never get big. If you can't conceive it, you will most assuredly not achieve it. So why not think big while you are dreaming? I guarantee you, there will be no harm in thinking big; you can always scale down your dreams later. Now is the time to go crazy with your dreams. Let's say you want to create a corner bakery. That is great, but maybe you want to own a chain of bakeries across the country. If you truly want to own only one store, then that can be your dream.

Get Out of Your Comfort Zone

Your comfort isn't likely to create a prosperous life for you. If you have a fear of speaking, for example, but you really want to touch millions of people with your teachings, then you might have to step out of your comfort zone to share your ideas. If you want to be a famous actor, then you better get used to auditioning and getting rejected. It's part of the process. Fear can stop you from even allowing your imagination to start working. It will shut that creative part of you down so fast that your head will spin. Remember, this exercise is just in your mind, so let go of fear and think big.

Be in the Present

Forget about your past. It isn't a predictor of the future. Learn from your experiences but don't live in them. If you were into drugs, did someone wrong, or ripped someone off, that doesn't mean it's who you are today. Leave that baggage in the past and focus on who you are today. It might sound strange to talk about being in the present when we are dreaming about the future. Just remember that you are here in this moment. You can dream about what you want to manifest, but remember to stay grounded in the present when you are thinking about what you want to create.

Don't Censor Yourself

If a thought comes into your head and it is in alignment with your core values, don't censor it. Go with it and turn it into a dream. You can always discard the thoughts you don't want to turn into dreams, so don't be afraid to explore things in your mind. It really isn't hard to delete a dream.

Don't Question Yourself

Continually questioning yourself and your abilities won't help when you are in the early stages of manifesting. Don't question whether you have the talent, money, or skill to do something. If you have a burning desire about your dreams, that might be all you need. But if you find yourself questioning your dream repeatedly, that might indicate your dream isn't in alignment with your core values. Check on this, and if it is in alignment, get rid of your self-doubt. You have nothing to lose at this stage.

Finally, Have Fun!

When you are working on creating a prosperous life, this is by far the most fun part of clarity, so have fun with this and enjoy the process. This is your time to knock down the boundaries and go crazy with the possibilities of what your life can truly be.

Tapping into Your Imagination

Guided Meditation

The best tool I have found to tap into my imagination is guided meditation. It is simple but very effective for dreaming. Sitting quietly and allowing your thoughts to pop into your mind space, while being fully relaxed, is absolutely the best method you can use to reach deep into your thoughts. Adding the guided piece to your meditation makes your dreaming even more effective. I am going to help you with this part. While meditating, I am going to have you ask yourself a series of questions that will spark your brain into a more structured way of thinking. This will allow you to get a bit more out of the dreaming process.

While we are doing a guided meditation, it is important to capture your thoughts on paper so we can refer back to them. We will stop after each question or two, allowing you time to write down your thoughts.

Journaling

My other favorite tool to tap into my imagination is writing in my journal. Call me strange, but I carry my journal everywhere. Sometimes I write just one page, and sometimes I write ten. It all depends on my mood. While the journal isn't the only thing I use to capture my dreams, it is a great tool to do so. This way, I get to jot down whatever thought pops into my mind. I also use my journal for working through a particular dream with more details (again just the "what," not the "how").

Exercise: Mastering the Art of Dreaming

Below are two different exercises to choose from: unstructured dreaming and structured dreaming. You are welcome to do both, but most people find that one or the other works best for them, because people think differently. Some are free flowing and just want to write down random ideas and thoughts while others love structure and guidance. Try them both and see which works better for you.

Unstructured Dreaming

Step 1: Find a quiet and relaxing place where you can't be interrupted during this process. Grab a nice cup of tea. Make certain you have a pen and paper beside you.

Step 2: Close your eyes and take some deep breaths. Focus on your breathing for a few minutes and get in tune with your body, letting your brain calm down. Let all the stress of the day melt away. If you are really tense and stressed, take as long as you need to begin to feel relaxed and calm.

STEP 3 – GET CLEAR

Step 3: When you are fully relaxed, ask yourself, "What is one thing that will move me closer to an even more prosperous life?" Or, put another way, "What is one thing I could create in my life that would make me happy or feel more fulfilled?"

As that thought enters your mind space, let it hang around there and take shape. See if you can add some detail to that thought or idea. When you are able to manifest this, how will it make you feel? How will it make others feel? How would it change your life for the better? How will this idea or thought allow you to grow?

Step 4: After working with this one idea or dream, take a few more deep breaths, open your eyes slowly, and jot down your first dream. Add a couple of bullet points with some details about what the dream is. Next, jot down how the idea would make you feel if you manifested it in your life. And finally, jot down how the idea would change your life and help you grow. Here is a handy template:

Idea or Dream	
A few details about the dream	
How will this change my life and allow me to grow?	

Step 5: Now repeat the process for your second dream. Get back into that comfortable and relaxed place. Close your eyes and take a few deep breaths. This time it will be much faster to get back into that relaxed state. Just sit back and let that next dream pop into your mind space.

People ask me all the time how many dreams they should create. I think it is up to you. Some people can handle only a few dreams at a time, while others want to figure out their entire lives all at once. I suggest no more than ten dreams for most people. If they are big dreams, like starting a business, developing a relationship, having children, buying a home, or making a million dollars, managing all those dreams at once can be quite daunting. If your objective is to get clarity around every aspect of your life, you can go with more dreams. But for most people, I suggest working with three to seven dreams.

Structured Dreaming

Structured dreaming provides you with a bit more detail on your dreams without interrupting your creative process. The big difference with this exercise is that you are going to focus on each area of your life rather than just randomly come up with dreams. Aim for one or two dreams for each area of your life but remember to build only as many as you feel you can handle. You can always create more later.

Step 1: Just like before, find a quiet and comfortable spot, and get relaxed and ready to meditate.

Step 2: Close your eyes and take some deep breaths. Focus on your breathing for a few minutes, get in tune with your body, and let your brain settle down.

Step 3: Pick the first area of your life you want to focus on and build your first dream. Again, here is the list:

- Relationships and Family

- Career

- Money

- Physical Life and Health

- Growth and Learning

- Spiritual Life

- Giving Back

Step 4: When you are fully relaxed, ask yourself, "What is one thing that will move me closer to an even more prosperous life?" Or, put another way, "What is one thing I could create in my life that would make me happy or feel more fulfilled?"

As that thought enters your mind space, just let it hang around there and take shape. See if you can add some detail to that thought or idea. When you are able to manifest this, how will it make you feel? How will it make others feel? How would it change your life for the better? How will this idea or thought allow you to grow? If you would like, start to fill in the thought with some details. Think more about what this idea is and how it can impact your life. Ask yourself, "How would this idea change my life for the better? How will this idea or thought allow me to grow?"

Step 5: After working with this one idea or dream, take a few more deep breaths, open your eyes slowly, and jot down your first dream. Add a couple of bullet points with some details about what the dream is. Next, jot down how the idea would make you feel if you manifested it in your life. And finally, jot down how the idea would change your life and help you grow.

In this exercise, I also want you to decide when you would like to manifest this dream. Think about when you would like to begin working on this dream and when you would like to fully manifest this. I have found this very useful because not everything you dream about will be something you want to put into action right away. That is okay. Most dreams have to sit in your brain for years before you take action on them.

Repeat the dreaming process for each area of your life, stopping the meditation each time to jot down your dream and some details.

Use the template below to complete the exercise for each area of your life.

Relationships and Family

Idea or Dream	
A few details about the dream	
How will this change my life and allow me to grow?	
Begin date or date to manifest	

Career

Idea or Dream	
A few details about the dream	

How will this change my life and allow me to grow?	
Begin date or date to manifest	

Money

Idea or Dream	
A few details about the dream	
How will this change my life and allow me to grow?	
Begin date or date to manifest	

Physical Life and Health

Idea or Dream	
A few details about the dream	
How will this change my life and allow me to grow	
Begin date or date to manifest	

Growth and Learning

Idea or Dream	
A few details about the dream	
How will this change my life and allow me to grow?	

STEP 3 – GET CLEAR

Begin date or date to manifest	

Spiritual Life

Idea or Dream	
A few details about the dream	
How will this change my life and allow me to grow?	
Begin date or date to manifest	

Giving Back

Idea or Dream	
A few details about the dream	
How will this change my life and allow me to grow?	
Begin date or date to manifest	

Check out **KenBurke.com** for the Companion Guide that
contains useful worksheets for this exercise.

CHAPTER 18

Create Your Personal Vision

Now you are getting down to business. You have all the main pieces for high-level clarity: values, passions, talents, and purpose. You dreamed about what you want if you could have anything to make your life prosperous. Now let's take all this great thinking and start applying it to your life right here and now.

Your personal vision sets your intention of what you want to achieve in your life. Intention is a critical component to manifesting. Your intention tells your brain exactly what you intend to do. Your intention can also tell the world what you intend to manifest.

What Is a Personal Vision?

A personal vision seems simple on the surface, but it is extremely powerful in getting you to focus on what is important in your life. A personal vision is really just your dream articulated in a way you and possibly others can understand. A vision is something you see in your mind's eye and feel in your heart. It's something that is so clear to you that you can't help but act on it. For me, a vision is also the knowledge of what I need to do to live my prosperous life.

Some people think a personal vision is a single vision statement for your entire life. While you should have a vision for your life, I have found it much more effective to have a personal vision statement for each area of your life. It can also be effective to create a vision for each major thing you want to manifest.

A vision can be expressed in a number of different ways. I think it is wise to create an actual vision statement for several reasons. First, it forces you to really think through your vision and commit to it. Second, when you write it down, you can refer back to it, allowing you to internalize it and make it part of your daily life. Third, it becomes something you can share with others, which also helps you reinforce it and take action on it. We are going to go through the process of creating vision statements for the things you want to do to make your life prosperous.

With nearly everything I have done in my adult life, I have created what I wanted to manifest in my mind's eye first and then in words. When I started high school, it was clear to me that I wanted to go to college and major in business. I could see myself graduating with a business degree and becoming a successful entrepreneur. I believed that to be a success in business, I had to get my MBA, so that is what I did. As I was working on that, my vision was clear that I was going to start my own business right after college. My vision continued with starting my own high-tech company. At the beginning, I must say I did not have a vision around how big it was going to be. I always knew it would be successful, but I was definitely not clear on exactly how to do it or how big it would be. My vision was refined as the business grew, and it became clear it was going to be a major player in the e-commerce software space.

It is my belief that without a vision statement and your ability to see what you want, you will struggle to manifest it. There are lots of people who are good at dreaming about what they want, but so many dreams go unfulfilled. A vision statement is the first big step to take you from just dreaming to doing.

Components of a Personal Vision

There are two primary components to a personal vision: the "what" and the "why."

What You Intend to Manifest

This is made up of the most important dreams you have in each area of your life. These dreams must be aligned with your values and purpose; otherwise, they will be much more difficult to achieve. I recommend that you look at no more than the top three things you want to create when coming up with your personal vision. It is easy to get overwhelmed if you try to cram everything you can think of into your vision statement. I have seen many vision statements that contain only one thing. That is okay. That's all you need for a vision statement.

Why You Want to Manifest It

For a vision to come to life, you have to understand why you really desire it. Try filling in this blank for each of your vision statements: "By manifesting this vision, I will experience more _____ in my life."

Here are a few examples of personal vision statements for different areas of life. I like to start vision statements with, "My vision is ..."

Area of Life	Personal Vision Statements
Physical Life or Health	My vision is to create a healthy and fit body I can look at and be happy with. I'm not looking for perfection or an ideal weight but rather a body I feel comfortable and confident with in my day-to-day life. I envision maintaining this healthy and fit body for many years to come.
Relationship	My vision is to create a loving relationship with my ideal partner, whom I consider not only my lover but also my best friend. We love being together each and every day. We love to travel together and experience new adventures. We equally care for each other and love supporting each other through this thing we call "life." And we both truly want to be together for the rest of our lives.
Money	My vision is to become financially independent and to do exactly what I love doing, which is creating art for people all over the world to enjoy. I want to have a collection of galleries in key spots throughout the world, selling my paintings. I want my paintings not only to make me over $1 million a year but also to inspire people who view my work.

STEP 3 – GET CLEAR

Career   My vision is to change my career from my uninspiring job at the bank to becoming a travel blogger, writing about all the amazing places I will see all around the world. I want my travel blog to educate and inspire my audience to travel to these amazing destinations and to make the most of them.

Learning   My vision is to learn to play the piano so I can play beautiful music for myself, my friends, and my family.

Every well-run business has a vision statement. CEOs and executive management teams spend lots of time crafting these apparently simple statements of intent. But they are anything but simple, because they set the directions for entire companies. Arguably, this is the most important statement a company can come up with. The vision statement provides laser-like focus and incredible direction to both the management team and the entire employee base. From the vision, everyone in the company knows what the company is working to achieve. A vision can be inspirational to everyone associated with a company.

What Does a Personal Vision Do for You?

While I think a personal vision is one of the keys to manifesting, here are some more tangible things a personal vision can do for you.

It Creates Focus

Many people get overwhelmed with all the choices of things they can do with their lives that they end up not making any and therefore not manifesting what they truly want. One of the important keys to manifesting is that at some point, you just have to pick a direction and take action toward it. It really is that simple. A vision statement allows you to focus on what you want in any aspect of your life. With this focus, you can take action toward something rather than just wallow in a pit of confusion. If you don't have focus in your life, it is hard to manifest.

It Sets Intention

This is your commitment that you will, in fact, take these actions. Intention is an extremely powerful tool in your manifesting arsenal. Not only does it provide you with that internal motivation and drive that says, "I am going to do this," but it also sends the same message to other people. You will have a higher likelihood of taking action on something if others know about your intention as well. Also, if other people know and understand your intention, they can help you. And finally, intention is something you give to God or the universe. Just putting your intention out into the universe creates an energy that will help you manifest.

It Improves Decision-Making

Your vision statement will provide you with a framework for making decisions. When faced with a choice, ask yourself, "Is this decision I am about to make in alignment with my vision statement?" Your statement is something you should refer to again and again. Keep it on your refrigerator, tape it to your mirror, place a note card by your bedside, or even write it as the first page in your journal.

More importantly, your vision statement will help you as you are making decisions in your life. "Is this decision I am about to make in alignment with my vision statement?" Check in to make sure the decisions you are making are supporting your vision.

It Increases Motivation

A key component to a vision statement is the "why," and the answer to this question will provide you with some serious motivational power. I also think the acts of getting focused, setting a direction, knowing your intention, and making decisions toward what you want to manifest provide incredible motivation. All this will lead to results, and there is nothing better for your motivation than starting to see results from your actions.

Guidelines for Creating Your Personal Vision

Think Big

Most people tend to limit themselves because they want to ensure success. While a vision statement should be realistic, it should also push you to greater heights. I always say that if you don't think big, you most assuredly won't get there. You don't need to play it safe with a vision statement.

STEP 3 – GET CLEAR

Think Broadly

Through most of this book, I suggest you be specific and focused. But with a vision statement, I want you to go more broadly. Cast a wider net. Unlike a specific goal, a vision sets your direction. Take this opportunity to broaden what you want to manifest.

Think Long Term

Vision statements can look out a few years to many years. For example, if your vision is to build a large and successful business, that might take ten-plus years to accomplish, but that's okay. Just make sure the vision statement is guiding you in the right direction. Maybe you have a vision of raising a happy and well-adjusted child. This might take twenty-plus years to achieve. There is no hard-and-fast rule to the time frame. It all depends on what you are trying to manifest.

Think Detailed

This might seem counter to what I said just a moment ago, but the more you can color in the picture of your vision, the better. A vision must be detailed enough to properly articulate what it is you want to manifest.

Exercise: Creating Your Personal Vision

For this exercise, we are going to focus on one area of your life. Pick the area of your life you feel needs the most attention.

Step 1: Select One Area of Your Life to Focus On

What area of your life are you struggling with the most? In what area of your life do you experience the most pain? In what area of your life do you see the most opportunity for growth? What area of your life gets you most excited? All these can be used as clues as to what to start with.

Step 2: Select a Dream You Want to Manifest

Look inside your heart and determine which dream is most important for you to manifest. Remember, you can't realistically manifest everything at once, so try to pick just one. If you did the earlier exercises, take a look back at how you ranked your dreams for some guidance. If you want to get a bit more spiritual, ask yourself, "What am I being called to do?" Is there something in your life the universe is pushing you to manifest?

Step 3: Passion Test

I want to make certain you are super passionate about the dream you want to manifest. Go back and review your passions from top to bottom and test how your dream fits into your passions. Is this dream in alignment with your passions? Is this dream something you can get really excited about? Do you have a burning desire to achieve this dream?

Step 4: Talent Check

Go back and review your biggest talents. Does this dream use your most valued talents? You don't need to have expert skills in what you are trying to manifest, but your dream should make use of your best talents.

Step 5: Value Check

Next, take your dream and make certain it is in alignment with your values. This is a really important step. You might assume that if it is your dream, then of course it is in alignment with your value system. But dreams and values are often in conflict. Revisit your hierarchy of values and ask yourself, "Is the dream I want to manifest in alignment with each of my most important values?"

Step 6: Visualize What You Want to Manifest

This is my favorite part. It's your chance to give your dream some form and substance. Find a quiet place and close your eyes. Let your mind go free of all your thoughts for a moment. Ask yourself, "What does this dream look like in one year, two years, three years?" Start to fill in the details of your dream. What is the end of your dream? How will your dream change your life for the better? How will you feel when you achieve this dream? What do you look like? Imagine how it will feel when you have manifested this dream.

Step 7: Write Your Vision Statement

You are finally ready to write your vision statement. This step should be really easy since you have done all the prep work. All you need to do is state your vision as if you were explaining it to your best friend in about a minute. Your vision should be clear and concise, but it should also draw the picture of what you want to manifest. It can be just one sentence or a few short paragraphs. Your vision statement is designed to make your dream real. Check to make sure when you read this statement that you get really excited about it. If you are excited, then you have a good vision statement that will guide you into the future.

To help you with this exercise, I am going to walk though it with one of my dreams.

Step 1: Area of My Life

Career

Step 2: Dream I Want to Manifest

My dream is to create a different kind of venture company, which would be a collection of highly entrepreneurial companies, where I design each of the companies and mentor the entrepreneurs, along with my team of experts. The dream is to build a vast collection of intriguing companies that do good things for the world.

Step 3: Passion Test

I am very passionate about growth. This includes both growth for myself as well as growth for the businesses and the people I am involved with. I am also passionate about learning new things as well as teaching new things to other people. This dream is really a combination of all my passions.

Step 4: Talent Check

My God-given talents are my abilities to communicate, inspire, teach others, and mentor them to be successful. This dream is in direct alignment with my talents.

Step 5: Values Check

My highest value is to make a difference in the world through my working and teaching, educating, and mentoring people. This is in exact alignment with my highest values

Step 6: Visualize

I visualize a bunch of companies filled with eager and talented entrepreneurs, all striving toward building highly successful companies and learning from me, my executive team, and each other. I see that my venture company has fifty-plus individual companies inside it, all working together to create something truly special.

Step 7: Vision Statement

My vision is to create a venture company that creates and grows intriguing businesses with highly motivated and talented team members. They learn from me, my executive team, and each other on how to grow very successful businesses that help the world become a better place. I want to build many businesses that in combination do at least $1 billion in total sales over the next fifteen years.

Further Vision Statements

Once you have your first vision statement, continue creating personal visions for each area of your life. Make sure you don't get overwhelmed, though. You don't need to develop a growth plan for each area unless you feel compelled to. Remember, you can execute only so many things in your life at one time. Pace yourself and bite off what you feel you can chew.

CHAPTER 19

Step 5: Create a Growth Plan

Let's face it: we spend more time planning our summer vacations than we do planning our lives. But if you want to manifest anything in your life, you absolutely need a good plan. Heck, you need a great one.

There are a lot of people out there who just wander through life, letting it happen to them. From my experience, this is where people get stuck the most. People are pretty good at dreaming about their lives and ideas, but when it comes to putting those dreams into action, things fall apart. This is where a solid growth plan will allow you to get the final bit of clarity needed for action. Letting your brain work through your plans ahead of time will help you immensely in the actual execution.

The quality of your planning will determine to a large degree the quality of your life. Your growth plan is going to provide you with the road map to manifesting whatever you want in your life. The clearer and more specific you are with your growth plan, the more likely you are to manifest what you really want.

So why don't more people sit down and build out plans? First, if you haven't done the other steps I outlined in the clarity model, it's hard to just begin building a plan. But with your values, passions, and talents identified, and after some broad dreaming, it's really just a matter of narrowing things down. Second, some people just don't know how to do it. Don't worry, because I will give you a framework and a bunch of tools for getting really good at planning. Third, people just don't want to take the time. It sounds like such a big, intimidating task that people would rather not embark on it. Fourth, fear is a big roadblock to your growth plan because it forces you out of your comfort zone and into a place where potential "failure" can happen. Of course, by now, you know that failure does not actually exist.

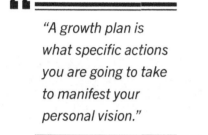

"A growth plan is what specific actions you are going to take to manifest your personal vision."

If you were running a business, you would never operate that business without a plan. Your business would be challenged to be a financial success. I have seen enough businesses in my time, and very often the quality of planning determines how successful the business is. Well, the same holds true for you. If you think more about what you want to accomplish about it, manifesting can become a whole lot easier.

Benefits of a Growth Plan

Here are some of the benefits a great growth plan brings.

Benefit 1: It Creates Focus

Focus is one of the most important keys to clarity, and a growth plan allows you to get down to the details of how you are going to manifest your dreams. It will take your dream from the general to the specific. The more specific you get, the more focused you will become.

Benefit 2: It Makes Things Seem Less Overwhelming

I have found that if I can work my dreams out in my brain first, the actual execution doesn't seem so overwhelming to me. When I can get a handle on the steps needed to start a business, develop a relationship, lose weight, make lots of money, or learn something new, I start to feel more confident that I can actually achieve my dream. A well-developed growth plan will ease your anxiety and show you there is a pathway to fulfilling your dreams.

Benefit 3: It Helps You Make Decisions

Building your growth plan will force you to make decisions. This is a good thing — a *very* good thing. This is exactly what you need to do to manifest your dreams. There are way too many things out there in the world to do and too many directions you could take that will paralyze you if you don't make decisions. Some people don't like making decisions because they believe it is limiting. They think that by making a decision about something, they are giving up something else. Not at all — you are allowing yourself to manifest more of what you truly want. I would suggest that by not making decisions, you are in fact limiting yourself much more because you never act. If you don't act, you will remain stuck.

Benefit 4: It Gets You to Take Action

Since a growth plan helps to create much more clarity and focus, makes you feel less anxious and overwhelmed, and helps you to make decisions, you will have a much higher chance of taking action.

Strategies to Create a Winning Growth Plan

Break Things Down into Small, Bite-Size Pieces

This tool is incredibly simple and amazingly powerful. Most of us start off with a pretty big dream of what we want. The more life-changing the dream, the more overwhelming it can be. Just take whatever you are trying to manifest and start breaking it down into pieces by asking yourself, "What actions do I need to take to manifest this dream?" Start with the biggest actions and put them into categories, if needed. This creates the major "buckets" you need to focus on. If needed, break down each category into subcategories. Continue until you get each category down to a list of actionable items. If any of these items still seem overwhelming, break the group down even further.

Ask Good Questions

The higher the quality of questions you ask about what you want to manifest, the better your growth plan will become. This step gets missed by lots of people who don't follow a more formal process. Spending some time thinking about asking the right questions will pay dividends as you work to manifest what it is you want. As you ask questions, your brain will start working to answer them.

Talk about Your Dreams

Share your dreams with other people and let them ask questions. I am always amazed by what great questions people come up with; answering these will propel you forward. I am a big proponent of sharing your dreams with others because of the feedback I can get from them. Remember, don't internalize their judgments about your dream. Rather, look at their input as data points you can choose to use or discard.

Be Specific

If an action is too big, too overwhelming, or even too frightening, break it down until it becomes very tangible and achievable. Saying you want to make a million dollars isn't very tangible. How the heck are you going to make that happen? To make it real, you must get very specific on exactly how you are going to achieve it. I assure you that this dream is extremely achievable as long as you define the exact steps from where you are today to the realization of that dream.

Work from the Present

You have to start manifesting from where you are today, not where you were in the past or where you think you are going. So don't say, "When I am this or that, then I can begin to achieve this dream." This will kill your dream for sure. I used to say, "When I have a great body, I will start dating." That is working from the future, and you will never start dating with this way of thinking because you have a huge undefined hurdle in the way. If having a great body is important to your dating, then make it part of your growth plan.

Focus on the "What," Not the "How"

We have talked about this one before. Don't get too caught up in how you are going to do something. Focus on what you need to do. Once you know what you need to do, the "how" typically comes to you. Just ask yourself a very simple question when you get this point: "How am I going to achieve this?" That's it.

Don't Create Time Limits

Deadlines can be helpful but don't be obsessed by them. Remember that the true journey is about growth, not achievement of some "thing"; the growth and learning *are* the thing. As you start executing your growth plan, you will learn new things and possibly head into a new direction that might be much more positive and productive to your dream. Allow yourself the time to make these new discoveries and allow yourself to modify your growth plan as you are executing it. Nothing is written in stone with growth.

Visualize

You have to see it to believe it. If you can see it in your mind's eye, you have a much greater chance of manifesting it. Just get that picture in your head of where you want to be, then start filling in the details just like you do with a painting.

Get Your Ego Out of the Way

If your growth plan is filled with ego-driven things like how much money you'll have or how beautiful you will look when you are thin, you are probably going down the wrong path. Your ego can't drive your growth plan. Remember to look back at your purpose and reground yourself on why you are really here on this earth.

Stay Loose

Don't be a perfectionist when trying to manifest your dreams. This isn't about perfection; it is about taking action and growing from that action, which will lead you to new distinctions that will allow you to take more action. If you try to perfect each step of your dream, you will never get to the next step because perfection really doesn't exist. Also, be aware of overthinking. You can think so much about your dream that you end up never actually taking action. Don't fall into this trap.

STEP 3 – GET CLEAR

Don't Get Bogged Down by Your Current Reality

Your current reality isn't a predictor of your future reality. I have seen more people start out with virtually nothing and achieve incredible things. Remember, you are 100 percent responsible for your current reality and 100 percent responsible for changing it if you want to.

Identify Your Fears

The number one thing that will stop you from executing your growth plan is your fears. This could be the fear of failure, the fear of rejection, the fear of not being good enough, the fear of missing out, and so on. By identifying your fears, you will have the ability to face them and work to overcome them. After identifying them, create solid strategies for overcoming them. Just the fact that you are aware of your fears will help you start dealing with them. They will be your biggest roadblocks to realizing your dreams.

Roadblocks to Creating a Growth Plan

As you are working through your growth plan, watch out for some of the things that might get in your way of creating a solid growth plan.

Roadblock 1: Your Perfectionistic Tendencies

Don't be a perfectionist when trying to manifest your dreams; otherwise, you will never truly manifest them because you will be so obsessed with perfecting them. This isn't about perfecting them; it is about taking action and growing from that action, which will lead you to new distinctions that will allow you to take more action. If you try to perfect each step of your dream, you will never get to the next step because perfection doesn't really exist. I have a lot of friends who are perfectionists, and this affliction holds them back more than anything else. If you find yourself falling into this trap, acknowledge it first and understand that you could be doing more damage to manifesting what you want than helping it.

Roadblock 2: Overthinking It

Like perfectionism, overthinking your dream can be deadly too. You can think so much about it that you end up never actually taking action. You see, if you don't take action toward your dream, you will never start the learning process, which helps you get clearer about what you want (or don't want). Action is what provides you with the data points you need to take your dream to the next level. It's so much better to stop your brain from thinking and get your mind into doing.

Roadblock 3: Inability to Make a Decision

We talked about this earlier. You have to be able to make decisions, or you could find it hard to complete your growth plan. It is important to set a direction as part of your growth plan. Worry less about whether the decision is right or wrong; rather, make the decision. At least you have new data points that you are moving in the wrong direction, and now you know to correct your course. That is better than doing nothing at all, in my opinion. I have some tools for you in the "Taking Action" section of the book to help with making good decisions, so not to worry.

Your Fear of Failure

Fear is a big roadblock for lots of things, including building your growth plan. Your fear of failure might stop your planning process because you are thinking about all the things that could go wrong. Your brain will get caught up with this fear and stop thinking about the many ways you could succeed with your dreams. Fear of failure is a very powerful force, and it can be a killer to manifesting your dreams.

Roadblock 4: Your Current Reality

One thing that can get in the way of building an effective growth plan is your current reality (your day-to-day life). When you focus on where you are today, it can be hard to see the future ("the forest through the trees," as the saying goes). You can't see how to get from here to there, so you just stop, stall out, and give up on your growth plan. Don't let this happen. Your current reality is not a predictor of your future reality. I have seen more people start out with virtually nothing as it relates to a specific dream and achieve incredible things. Remember, you are 100 percent responsible for your current reality and 100 percent responsible for changing it if you want too.

I have heard it all. "I can't because … I am too poor, too fat, in a bad relationship. I have kids, I have no money, I am not cute enough, or I am not smart enough." All of these

STEP 3 – GET CLEAR

"I can't because" statements are crap. All this can be changed based on your mind-set and actions. I have seen poor people become rich, fat people become thin, people with no time make time, and so forth. It is all up to you, so don't let your current choices dictate your future actions.

Creating a Growth Plan

Let's get down to creating the growth plan that will help you organize your thinking and establish actions. As we go through the following, aim for just a page or two; if you have a complex dream that requires much more than that, you might want to consider breaking it into smaller plans. This should be a document you use and refer back to once you begin taking action.

I often think of a growth plan as something like a business plan. Your business plan outlines all the things necessary for you to build a successful business. It defines what you are going to do and, in many cases, how you are going to do it. It forces you to make decisions about things like what type of products or services you are going to offer, how they will be positioned in the market, what staff you need to run your business, how much money you need to start and continue operations, and so forth. You wouldn't start a business without a business plan, and you shouldn't start manifesting a dream without a growth plan.

One Very Important Thing

You should develop a growth plan for one dream at a time. I have found it much more effective to develop individual growth plans for each dream rather than one big growth plan for my entire life. For most of us, that would be too much to tackle. All right, let's get started!

Step 1: Choose a Dream

Ask yourself, "What do I really want to do?" What dream do you have an absolute burning desire for? Refer to either your ranked list of passions or your personal vision statements. Maybe it is starting a business, developing an amazing love relationship, losing twenty pounds, becoming a millionaire, buying a house, learning something new, or helping kids from an impoverished country. Is one of your dreams jumping off the page?

I have personally struggled with this. I am the kind of person who wants to do everything and all at the same time. I struggled to commit to writing this book. I was working full-time at my internet business, but I also wanted to start a chocolate company, and I wanted to learn to fly a plane, and I wanted work on a business plan for my next big internet business. I quickly became overwhelmed and froze up. I kept switching from dream to dream, none of which had a growth plan. After getting some clarity, I decided to focus on writing this book and running my current internet business. I told myself that after I finished, I could move on to other dreams.

Step 2: Find Your Starting Point

If you are ready to execute this dream, then your starting point is right now. You might be saying, "I want to start a business, but I am one hundred thousand dollars in debt." Your plan needs to start with how you first get out of debt. Maybe you want to learn how to cook or to speak a foreign language but can't start until you have more time. Your plan needs to start with how to free up more time. Maybe you want to make a lot more money but don't have the skills to do so. Well, then figure out what skills you need and get the training.

Step 3: Identify Your Dependencies

I want you to get very clear on the dependencies to getting started with growing your dream into reality. Ask yourself, "What are the things that are in my way?" You might be thinking, *I don't have enough time to start this.* Or maybe you don't have enough money. Maybe you are overweight. Maybe you don't feel you have the talent or skills you need. These are valid concerns; in this step, just become aware of them.

Guess what? These dependencies are your starting point for your growth plan. Therefore, most people don't actually get started working on their dream; their dependencies get in the way, and they can't figure them out. Don't worry about how long it takes you to work through your dependencies or how hard it will be. Pushing through these dependencies is where dreams are made.

Step 4: Fix Your Dependencies

For each dependency you have identified, you need to come up with a solution to eliminate it. Make sure you have a strategy to work around whatever is stopping you from manifesting your dream. Get rid of any of those nasty excuses for why you can't do something because there is no valid excuse if what you want to manifest is important enough to you.

Step 5: Identify Your Fears

Ask yourself, "What fears do I have that could stop me from achieving my dream?" Make a list of each fear that comes up for you and create a strategy for overcoming each one.

Step 6: Create a List of Actions

The only way you are going to achieve your dream is to do something to make it happen. Ask yourself, "What specific actions am I going to take to achieve this dream?" Try to list every action you can think of. The more specifics you have, the better chance you have of achieving your dream.

Step 7: Create Markers to Track Your Progress (and Reward Yourself)

Markers are a great way to understand where you are in the process of manifesting. These are defined milestones as you move along the path of manifesting. We discussed breaking your plan into bite-size pieces, and these provide natural markers for you. For each of these, ask yourself, "What is the action I need to complete to feel that I have manifested this particular set of actions?" Add these markers to your action plan.

Step 8: Visualize It

I think of this as the icing on the cake. I have found it immensely helpful to make sure I can see my dreams fully manifested. This will provide you with a clearer picture of where you are going as well as lots of motivation to get there. You can use this picture that you draw in your mind to go back to again and again while you are working on manifesting your dream.

To visualize your dream, do the following:

1. Close your eyes and take some deep breaths until you feel relaxed.

2. Draw a picture in your mind of your manifested dream.

   a. What does it look like when you've achieved your dream?

   b. How does this make you feel?

   c. How has this changed your life?

   d. How has this changed the lives of others around you?

Example: My Growth Plan

Just to prove that I practice what I preach, I am going to go through my growth plan for becoming a thought leader on growth and personal development. Since my growth plan is a work in progress, some of it has already been completed, while much has yet to manifest.

Step 1: Select the Dream

This wasn't easy for me. Since my early twenties, I have been fascinated with self-improvement. I listened to all the greats like Tony Robbins and Wayne Dyer. I had all the books and tapes. I dreamed of getting up on stage someday and talking to the masses about how to build a great life. While I'd had this dream for a long time, it wasn't taking much shape. I wasn't clear on any of the details. It was just something I thought would be exciting, but I was conflicted because I also had about fifty other things I wanted to do.

I had to go through a process to get this particular dream to stick so I could take action. For about a year, I bounced around from idea to idea, and then I just simply decided one day that this wasn't productive and that my true purpose in life was to help people live better lives.

Step 2: Find Your Starting Point

The starting point for me was writing this book. I felt like I couldn't be an effective thought leader without getting all my thoughts down on paper in an organized fashion. There are many thought leaders who have never written a book, but for me, I felt like it was extremely important. In addition, starting with a book would give me some credibility in this field. While I have been studying and living these principles for more than twenty years, a book is my platform to launch these ideas in a much more real way.

Step 3: Dependencies

Wow, this is such a powerful concept to include because I have quite a few dependencies in my way. Here is my list:

1. Finding the time. This was a big one for me. How was I going to find the time to write a massive book like this when I was running a company and responsible for employing 250 people?

2. Lack of focus. It is no secret that I suffer from ADD. My brain pops all around the universe and back in minutes. I can't hold a darn thought in my head without having a hundred more come in within seconds. Okay, maybe I'm not quite that bad, but you get my point.

3. Do I have what it takes to write a book? Who am I to write a book on personal development and success? Am I credible? After all, I don't have a PhD in psychology. This is a classic case of self-doubt.

Step 4: Fix Your Dependencies

Here are a few examples: I solved the time problem by writing almost the entire book while on airplanes. I think I drove the people sitting next to me crazy, typing away at all hours of the day and night. This also solved my ADD issue. On a plane, I am stuck in my seat with nothing to do but focus.

Step 5: Identify My Fears

Fear of failure is a big one for me. Would I even finish this darn book? Maybe I put all this work into it over many years and would never pull it across the finish line and get it published. Maybe no one would want to publish it.

There is fear in putting myself out there to be judged. I have exposed myself quite a bit in this book. I talk about myself, which I tend not to be that comfortable with, and I express many ideas that can be judged by my friends and family.

Getting rid of my fears was a bit more challenging. For my self-doubt fear, I just kept telling myself that I had a PhD in life. I knew the ideas in the book could change people's lives; I just had to keep reminding myself of that.

Step 6: Create a List of Actions

I have quite a long list of actions, but here are a few:

- Complete this book.

- Build a website to communicate my ideas.

- Start a podcast.

- Hire a PR specialist to help promote me and my ideas.

- Get speaking engagements (one a month).

- Create my own seminar series.

- Create an e-learning masterclass.

Step 7: Create Markers

I love creating markers so I can measure my success. I created a big marker after finishing each chapter. Since my example is a book, it makes sense to use chapters, but for whatever you are manifesting, there are natural breakpoints for you. Since my chapters are long and took me many months to complete, I created another marker I often celebrated. Every time I wrote ten pages on one trip, I considered that trip a huge success. Another marker I sometimes use is a time goal. On a long trip, if I could write for ten hours (five hours each way), that was a huge success.

Step 8: Visualize It

I often visualized the book sitting at eye level on the bookshelves of all the bookstores around the world. And on the book jacket bearing my picture (scary, huh?), the words *"New York Times Bestseller"* were right at the top of the book.

Now That You've Attained Clarity

Here's a quick review before getting down to the next order of business: The six steps in this chapter have helped you to identify your values, passions, and talents, and you've used those to determine your purpose, which led first to dreams and then to a clear growth plan with specific steps to attain those dreams. So now you've got clarity on who you are, what you bring to the table, and what to do with those insights. Guess what comes next? That's right, it's time to act.

Get the latest updates on the book, including articles and videos.

Visit **KenBurke.com**

STEP 4

Take Action

CHAPTER 20

Just Decide

You have reached by far the single most important section in the book: taking action. Everything to this point has been an introduction to living a prosperous life, but until you take action toward your purpose and dreams, nothing will really happen.

If you are like me, I am sure you have lots of dreams floating around in your head, but for some reason, you just can't move past the dream phase. Your dreams haven't become reality because there is something blocking you from taking action on a consistent basis. I hate to break it to you, but your dreams don't just manifest themselves; you actually have to do something to manifest them.

Some people will say, "Wait a minute. I know about the law of attraction, and it says that all I have to do is put the thought in my head, and somehow the dream will come true." But there is another part to the law of attraction; you must actually do something to manifest those dreams. You can't just sit there and wait for something to happen.

This sounds like such a simple concept, right? You might be saying, "You mean, all I have to do is to have a thought, then act on it, and I will get results?" Actually, yes. That's all there is to it. However, while it seems very simple on the surface, taking action is unquestionably the hardest thing for people to do. Just take a look at how many people you know who talk about their dreams constantly, yet they never seem to change their lives. One year goes by, then five, then ten, and nothing seems to change. They are still living the same existence. Those dreams they want so badly just never seem to materialize. They want to lose weight, write a book, start a business. So why are all these dreams not being realized? Are you one of these people?

Why is it so hard to take action? If you are like most people, there are a whole host of roadblocks standing in your way, and once you become aware of what they are, you can push right through them. In this section, I am going to share with you some tools that have worked very well to help me take action in my life.

Just like you, this is something I have struggled with all my life. I have so many dreams and things I want to do with my life that it feels like my brain is overflowing with desires, yet many of them remain on my list year after year. It drives me crazy. Does this sound familiar? Does it drive you crazy that your life isn't moving in the direction you want it to, despite your desires?

My Personal Story

I have many examples in my life to illustrate the above point, but the one I will share has to do with writing this book. It has taken me years, yet I have had the content of the book floating around since long before I started. I have been dreaming about getting this book in the hands of millions of people because I truly believe it will help them. I have had that burning desire to let the world know these ideas that I have been learning about for thirty years of my life. I have even had a clear vision on how I see the entire thing playing out in my life, yet I have struggled for years with getting the thoughts in my head on paper. I went for an entire year without writing one word. So even with a ton of motivation and a burning desire to help the world, I experienced many of my own roadblocks – all of which I created in my own head. Don't worry because I am going to cover all the roadblocks to taking action, and I'll help you identify them in your own life, and then I'll give you the tools you need to remove them.

Decide, Act, and Harness the Momentum Effect

It takes only a split-second to decide to take action on any dream, but you also need to be completely committed to your decision. To commit to the decision, you need to take one – just one – small step toward your dream. This will lead to a second step and then a third and a fourth. These small steps reinforce your decision to take action.

From my experience, taking the first step is the hardest one. For many people, including me, taking that first step equates to making the decision to completely follow through until the dream is fully realized. This belief creates a ton of fear, uncertainty, and doubt around that first step, and for this reason, most people never take it. But obviously, everyone who has ever manifested anything at all had to take that first step.

I believe that any action, whether its outcome works out the way you thought it would or not, pushes you toward your dream. If things work as intended, then you are encouraged to move forward in the same manner. If things work out otherwise, the action provides you with valuable insight as you take your next step. Harness that knowledge to move closer toward your dream.

It's important not to slow down once you get started. Actions create energy, and you want the forward momentum to continue. It's just like a train pulling out of the station. As the train starts out, it takes a lot of energy just to move a little way down the track, but once it picks up steam, it can cruise on that track with much less energy. It's the same with taking action. The more actions you take toward your dream, the more momentum you create. This is called the "momentum effect"; you might have also heard this phenomenon referred to as the "snowball effect." As the tiny ball of snow starts rolling down the hill, it does two things: it gets bigger, and it picks up speed. This is a good metaphor for your dreams. All your dreams start out with a single action — just one step to get them started. Once you take that first step and achieve that first action, the momentum effect kicks in, giving you just a little more energy to take that second step, just as it is with that tiny snowball rolling down the hill. As you continue to take action, your dream starts to take form, getting bigger with every action you take. As the momentum builds around your dream, you will find subsequent actions easier, and things will start moving faster.

Just One Hour

One of the best pieces of advice I've ever received arose while I was writing this book. I was attending a writing seminar from my favorite author, the world-renowned Wayne Dyer. And Wayne, who has written over forty books in his lifetime, said this: "If you want to complete your book and never seem to have the time to work on it, just take one hour a day in your writing space to write. It does not even matter what you write, just write. Even if you don't think your writing is that great, keep writing."

STEP 4 – TAKE ACTION

Well, I followed that advice, and it worked for me. I modified it a bit to work in my life. Instead of taking an hour a day, I took five hours a week and worked on this book. Your schedule might be different from mine, but one thing is certain: there is no way you will manifest you dreams unless you schedule yourself to put in the time.

Consistency

While I'm suggesting one hour a day, you can also do less. Even if it is only one hour a week, that would be great because you are putting some level of energy toward your dreams. If you can't devote at least one hour a week, maybe you aren't quite ready to manifest that dream yet. An hour here or there doesn't count; it puts you back in the dreaming stage. To move things forward, you need consistency, which is one of the keys to developing momentum. The more consistent you are, the more momentum you will create toward your dream. I know it is hard, so I suggest you schedule it. Put it on your calendar, and even if you sit there and stare out the window and think about your idea, you're putting energy into it. Eventually, you will go from staring to researching. Then you might even talk to a few people about your dream. Next, you might commit some of your dream to paper. That will be followed by more actions that lead you down the path. Remember, this is a journey that gets taken one hour at a time.

My Own Actions

I can't tell you how much this simple little technique has helped me in manifesting the things I've wanted. I literally schedule time to work on my dreams, such as this book. And in my businesses, I have experienced the momentum effect alive and kicking. Starting my own company became a dream of mine at the age of ten, when my dad almost purchased the local hardware store – it ignited an entrepreneurial spark in me. Nothing would have happened without action, though. Getting myself prepared to be an entrepreneur, I started my journey by getting a master's degree in entrepreneurship from one of the top universities that specializes in this, USC. This helped to create energy to propel me to take action to start my business after graduation. My first step in really committing to the business was renting a three-hundred-square-foot office in a local business park. This was a huge commitment, since it required me to invest actual dollars in my dream, which, in turn, led me to keep going. My next step was to work weekends writing a business plan, another huge action toward realizing my dream because it took quite a lot of energy and time to put together a fully baked business plan. With my own office and a business plan under my belt, I took the next action, which was to quit my current job. This was a gigantic step toward my dreams because it freed me up to dedicate 100 percent of my time toward my business. Moreover, I had $50,000 worth of college debt at the time and no income. Talk about motivation to succeed!

With the little money I had, I took the next step to build some marketing materials and exhibit at my first industry trade show. I remember it well: Internet World in San Jose in 1995, right at the start of the internet revolution. Those marketing efforts led to my first customer. While I earned very little money on that first sale, I didn't care because I was finally in business and had a real-life paying customer. Well, that customer led to another customer and another and another. Then, about six months after my official launch, I landed my first really big customer, Guthy-Renker, which was a large marketing company. That led to a huge contract to build a large-scale internet mall. (Remember, this was before Amazon.) This led to my company building more than 25,000 websites over the next ten years. But we didn't stop there. I took every dollar I had made from that and invested it in building a sales team, new technology, and other capabilities. All these actions helped create a successful, industry-leading software company worth over $100 million. And it all started with a single action.

This is how everyone in the world manifests things. Your dreams don't just happen; you have to make them happen. And making them happen requires some discipline on your part. And that, my friend, can be the difference between you and so many other people out there. We all have dreams, but few people act on them.

Exercise: Initiating Momentum

I want you to think of a time in your life when you experienced the momentum effect. When have you taken an action that led to further actions? Do you remember how difficult it was to take that first step? Did it become easier to take action once you started? Even if you didn't fully manifest your dream, did you make progress? Do you feel you are better because you took that first step? Did you grow from the experience? How did it make you feel to manifest whatever it was you created?

Let's get you on your way to manifesting one of your dreams. This exercise is rather simple but very powerful. It is designed to get you warmed up to taking action.

1. Select one of your dreams that you would like to manifest. It doesn't have to be a big

dream; it can just be something, anything you want to do. In fact, I would suggest you practice on something small just so you can see how taking one step can make a huge difference in your life.

2. Determine one action you can take toward moving that dream forward. I don't care how small the action is, just as long as you take some type of action. For example, let's say you want to start a bakery. Maybe your first step is deciding on a list of recipes.

3. Now write down five more steps to move you forward toward manifesting. Again, I don't care how small these steps are, just take them. For that bakery, it might be researching equipment or visiting a handful of bakeries in your area to check out the competition.

4. For each step, determine a timeline for taking action. Write that timeline down, committing it as a goal for you to achieve.

5. Now, commit to taking action on each item, and commit to the timeline.

After completing those actions, do you notice your dream has more energy around it? Do you feel you are on a path to achieving it? Do you feel momentum building? Keep it going. Use that momentum to propel you forward.

This seemingly simple exercise is very powerful. You would be amazed by how many people who want to manifest their dreams never even get up to bat. They never even take one step to realizing that dream. They might be really good at dreaming but do absolutely nothing to move their dream forward. If you are one of the few who completed the exercise above; you have done more than many people. Congratulations!

My advice to you is to repeat this exercise over and over again. After you complete your first five small actions, make a list of the next five, again with solid timelines. And remember my one-hour-a-day tip. Allocate one hour a day toward your dreams, and you will be amazed by how much progress you will make in a very short period.

CHAPTER 21

Roadblocks to Success

Taking action isn't easy. If it were, everyone would be doing it. And as you probably know already, this is the single-hardest thing for most people. I strongly believe this is what separates people who are living prosperous lives from those who are struggling. Understanding the roadblocks to taking action and how to overcome them will make it so much easier to take the action you need to achieve your dreams.

Roadblock 1: Fear of Failure

This is the big one. Nothing stops people in their tracks more than the fear of failure. Most people don't even get to the starting line because of fear. In many cases, the fear of failure stops people from having the dream in the first place.

Do you suffer from the fear of failure? Have you considered doing something new, like starting a business? Your brain likely goes right into fear mode, jumping right to thoughts of failure. *What will people think? How much money will I lose? Will I hurt other people in the process if I fail?*

I talk to so many people who dream about running their own businesses but never do, mainly because they are worried they will fail. This fear is something I'm well-acquainted with.

STEP 4 – TAKE ACTION

I almost didn't start my own business because of fear. I had just graduated with my MBA, and it took several years for me to work through the fear of dreaming about it at first and then the fear of starting it and then, once started, the fear of it being a success. Thank God I was too young and stupid to obsess about it.

The better question to ask is, to what degree do you suffer from the fear of failure? Which of the following best describes you?

- Does fear paralyze you so you can't even dream?

- Are you able to dream but can't seem to manifest that dream into actions?

- Are you able to dream and start taking actions but then come up against uncertainty that stops you in your tracks?

- Or are you able to overcome fears as they come up while taking action toward your goal?

It's important for you to determine where you are on the fear-of-failure continuum, since that will tell you how much attention you have to put toward solving this problem.

Solution: Change your perspective on the fear of failure. When you are living in an ego-driven world, failure is all around. You fail every day at something, according to the ego, because it's always comparing you against something or someone else. And there's always someone who has made more money than you, built a bigger business, is better looking, is smarter, and so forth.

In a spiritual world, can you really fail at anything? The answer is absolutely and unquestionably no. My surefire way of dealing with the fear of failure is to simply choose a new belief about failure. I hold the belief that it's impossible for me – or anyone for that matter – to fail. It's impossible because everything you do teaches you something. You are always learning. You may not learn the right way the first time, and you may experience further "failures," but you are learning.

With each and every experience you have, big or small, your brain is collecting and processing data. And you can't get rid of your experiences. Let's say you get into college and go for one year. After that first year, the university kicks you out because your grades are so bad. Did you learn anything from that experience? Absolutely. You might have learned that you don't want to be in college, that it isn't in alignment with your life's purpose. You might have learned what it feels like to do poorly at something, and you might have decided you don't like those feelings. Any new understanding you can take away from the experience is valuable.

Now you might be thinking, *That is easier said than done.* And you would be right. But give it a try, and after a while, that belief will take on momentum and become stronger until it is cemented into your personality. That is exactly what happened to me with this belief.

This simple but powerful concept helps reduce the fear of failure in my life. It makes it virtually impossible to fail because at every turn, I am guaranteed to learn something from my actions. One of the biggest fears was that my business would fail and lose lots of money, so I did everything to protect my wealth. Nothing felt better than winning a large account, and nothing felt worse than losing an account and taking a step backward. The ego hates to take a step backward.

Well, my worst fears came true. After growing a very successful company, many things happened, and I watched as it deteriorated to a fraction of its value over a span of eight years, leaving me with very little to show for it. As I watched my company crumble, but I learned the most valuable lessons of my life, including detachment and how to manage my ego. Over those eight years, I developed an entirely new perspective on life that has made me incredibly happy with my life and grateful for each day. While my life's work was falling apart, I was happier than I had ever been. All those years of being fearful – that I would have this huge failure on my record and have to start all over again – were gone. The fear just disappeared, and I understood that the value of the experience of my business were all the lessons I had learned. Not only did I learn those valuable lessons of life, but also in the process I learned how to become a better businessperson. And I realized I could take those skills and start another business in an instant with new confidence.

I ended up selling the company to a very large software company for over $100 million. So yes, after all that, I did make a large sum of money, but even more valuable were those lessons I get to take with me for the rest of my life.

Roadblock 2: Lack of Clarity

In the previous chapter, we spent lots of time on the importance of clarity, so you already know that if you don't have clarity on where you want to go, you won't get there. Imagine driving a hundred miles per hour down the freeway with your windshield completely covered with mud. Well, that is what it's like trying to take action with no clarity.

It is incredibly difficult to take action when you don't truly know what you want to take action on. You might have a vague idea of what you want to do, but you're fuzzy on the details. The less clear you are about where you are going, the less likely it is that you will actually take action. Your brain will translate your lack of clarity as risk, and with risk comes fear. Anything you can do to reduce that risk and fear will give you a much better chance of taking that next step. I see this all the time in business. Without a clear definition on what to do, employees will just freeze up.

However, many times when you are doing something new, you won't have perfect clarity but will still need to take action. If you have done everything you can to clarify what you are trying to do but are still not comfortable, that is okay. Just take the best action you can. Consider taking a smaller step than you might otherwise but make sure you take a step that moves you in the right direction. That step creates invaluable data for you to determine whether you should continue this course of action or try something else.

Solution: If you feel like you aren't completely clear on your next actions, go back through step three on clarity. That will give you everything you need. But here is a simple and quick exercise you can do to get instant clarity.

Exercise: Getting Clear

Here is a list of great questions to ask yourself when you are trying to gain clarity. Ask yourself the following:

1. What is the most important thing you want to accomplish in your life? There might be more than one thing on your list, and that is okay.

2. For each of the answers to question one, why is this so important to you? What benefits will you get from achieving it? What are you going to get from it? How will this create more joy and fulfillment in your life?

3. For each of the answers to question one, what pain will you experience if you don't achieve it?

4. Do an evaluation of your answers and see if you can pick one of those goals to go after.

Roadblock 3: Uncertainty

Generally speaking, people hate uncertainty, but if you are working toward a new goal, I guarantee there will be uncertainty. That is what growth is all about. When you have uncertainty, a few things happen. Risk enters the equation, and risk is usually followed by fear. (We seem to always get back to that darn fear.) The choice at this point is either to drop back and freeze or to work to gather more information to help reduce the risk.

Marry uncertainty and the fear of failure, and you will find yourself testing the bounds of your comfort zone, which is the only way to grow. And isn't that what life is really all about? Expanding your comfort zone can be challenging, but it will lead you to do more things, to live life at a higher level, and to fulfill those dreams.

Let's look at an example. Think back to high school and the first time you asked someone out. For most of us, this was out of our comfort zones. Remember the feelings that came from that? What comes to mind? Fear, perhaps. Maybe you were even sweating. But once you asked that special girl or boy out, were you more confident the next time you asked someone out? Even if the answer was no, you probably were more confident because your comfort zone expanded.

Solution: To cope with the issue of uncertainly, the first thing you need to do is to become aware that it is driving your inability to take action. For whatever reason, you feel that you don't have enough information to take that next step. I suggest you try to fill in the gaps with more information but limit that to only what is necessary, or you could run into a different problem — you could use research as a new excuse not to take action. (See the next roadblock.) Second, realize that taking a risk and living with some uncertainty are just part of the game. If you want to achieve new things, you have to be willing to accept some degree of uncertainly. I suggest you embrace that uncertainty and look at it as an opportunity for you to expand your comfort zone.

One concrete action you can take to combat uncertainty and to expand your comfort zone is to give yourself a good kick in the butt — or, if you aren't that flexible, then get someone else to do it. Find a really good friend and describe what you are trying to do. Explain that you are stuck, that you think it is your darn comfort zone, and that you are a bit fearful of failing in some way. The key here is to pick someone you trust who doesn't suffer from the same fear you have. I have used this technique many times on myself, and it works really well. Friends can be a great help with your personal development if you know how to ask.

STEP 4 – TAKE ACTION

Roadblock 4: Analysis Paralysis

Boy, oh boy, have I seen this one in my day! This is the syndrome of those who keep analyzing and reviewing a certain situation without ever making a decision or taking real action toward the goal. They are paralyzed by the process. They get stuck in an endless loop of analysis and never feel like they have enough data to make a decision. Does this sound like you? Maybe you know someone like this. I certainly do.

The belief here is that more information means less risk. So, if you are risk averse, you might well find yourself gathering data rather than taking the risk. Why does this happen? No surprise – it comes down once again to the fear of failure. Instead of taking risks and creating the possibility of failure, those suffering from analysis paralysis continue to live in a world of research data, conversation, and review. I am all for effectively gathering information so I can make an informed decision, but there is a limit to how much information you really need.

Solution: First, know yourself. Awareness about who you are is critical here. Are you the type of person who loves to do lots of analysis? If so, be aware that you are prone to analysis paralysis. Know that this is powerful because you can take corrective action. Next, remind yourself that the act of taking action will give you more real information than sitting there, thinking about it. Break out of analysis mode and take some action toward what you want to achieve, and you will get that data you are seeking. Remember, you can always pull back, change course, or just completely stop anytime you want. Few things in life are irreversible.

Again, it can help to take a small step forward, if possible. Even that small step will help you start gathering more information. Now keep doing this. Take an action, gather some data, and take some more action. The good thing is, by taking a little action, the momentum effect will kick in, and you will be more motivated to take the next step.

Roadblock 4: Overwhelm

This is a very common roadblock. When you start doing new things, it is easy to feel overwhelmed with the sheer size of the task in front of you. You might be trying to do something quite large, like starting a new business or getting a college degree. And just the thought of this overwhelms you to the point that you can't take action. This happens for a couple of reasons. One, because of the fear, you won't be able to complete the task. And two, because with large or complicated tasks, it can be difficult to figure out where and how to start. But I am here to say there is nothing too big for you to achieve. No goal is so large that you can't meet it.

Have you ever felt like this? Have you had something you wanted to learn, do, or be but never got started because it just seemed too big? For me one of the things that seems overwhelming is learning a foreign language. I would love to add this to my skill set, but the thought of many hours of study in an already busy life keeps stopping me from taking action. It could take me years to really learn a language, so instead of trying, I just keep putting it off. Does this sound familiar to you?

Solution: To combat feelings of being overwhelmed, first ask yourself this: Have you ever embarked on something really big and achieved it? If yes, think back to when you first started out. I'll bet you had doubts about whether you could meet your goals. Now think back to how it felt after you achieved your goal. It doesn't seem so overwhelming now, right? Commit those feelings about your achievement to memory and go back to them anytime you feel overwhelmed.

If you don't have a success story like that in your past to draw upon, try the following. Get out a piece of paper and break down your goal into smaller, bite-size pieces. I like to put my main goal in the middle of the page and draw a circle around it and then connect smaller tasks in smaller circles to it with lines. This is called a "mind map," and it's one of my favorite tools around. You can even download free software to help you with this. Just do a Google search for "mind map."

Breaking things down into smaller pieces makes the entire process much more manageable. Commit to taking on one of those smaller tasks, and once you complete that, move onto the next. It sounds simple, but the momentum effect will kick in, and you will be on your way to achieving your larger goal.

Roadblock 5: Failing to Take Responsibility

As I'm sure you know by this point in the book, you are 100 percent responsible for everything that happens in your life. But for many, this fact can remain a challenge in certain situations, and instead of taking responsibility, they play the victim and blame others. The key sign you are playing the victim is that you are blaming someone or something else for the current situation you find yourself in. You might say, "I can't start a new business because my wife or husband won't let me," "I am overweight because my friends make me go to restaurants all the time," or "I am not successful because my parents didn't encourage me when I was a child."

STEP 4 – TAKE ACTION

Do you know someone who lives his or her life being a victim? I know I do. Do you think the person's ego plays a role in this? You better believe it does. Playing the victim is a manifestation of the ego, which is trying to deny any possible association with failure. The ego will fight like hell to avoid responsibility for anything remotely bad.

So how is this related to taking action? It's very hard for you to take action when you are busy blaming others. If you are blaming others, then you aren't the one who has to take action; the other person is. You remain frozen while you blame others for your challenges and failures.

Solution: The solution to fixing this affliction is simple to state but hard to execute. First, you must acknowledge your tendency to play the victim. This behavior is a virus in your life, and the sooner you can identify it, the sooner you can rid yourself of it.

It can be hard to spot this with certainty in yourself, so even if you just have a suspicion that you are blaming someone, catch it and immediately tell yourself you are 100 percent responsible for everything in your life. If you are struggling with this one, a good friend can come in handy. Select someone you trust and ask him or her whether the person feels you are acting like a victim. The feedback just might snap you out of this behavior. And I assure you that life is so much easier if you just take responsibility for everything in it.

Roadblock 6: Limiting Beliefs

Limiting beliefs are the beliefs living inside you that stop you from taking action. They are the voices inside you that say, "I can't do that because ..."

What makes them particularly bad is that you don't even realize they're there. You are so used to the voice inside you that stops you from even thinking about something you might want to do. Limiting beliefs can shut you down before the idea even forms into a dream or goal.

I call these the "silent killer" because many of these beliefs live in our subconscious minds. These aren't beliefs you really think about. You might not even know you have them. For example, there are people who believe having money is bad. You might even believe this but don't know it. It sounds crazy because you might be striving every day to make more money. But is it possible you have a belief in your subconscious mind that says, "Money is the root of all evil" or "People who have lots of money are bad people"? You could even hold the belief that you don't deserve to be rich. This can be true, even though your conscious mind seems to desire money.

If you have wondered why you can't get off the ground with something you want to achieve, it could be that you have beliefs somewhere inside you that just won't allow you to move forward. Where do these come from? Just like many things in life, limiting beliefs come from our childhood. Now, before you go and call your mom or dad and yell at them for creating all those limiting beliefs, you should realize that not all of them came from your parents. Limiting beliefs can come from anyone who was influential during your childhood, including teachers, coaches, siblings, and friends. Just living in society can also create limiting beliefs from sources like television, magazines, and the internet. You aren't alone, though. We all have them.

Here's an example. Today, I was talking to a good friend of mine who over the past few months realized after thirty years that what had been stopping her from living her life to the fullest were limiting beliefs. She'd grown up with alcoholic parents, and her childhood was filled with doubt in her abilities. She was constantly told she wasn't good enough and would never amount to much. Well, those statements turned into beliefs at a very young age and have been limiting her thoughts, behaviors, and actions ever since. Now that she has broken through her limiting beliefs on her self-worth, she is unstoppable. She is taking action daily and crashing through the barriers that have so long stood in her way. Those limitations were all in her head.

Solution: The first step to solving this problem is to identify which limiting beliefs you possess. This can be tricky because some of these beliefs are hidden, so they can be hard to find. Let's start by looking at some common limiting beliefs.

- "I have been fat all my life, so I will never be thin."
- "I never went to college, so there is no way I could do that job (or run a company)."
- "I am ugly, so I will never find my dream guy or gal."
- "I will never be rich because I am not smart enough."
- "I will never have a good-paying job because I have no talent."
- "I am not smart enough to write a book."
- "I will never be a good parent because I am too selfish."
- "I will never be rich because I think rich people are rotten to the core."
- "I will never get that promotion because I don't work hard enough."
- "No one likes me so I will never have friends."
- "I will never be good at sports because I am slow and uncoordinated."
- "I will never be famous because I am not talented."
- "Why get a good job that challenges me when I will just fail at it?"
- "I will never get great grades in school because I am not smart enough."

STEP 4 – TAKE ACTION

And the list goes on and on. There are literally millions of limiting beliefs out there. To identify yours, let's look at some of the symptoms that might give us some clues that we have a limiting belief lurking around.

- Doubting yourself: What are those areas where you question yourself and your abilities? When you say, "I can't do something because . . ." that is usually a sign there is a limiting belief beneath that statement.

- Being stuck: You know that yucky feeling of being stuck and not knowing why? It feels like your life (or one area of your life) has stalled out, and you can't figure out the reason. If you find yourself not being able to take action, then you might have a limiting belief blocking you.

- Inability to dream: For some reason, you don't even allow yourself to dream big. Every time you try to think bigger, your brain stops you dead in your tracks. The thoughts just won't come through, but you know there is a desire there.

- Inability to get clear: You keep trying, but you just can't allow yourself to think clearly about something you are trying to achieve.

- Starting and stopping: Have you ever started something only to stop working on it? Then you push yourself to start again, only to stop shortly thereafter?

When you find yourself in one of these situations, I suggest asking, *What beliefs do I have that could be causing me to be blocked from achieving?* Write down your answers. Once you are aware of these limiting beliefs, you have a much better chance of resolving them for good. Now, you might have to ask this question over and over to get rid of even one limiting belief, so don't give up.

I have found it helpful to ask this question in relation to the thing I am trying to achieve. Trying to identify all the limiting beliefs you have might be a daunting or impossible task, so limit your questioning to a particular goal. Resolving a limiting belief can be easy for some and challenging for others.

The good thing about beliefs is that they are just thoughts, and thoughts can be changed in an instant. Your limiting beliefs might have been embedded in your brain for many years, though, so that fact can present challenges. But none of them are too embedded to transform if you work methodically to rid yourself of them. Here's how you resolve them.

- Create a positive belief. After you identify the limiting belief, replace it with a new, positive belief that moves you toward your goal. This new belief needs to be powerful, strong, positive, and most importantly, something you can believe in your soul. Let's say you have been struggling in your dating life. Maybe your limiting belief is, "I will never be successful at dating because I am not attractive." Replace that with a different, positive focus. "I will be very successful at dating because I have a beautiful, loving soul, which makes me extremely attractive." Who wouldn't want to date someone like that?

- Reprogram yourself to accept this new belief. Keep in mind that you have had this limiting belief for most of your life, so it isn't going to vanish overnight. While we have the power to change it in a second, things that are embedded deep inside of us aren't easy to get rid of. Be patient! Take the new belief and each day read and repeat it to yourself. Better yet, do it multiple times a day. If you are speaking it aloud, say it with incredible passion and enthusiasm. Do this every day for thirty days. At the end of this period, your brain will have forgotten about that yucky limiting belief and will take this new belief in place of it. If you still haven't been able to crush that limiting belief, do it for another thirty days. If you keep working at it, that belief will be replaced.

Here are a few more techniques you can use to help reinforce that new belief.

- Write your new belief on the refrigerator.

- Write down your belief, take a picture, and make it the background image on your phone.

- Write it on a sticky note and attach it to the side of your computer screen.

- Write it down on a note card and put it in your pocket.

Above all, remember this, the king of all beliefs: *I have the power in me at this moment to achieve anything I want to achieve.* Work on holding this belief at all times. I believe this with all my heart. It guides my life every day. I know there is absolutely nothing I can't achieve. If you need a new belief to replace one of those limiting belief and can't think of one, use this one.

STEP 4 – TAKE ACTION

Exercise: Identify and Resolve Your Limiting Beliefs

I encourage you to do this exercise. Let's work on getting rid of one limiting belief in your life.

Identify the following:

1. Pick a goal or something you want to achieve in your life. It can be something small or something you've been struggling with for many years. For an example, I am going to pick a goal of losing twenty pounds because for some reason, I feel like I always need to lose twenty pounds.

2. Ask yourself, "What beliefs do I hold about [my goal] that is stopping me from taking action (or achieving my goal)?" In my case, I would ask, "What beliefs do I hold about losing ten pounds that are stopping me from losing the weight and achieving my goal?"

3. Write down any beliefs that come to mind. Even if it doesn't make sense in the moment, write it down. For my example, here are some of my possible limiting beliefs:

   a. "I have been called overweight all my life. It is just who I am."

   b. "I have tried a million diets, and none of them work. I think it must just be bad genetics."

   c. "People see me and know me as a happy and fun person, but if I lost the weight, they would see me in a different way, and that wouldn't be good."

4. If you are struggling with coming up with a limiting belief, you might want to consult close friends or family members. Tell them your goal and your struggles and ask them this question: "What beliefs do you think I hold that are standing in my way from achieving my goal?" You might be surprised with what they come up with.

Resolve:

1. Choose one of your limiting beliefs you feel is stopping you from achieving your goal. For example, I am going to pick "I have been called overweight all my life. It is just who I am." Let's change that to something else.

2. Create a new belief to replace this limiting belief. Make the statement positive and powerful. My new belief is that I am beautiful inside and out, and I'm working each day at becoming even better.

3. Reprogram your brain by repeating this belief multiple times a day for thirty days. Go beyond just repeating it and write it down each day. Paste a note on your computer, phone, or refrigerator. Add some passion each time you say it.

4. If your limiting belief still exists, repeat it until it is resolved.

Now that we have a good handle on our limiting beliefs, gear up for one more exercise that will blow away any of your roadblocks so you can take action.

Exercise: Busting through Your Roadblocks

Most people have no clue what their roadblocks even are, but you are different. You just learned about the major roadblocks that stop people from taking action. Now I want you to get good at identifying your roadblocks and applying the techniques on how to overcome them. Remember, awareness is the first step to everything. Let's work on getting aware of what your roadblocks are because then we can work to overcome them.

1. Come up with one thing you have been wanting to take action on but just can't. If you are like most people, I am sure you have a big list. I suggest you pick something that is meaningful to you. You are more likely to have roadblocks there.

2. Go through the list of roadblocks and ask yourself if any of them apply. Write down the roadblocks that could be stopping you from taking action. Consider the following:

   - Do I fear that I might fail if I take action in this area?

   - Am I suffering from a lack of clarity in what I want to do?

   - If I took action, would that action be outside my comfort zone?

   - Is there just too much uncertainly around what I want to do?

   - Am I unable to take action because I need more data before I can move forward?

- Am I being a victim or failing to take responsibility in any area?

- Am I overwhelmed with the idea of taking action on this goal?

- Do I have beliefs from my past that are stopping me?

3. For each of the questions you wrote down or answered yes to, work to identify the why behind each of them. Why are you overwhelmed with this goal? Why are you fearful?

4. Reread the solution for each roadblock. Next, figure out what actions you need to take to remove or minimize this roadblock. Do you just need to change your perspective on the situation or maybe something more?

5. If you are really having fun with this exercise, then repeat it. Pick another thing you want to take action on and run through the exercise again.

Make a Decision

At the end of the day, all these roadblocks are very real, but you can take action in a nanosecond. All you have to do is decide. Forget everything else and cut straight to the finish line by simply deciding you are going to do something. I refer to this as the "brute force" approach, and there is nothing wrong with a little brute force.

Let's see how this works in action. Have you ever gone on a diet? Like almost everyone, of course, you have. And what was the difference between the moment before you decided to diet and the next moment, when you actually started dieting? That's right – you decided that enough was enough and that it would be the day you'd start. It was just like a light switch. One day you were eating crap, and the next day you were eating better.

Once you made that decision to take action, didn't you feel better? You were suddenly on your way to achieving something you had been wanting to achieve. If it wasn't a diet, maybe it was a decision to start a business, go to college, or even get a divorce. Once that decision was made, you could start taking action to move forward. Many times, making the decision is the hardest part, but once you do, it will set you on a new path and propel you to new heights. I guarantee it.

I challenge you to give this a try today. Come up with one small and simple thing you have been wanting to do and make the decision to take action on it. "I have decided to start_____ today!" Here are some ideas to get you thinking:

- "I have decided to start volunteering one day a month for a local charity."

- "I have decided to start walking briskly for thirty minutes a day."

- "I have decided to start having my family eat dinner together one day a week."

- "I have decided to start saving or investing 10 percent of my income."

Now commit to this action. You will be surprised by how easy that light switch can be turned on to set you up for success in the future.

The incredible Dr. Wayne Dyer taught me the concept of a "quantum moment." It is a very simple concept. There are times in your life when something very meaningful or dramatic happens, and it is during these moments when you make the shift into a new reality. Your life literally changes in an instant because of this major event. Unfortunately, the event that happens to motivate this change is usually bad, not good.

This happened to someone very close to me. One day, she was diagnosed with heart disease. She had struggled with being considerably overweight all her adult life, but after receiving that diagnosis, she made the decision that moment to change her life, and she probably saved it in the process. Within a year, she lost over one hundred pounds, and she has kept it off for years now. There are so many examples of quantum moments, but here are just a few:

- Death of a loved one

- Loss of a business or bankruptcy

- A car accident

- A near-death experience

- Failing out of school

- Any major failure in your life

STEP 4 – TAKE ACTION

Unfortunately, most quantum moments are negative experiences. My question to you is this: Why does it take something bad to motivate you to take action? Can't you create a quantum moment anytime you want? Just imagine the scenario and tie strong emotions to it.

Now this isn't easy for most of us to do. I understand that. But if you commit and work hard at it, you'll be able to skip the negative quantum moment and move straight into taking action. Just decide! It really takes only a nanosecond. It will be the most freeing thing you do. You will feel so amazing after making that decision to diet, start a business, get a divorce, get married, save money, or whatever you want to do.

CHAPTER 22

The Taking-Action Toolkit

I have created a handful of amazing tools to help you take action more easily and quickly. Once you are clear on where you want to go and you identity and resolve the roadblocks stopping you (for example, fear), then it really is just a matter of making a decision and having a solid plan.

The tools included in this chapter help you to do just that. First, let's remove one of the biggest barriers to taking action, which is indecisiveness and your inability to choose a path and commit to it. Next, I will share some planning tools I have used to make it easier for you to act step-by-step toward whatever you want to manifest. Remember, these are small, decisive steps with a clear direction on where you want to end up.

Also remember that with each action you take, the more momentum is created toward your overall goal. The hardest thing is to start, but once you get some momentum, you can really take off.

The Ultimate Taking-Action Tool

Now it's time to pull everything together with a framework for taking action. If you follow this step-by-step plan, it will guide you through the entire process and make sure at the end you have nothing preventing you mentally or physically from taking action. It's a six-step process.

- Step 1: Get Clear on What You Want to Do

- Step 2: Make the Decision

- Step 3: Create the Plan

- Step 4: Blow Away Your Blocks

- Step 5: Create Momentum

- Step 6: Measure and Adjust

While you go through this process, make sure you keep in mind all the principles we have discussed throughout this book about living a prosperous life. If you do, you will absolutely be making real progress toward your prosperous life by the end of this chapter.

Step 1: Get Clear on What You Want to Do

Everything starts here. It's nearly impossible to take meaningful action of any kind unless you know what you want to do. It's like getting into a car and driving, but you have no idea where you are going. I assure you, it will be hard to get there if you don't know where *there* is.

The clearer you are on what you want to do, the more likely you will take action and more importantly hit your goals. Here is the great thing: all the information you need to get clarity is already inside you. If you have even the smallest seed of desire to take action in a particular area of your life, then you have everything you need to get the clarity you need to make it happen. I will tell you that once you get clear on what you want to do, everything becomes much easier.

We devoted the last chapter to attaining clarity, starting with a careful look at who you are and then ending with a specific growth plan. Well, it's time to take that plan back out and convert it into action. If you're not ready to do that, then return to the last chapter and run through its exercises again. If you are ready, then read on.

Step 2: Make the Decision

By now, you know what you want to do. If there's a clear path forward, then jump to the next step. But if your situation is complex, you might need a sophisticated decision-making tool to help you get to the answer.

Well, I present to you the Multi-Attribute Decision Matrix (MDM). It's a tool I've been using for years. It has a fancy name, but it's a really easy tool to use. The MDM allows you to rank a host of possible actions. All you have to do is evaluate those actions against a list of weighted decision criteria that are important to you. The MDM will produce a score for each, helping you to sort through all your possibilities. Here's a warning, though: the MDM isn't for everyone. Some people will love it, and others will hate it. People who tend to be logical and unemotional in their decision-making will love it. People who tend to be more emotionally driven won't like the straightforward approach. This second group tends to struggle a bit with the results. Regardless of which group you fall into, though, I think this matrix will help clarify your thinking.

The Matrix Explained

I'm going to review each piece of the MDM. You can also download a copy of the MDM at KenBurke.com. I suggest you read through the explanation, so you understand how to complete the matrix. If you don't want to download the Microsoft Excel spreadsheet from my website, I suggest you build the model in Excel. Alternatively, you can absolutely do this with a piece of paper and a calculator.

Check out KenBurke.com for the Companion Guide that
contains useful worksheets for this exercise.

Step A: Outline the Possible Actions

Think about what you are trying to achieve. It could be anything from starting a new business to deciding whether you should marry someone. The list of possibilities could be as simple as yes and no, as with the decision to marry, or it could be a more complicated list of alternatives, as with deciding which kind of business to start. For example, here are some business ideas I've been personally considering:

STEP 4 – TAKE ACTION

- Software company

- Fashion company

- Chocolate company

- Technology services company

- An e-learning company

Step B: Define the Measuring Criteria

Next, define the things that are most important in making this decision. What are the things to consider? These are what we call the criteria. Create a list, stating each item in its most ideal form. For example, here are the criteria if you're considering starting a business:

- Low startup capital required

- High revenue potential

- Low complexity of business

- High value in ten years

- Level of interest

- Your knowledge in this field

- Positive impact to people's lives

If you state them in this form, a high ranking for each criterion will indicate a positive effect and create a standard basis for comparison.

Step C: Weight the Measuring Criteria

Assign a weight to each criterion based on how important it is to your decision-making process. I suggest you use the simple one-to-ten scale, with ten being extremely important and one being very unimportant. Continue with our business example and fill in the weights from my own perspective:

Criteria	Weight
Low startup capital needed	7
High revenue potential	9
Low complexity of business	5
High value in ten years	10
My level of interest	9
My knowledge of the chocolate industry	4
Positive impact to people's lives	7

We will come back to these weights after we score each criterion in the next step.

Step D: Score Each Action for Each Criterion

Now the fun begins. Score each possible action as it relates to each criterion. Going back to our starting-a-business example, let's take each business and score it against one of the criteria.

Possible Action	High Revenue Potential	Low Complexity
Software company	9	2
Fashion company	7	7
Chocolate company	5	8
Technology services company	6	6
E-learning company	3	10

You can see how the scores vary widely based on each criterion. Sometimes there is a lot involved in making these decisions.

Step E: Do the Math

Next, multiply the weight for each criterion by the score you gave each possible action. Remember in step C that I assigned a weight of "9" to the criterion high revenue potential? So I'd take that 9 and multiply it by each of the scores I gave to each type of possible company.

STEP 4 – TAKE ACTION

Possible Action	High Revenue Potential	Weighted Score
Software company	9	81
Fashion company	7	63
Chocolate company	5	45
Technology services company	6	54
E-learning company	3	27

Complete this for each criterion and then add the scores for each possible action.

Step F: Interpret the Results

This is a easy step. While nothing is cut and dry, you will get weighted scores for each decision or action. It is up to you to determine whether the highest score is the best decision or action for you. Either way ...

You must make a decision now!

That's right. The brainstorming and planning are over. You can't move to the next step if you don't have your decision made.

Right after you make a big decision, there will be this period where you question your decision and maybe even obsess over it until you start taking action. I assure you, once you start taking action, though, you'll discover more clarity and therefore less anxiety. Think about making the decision to go skydiving, for example. Some people would go back and forth on it for years. Up to the point you actually jump, you would question your decision. *Really, should I do this? Why am I here?* But once you jump – or land safely, I should say – you are not only relieved but also exhilarated. You can't believe you did it. And of course, there's a huge sense of accomplishment. More importantly, you now have much more data to determine whether you should try it again or not. As I have said before and will say again, the mere act of taking action gives you more information and clarity to make your next moves.

You will question your decision to take a certain action over and over, but it's critical at this point to commit. Start taking action so you can get more data and get further clarity.

To help you strengthen the decision you just made, come up with five positive things you will get out of moving forward with your decision. Come up with the things you value the most. Maybe they are money, knowledge, better looks, more energy, better health, satisfaction, joy, a new car, or something else. But don't stop there. Come up with another five things if you can. And for even more bonus points, do it one more time. This strategy will help your brain override the fear and uncertainty with all the benefits you will get. Then every day, every hour if you have to, reimagine all those positive things you came up with. Write them down and carry them with you. This step really works.

Step 3: Create the Plan

Most of us have been told to create a plan when we are setting goals, but few of us do. I assure you that you will be much more likely to be successful at achieving your objectives if you follow the sure-fire framework below. I have been using this plan for many years, and it works great.

The What, Why, How, and When Plan (WWHW)

There are lots of frameworks for planning and goal setting. Please feel free to use any method that will get you to the results. That is all I care about. The WWHW framework is one I created based on something I have been using in my business for many years; it has allowed me to achieve a great deal over the last twenty years.

I believe the key to success is breaking down what you want to achieve into small, bite-sized pieces. Please note that in this plan, I call whatever you are trying to achieve an "initiative." The more you break down your initiatives, the more likely you are to take action on them. Makes sense, right? When something looks less intimidating, you are more likely to do it. You can create many initiatives that all add up to the bigger initiatives you are trying to achieve. Keep it simple, and you will be much more likely to succeed.

Define the What

Key initiative: We have worked a lot on getting clear and defining what we want. Write down your answer from step one of this chapter — your key initiative. Now define that initiative in one sentence, incorporating specifics and concrete actions. The more vague the key initiative is, the harder it will be to achieve it. Here are some examples of good and not-so-good key initiatives:

Not Good	Good
Lose weight or look better.	Lose twenty pounds in the next six months.
Start a business.	Create a chocolate company and generate $250,000 of revenue within the first year.
Buy a house.	Save $100,000 within two years for the down payment on a new home.
Learn Spanish.	Learn conversational Spanish within six months and become fluent within one year.
Find a new job to make more money.	Find a job in project management that makes 20 percent above my current salary.

Do you see the difference? The good initiatives are more specific and usually have a time frame or some measurement associated with them. Be specific but also keep them general enough so you can define the actions necessary to achieve them.

Sub-initiatives: The secret weapons in your plan are effective sub-initiatives. These are the bite-sized pieces. The smaller, more defined initiatives are directly associated and linked with the key initiative.

How much should you break things down? If the key initiative has multiple parts or layers of actions under each part, then break it down into sub-initiatives. Each sub-initiative should consist of a simple action that doesn't take more than a couple of months to achieve. Make these even more specific than the key initiative and include deadlines.

Let's look at some examples using the chocolate business and the revenue goal above. Here are my sub-initiatives:

- Build a business plan.

- Secure $500,000 in funding.

- Learn to make amazing chocolate.

- Create chocolates and packaging.

- Create an e-commerce website.

- Select location in San Francisco.

- Design and build out a store location in San Francisco.

- Hire and train staff.

- Set up manufacturing.

- Develop a marketing and promotional plan.

- Prepare for the grand opening.

- Elicit customer feedback, measure success, and adjust.

These are all the essential steps in starting a business. Some of these sub-initiatives could be broken down further, of course, but for this example, we will stop here.

If you find you end up with more than about twenty actions per sub-initiative, you might be looking at multiple initiatives. Continue to categorize things until each initiative looks achievable; this is the key. If you can start making measurable progress, you'll be highly motivated to continue. Also, you can create as many sub-initiatives as you want. If a sub-initiative is too big, then create another layer — a sub-sub-initiative. For example, in the sub-initiative about designing and building a store location, there will be hundreds of steps, of which there will be sub-steps. Create as many layers of categories as you wish, but make sure it all looks specific and achievable.

Initiative map: I talked about mind mapping software earlier; tracking and visualizing initiatives are great applications for it. Here is a list of mind mapping software I recommend. Mindjet Mind Manager is the one I use and absolutely love, but it is pricey.

As an alternative, get out a piece of paper and a pen, and follow along. These maps are simple, and you really don't need software unless your initiatives are very complex. Let's do a simple mind map for the business initiative.

STEP 4 – TAKE ACTION

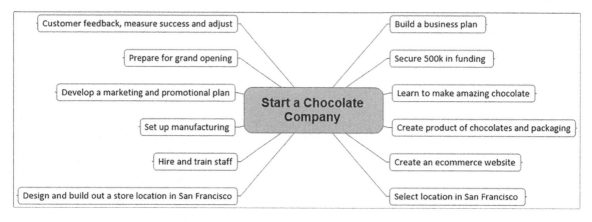

From this, you could go further and list every action beneath each sub-initiative. This is where the software programs come in handy. This allows you to not only visualize but also adjust things easily and quickly.

Achievement map: On a higher level, you can also map key initiatives in all the areas of your life and work on multiple ones at the same time. Just don't overdo it; you could lose focus and end up overwhelming yourself and achieving little. I create an achievement map each year, and I have found these maps very useful to guide me in all my key initiatives. I put all those things I want to achieve over the next year. I know some initiatives will span multiple years, and that is okay. Any initiatives I want to make progress on also go on my achievement map. You can include all aspects of your life: relationships, finances, career, spiritual life, physical life, learning, and so forth.

Let's look at my achievement map. Here are my key initiatives over the next year.

- Complete the writing of this book and publish it.
- Create a platform for the book.
- Start my business venture company (Extraordinary Ventures) and create and fund two startup companies.
- Travel to four new countries.
- Get toned by losing ten pounds and increase the intensity of my workouts.
- Meditate three times a week for thirty minutes.
- Buy a house.
- Develop a meaningful love relationship.
- Take cooking classes and cook something new once every two weeks.
- Become conversational in Spanish.

Here is my achievement map:

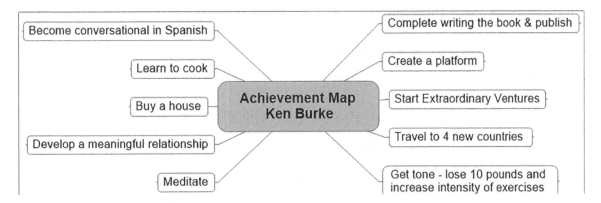

For each one of these, I have detailed sub-initiatives and a ton of actions outlined for each. The map is quite large, so I didn't include the whole thing, but you get the idea.

State the Why

Now that we know the what, one of the best ways to make sure you are completely committed to your plan is to understand why you want to achieve this initiative. The why is extremely important for creating extra motivation for you to take action. The clearer you are, the more likely you are to actually act. Ask yourself the following:

- Why is this initiative so important to me?

- What benefits will I get if I take this initiative?

List as many benefits as you can think of; the more you come up with, the better. And for each one, tie a feeling or emotion to it. What feeling or emotion will each trigger?

It is equally important to ask yourself how you will feel if you don't achieve it. How bad will you feel if you don't succeed? It is important to consider both the positive as well as the negative.

As Tony Robbins teaches, to take action, you have to both build up lots of pain for not doing something and just as much pleasure for doing it. It is a double dose of motivation to kick you in your butt and get you moving.

I highly recommend you write the why down next to each initiative you are going to achieve. Certainly, writing down the benefits as well as these positive and negative emotions is also important. For the chocolate company, consider this:

STEP 4 – TAKE ACTION

Why is building a chocolate company important to me?

- I want to build products that make people happy.

- I want to build a high-end branded company.

- I want to express myself creatively.

- This will challenge me to grow and learn new things.

What are the benefits I will experience from starting this chocolate company?

- Money: The business could be very profitable, allowing me to provide for my family.

- Learning: I will learn a ton by building a brand from scratch.

- Social: I'll increase my social interactions, and I'm happier when I am around people.

- Fun: This will be a fun business to create and manage.

- Creativity: I can be creative daily, which I love.

Determine the How:

The how is where we take each initiative and sub-initiative, and identify their action steps. This is my favorite part of the whole process!

For years, I have been using what I call "action cards," which are really nothing more than pieces of paper or index cards (I use cardstock paper folded in half). Here are a few steps to guide you:

1. At the top, write down the initiative or sub-initiative.

2. Write down all the actions needed to achieve this initiative. It is important that you do this for each sub-initiative.

3. If you have lots of actions (more than twenty-five), break things down into multiple sub-initiatives on multiple action cards. You can also group similar actions into categories to help maintain organization and to keep you from getting overwhelmed.

4. Actions must be as specific and well defined as possible.

Coming up with the how isn't very difficult. First, define everything you need to do. Second, break the actions into achievable, bite-sized pieces. Each small action you achieve gets you closer to achieving your initiative. Here's an example using the business plan initiative for the chocolate business:

Key Initiative: Starting a Chocolate Business

Sub-Initiative: Build a Business Plan

Actions:

- Build a competitive binder, looking at each of the major competitors and their strategies.

- Research positioning and pricing strategies in the industry.

- Research size and growth of industry.

- Determine competitive advantage of the business.

- Meet with ten chocolate chefs to research the manufacturing process.

- Build a three-year financial model for the business.

- Develop an initial marketing plan to promote the business.

- Determine the most cost-effective way to build and market the e-commerce website.

- Develop the initial product mix, including chocolates and packaging, and other products sold online and in the store.

- Determine the cost structure for all products.

- Determine the feasibility of the business after research is completed.

- Write the actual plan (keep to twenty pages).

- Build an investor's presentation deck based on the plan.

Figure Out the When

A fundamental of every goal-setting activity isn't just creating the initiatives and actions but also defining when you expect to achieve them.

STEP 4 – TAKE ACTION

Time is a fantastic motivator. Creating the when is important for two reasons. First, nothing drives people more than deadlines. These deadlines can help push you along and keep you on track. There is also a certain sense of achievement for each action you complete. Those little successes can be very motivating and keep you on the path to success. Second, including the "when" in your actions is a great way to measure how you are doing. This allows you to adjust your entire plan if things fall off the rails. Here are some quick guidelines to assign dates to your actions:

- While dates can push you through the process, it is also important to make them achievable. If you are always stressed out or not enjoying the process, you are less likely to keep going. Don't always be in a hurry.

- Don't be afraid to adjust the dates. I would much rather you have a realistic plan rather than creating something you know is impossible to do.

- But if your dates are so far apart that achieving the initiative is going to take forever, then break your initiative into smaller pieces.

- Keep in mind that life is a journey, not a destination. Enjoy the process.

I strongly suggest that you don't create initiatives that go longer than six months. I have found in my twenty-plus years of being in business that things that last more than six months tend to lose energy. If you do have a key initiative or sub-initiatives that are that big and require more than six months, break them into smaller sub-initiatives and focus on one at a time.

I also recommend creating an overall timeline for your key initiative. In my business, I would never do a project without a Microsoft Project plan. In fact, I require one of these before I approve funds for any project my executives want to do. I'm not suggesting you run out and build a complex Microsoft Project plan for everything you want to achieve; in fact, that would be overkill for most initiatives. But the importance of visualizing your actions and initiatives on a timeline might be helpful to you.

Simply take the major milestones (this could be each action, group of actions, or sub-initiatives) and draw a line for each from the start date to the end date. You can divide your chart into days, weeks or months, depending on how long your initiative will take.

This will show you two things. First, the existence of any dependencies – the need to complete one action before starting the next. Second, whether things overlap. If they do, you might need to adjust the dates.

Step 4: Blow Away Your Blocks

Earlier in this chapter, we reviewed the potential roadblocks to decisive action. In this step, I'll take you through two exercises that will absolutely blow away any roadblocks standing in your way.

Exercise 1: Identifying and Eliminating Risks

The number one reason people are stuck and don't take action is fear. This is one of the most powerful emotions we have. Instead of facing our fears, most people just remain stuck.

The most common fear is fear of failure. We think if we do something we have never done before, there is a high likelihood that we will fail at it. And as you know from earlier in the book, the ego plays a big role in creating fear. The ego never wants to look bad, so it creates this fear of failure if the future outcome is unknown. It really is just a protection mechanism.

One easy way to quickly blow through roadblocks is to first identify any risks associated with the actions you are planning. Write down all the risks you can think of. Ask yourself the following:

- What are the risks associated with this action?

- What bad things could happen if I do take this action?

By writing them down, you'll get them out of your head, and your brain can begin to process them and see how serious they really are. In many cases, when they are in your head, they are more exaggerated than when they are on paper.

Next, I want you to rate the fear based on two criteria. First, what impact does the risk have on your life? Is it really no big deal, or would it be devastating? Second, what is the likelihood this fear could come true? Rate these on scales of one to ten.

For those risks with low scores, just take them off the list. They aren't that important and won't cause you many challenges. For those with the highest scores, work to neutralize the risk. That means for each risk, come up with one or more actions you can take to reduce or eliminate that risk.

You won't be able to reduce or eliminate every risk, but anything you can do to reduce the overall risk will make it more likely you will act.

STEP 4 – TAKE ACTION

My risk (or fear) in starting the chocolate business is that it will be a horrible failure. Let's go through the steps:

1. Identify the risk.
2. Score the risk based on its impact.
3. Score the risk based on its likelihood.
4. Determine what actions I can take to reduce or eliminate the risk.

Risk or Fear	Impact Score	Likelihood Score	Actions
Lose lots of money.	9	6	Minimize initial investment and test the concept before going all in.
Waste years of my life.	7	3	Create a belief that states you can't waste any time if you learn from the experience. All this moves you towards learning your lessons.
Be embarrassed.	2	7	Work on my ego.
Don't have enough knowledge or experience.	5	5	Access the level of knowledge I need. Get a mentor who knows the business.
Customers hate my product.	6	1	This is unlikely because everyone loves chocolate. Remove from list.
Make enemies.	2	2	Remove from list.
Lose my family or friends because I have no time for them.	8	7	Set a life rule that says you can work only sixty hours a week.

Check out **KenBurke.com** for the Companion Guide that contains useful worksheets for this exercise.

While this is a pretty easy and quick exercise, it can be powerful to realize that most of the risks you face aren't as insurmountable as you think. Some risks are unimportant, while others can be handled by changing your perspective on them or taking action to reduce or eliminate them. Let's look at a more comprehensive exercise to help you get unstuck and to remove any of those nasty roadblocks in your way.

Exercise 2: Busting through Your Roadblocks

In this exercise, you'll develop your ability to identify your roadblocks and apply techniques on how to overcome them. Remember, awareness is the first step to almost everything we work on together. Let's work on getting aware of what your roadblocks are because then we can work to overcome them.

1. Come up with one thing you have been wanting to take action on but just can't. Pick something meaningful. You are more likely to have roadblocks there.

2. Go through the following list of roadblocks and ask yourself whether each applies. If so, write them down.

   a. Do I fear that I might fail?

   b. Am I suffering from a lack of clarity on what I want to do?

   c. If I took action, would that action be outside my comfort zone?

   d. Is there too much uncertainly around what I want to do?

   e. Am I unable to take action because I need more data?

   f. Am I being a victim or not taking responsibility for my entire life in every situation?

   g. Am I overwhelmed with the idea of taking action?

   h. Do I have beliefs from my past that are stopping me from taking action?

3. For each of the questions you wrote down or answered yes to, work to identify the why of each. For example, why are you overwhelmed? Why are you fearful?

4. Now reread the solutions section for that roadblock. Next, figure out what actions you need to take to remove or minimize this roadblock. Do you just need to change your perspective on the situation or maybe something more? This is your chance to finally

resolve your roadblocks. I assure you that if you don't do this now, the roadblock will continue to creep up in your life. So why not just resolve it now? You will feel so much better.

5. If you are making progress with this exercise, then do it again. Pick another thing you want to take action on and run through the exercise again.

Step 5: Create Momentum

Now let's supercharge your actions by creating as much momentum as possible. This can help get you off the ground with your decision as well as push you forward. The more momentum you can create, the more likely you are to achieve your goals.

Once you begin taking action, fear can set in. Remember, fear is just your ego protecting itself, but the ego is very powerful. Once you begin taking action, you will start to question your decision. "Am I doing the right thing?" "Is this the right time for this?" "Do I know what I am doing?" Creating massive momentum is one of the best ways to combat this fear. This momentum will build up and crush the fears and all that questioning.

Creating momentum is all about generating energy to drive you toward achieving your initiatives. Below are some techniques that will help you create energy around your actions. Even a little extra energy could be just the thing that pushes you forward enough to get things moving. Have you ever helped a friend push-start a car with a dead battery? As you begin, the car at first is really heavy and hard to push, but as you get a bit of momentum, it gets easier, and suddenly, the engine kicks in, and the car takes off. Well, you are doing the same thing with these techniques.

Momentum Tip 1: Take Action to Create More Action

The best way to create momentum is to take action. Action begets more action. This is why I have been pushing you very hard to get started doing something, anything, toward your goal. Even very small actions can help start the engine. One technique I use to get myself to take action is to research and increase my knowledge on the topic. Pick up a book and start reading or jump on the internet. While this might seem passive, it helps get you engaged in the process. For many people, it is also a way of dipping a toe into the water. You say to yourself, "I am just doing a little research. What can that hurt?" And your fears will subside a bit.

Momentum Tip 2: Break It Down

I've said it before, and I'll say it again, because this is one of the best techniques for getting yourself to take action. Breaking your larger action into small, bite-size pieces will really help.

Momentum Tip 3: Talk to People

Communicating your intentions makes it more likely that you will take action. Just talking about what you want to do gives it energy. In fact, talking is another form of taking action. As you discuss your goals with others, they will give you encouragement, feedback, and ideas about your actions. And once your intentions are out there, these same people will hold your feet to the fire by asking you, "How's it going?" When you have to report back to people on your progress, your ego doesn't want to say, "I am a failure and have done nothing." This is one place where ego comes in handy to push you a bit.

One caveat: make sure you talk to people who are positive and supportive. People who are negative toward you and your intentions will create negative energy and doubt. Don't let that happen. Avoid them and don't let them take you off your game.

Momentum Tip 3: Find a Mentor

Track down someone who has already gone through what you are attempting and solicit their guidance and direction to guide and inspire your actions. Just knowing you have someone by your side who has lived through this will diminish your fear. A mentor also gives you energy and can give you a little push when you need it.

Momentum Tip 4: Build a Trusted Support Network

While a mentor is someone who has seen the movie and lived through the actions, your support network is made up of those who encourage you and give you positive energy. Select people who aren't in competition with you either literally or in life. You know those people who are always trying to be better than you? Leave them out of your network. Also, I suggest you pick some people who are close to you and whom you trust but also pick some people who aren't as close but have some knowledge about the things you are trying to achieve. Here are some examples:

Family: The most obvious is family. However, these folks don't always make the best support network. My advice to you is to pick your family members carefully. And don't feel obligated to have a family member in your support network just because he or she is family.

Friends: The same rules apply to friends as they do for family. Select your friends carefully. Select the ones you believe can add value to your attempts to achieve your goals.

Spiritual Advisers: I always think having someone on the spiritual side to support you is a great thing. This person can be a religious leader in your place of worship or even an energy clearer, clairvoyant, yoga instructor, or meditation coach.

Professional: These people can be extremely valuable in supporting you. Depending on the initiative you are working on, this could be your psychologist, CPA, real estate agent, financial adviser, business coach, life coach, personal trainer, and so forth. The only word of caution here is to make sure to check that they are interested in helping you achieve your initiative. Will they financially benefit from your achievements? Will they gain in status? Even if the answer is yes, they still may be just fine. It is always good to understand their motivations as you add them to your support team.

Managing Your Support Network

Once you have formed your support network, you can decide how formally or informally you want to use them. A more informal method might be just checking in with them once in a while. A more formal method might be gathering your entire group together for regular updates and group coaching sessions. If this seems a bit much for you, then find something in between that works.

If they are part of your support network, it's important to keep them engaged. Communicate with them and make them part of the process. When you achieve your goals, they also get some satisfaction out of it because they helped you. Be sure to provide them updates on how you are doing. They want to know.

The size of your support network is up to you. Some people love lots of people all around them and can process the feedback well, while others like only a few. I would say not to have more than ten people in your network for any individual initiative you are working to achieve. Any more, and they can become hard to manage.

Momentum Tip 5: Meditate

I recommend that you meditate for many reasons. There are so many benefits that will help you in all aspects of your life. You will create more momentum and energy toward your actions if you are relaxed, calm, and focused on the end game. If your energies are scattered all over the place, which is typical when you are doing something new, it's harder to maintain the momentum you need. Having your energies aligned with your goals and staying highly focused on achieving them will give you that extra boost you need.

Momentum Tip 6: Understand the Why

Make sure you thoroughly understand why you are doing what you are doing. The clearer you are, the more your energy will be aligned with the end goal. It is the difference between driving down a bumpy road with lots of potholes and driving down a nicely paved road. You still might get there, but it certainly is lots easier and more comfortable if you know why you are doing it. This also helps you stop constantly questioning your decisions.

Accelerate Your Actions

Do you want to create more energy and momentum, push harder to take more action, and move faster toward your goals? The sooner you start seeing results, the more energy you will want to expend. Let's say you are going on a diet. When you lose those first five pounds and start to see your clothes fitting better, there is an excitement that comes over you. It's working. And what do you want to do when something is working? You want to do more of it.

Step 6: Measure and Adjust

Finally, we are almost done. We have our plan and are executing it. Everything is perfect. What more could I want from you? Well, after you start executing, you have to put in mechanisms to measure whether you are achieving your objectives. This is a basic principle of goal setting, but many people forget to adjust their actions based on what they are learning and the clarity they are getting along the way. You should even be prepared to redo your action plan if necessary.

Measure: If you created a strong plan, your goals will be stated in definitive and specific terms, which allow for measurements. One of our examples was "I am going to lose twenty pounds in the next six months." Well, if you get on the scale after three months and find you've lost only two pounds, you know it's time to reassess your methods.

Measurements also help reinforce your goal and, in many cases, can push you a bit harder to obtain something that is very defined. If, after three months, that scale says you've lost nine pounds, you know you're very nearly on the right track; you just need to make those last couple of adjustments. In this way, measurements can give you tremendous guidance.

Here is an example from my own life. For years, my goal was to sell my technology software company. When I took back control of the company two years before it actually sold, I set a measurement of not just selling the company but selling it for over $100 million. Remember, at the time I took back control from the prior CEO, the company had an offer on the table for $30 million.

I communicated my goal to all my stakeholders, including my board, all my investors, my executive team, and most importantly, my investment bankers. The first year back, I needed to fix lots of things to get the company back on track and to increase its value. The second year I worked to position the company for sale. Mind you, it takes a while to sell a company for $100 million, so a year goes by fast. The end result from creating this measurement was that I sold the company for $103 million. If I hadn't set that measurement, we would have likely sold the company for $80 million. But I was so committed to my measurement that when the buyer came along, all my stakeholders were so convinced it was worth what I thought that the buyer really had no choice in the matter.

Adjust: Remember not to be afraid to adjust both your action plan as well as your measurements if you need to. Adjusting is an important and necessary part of the process. I suggest breaking up what you want to achieve into pieces (as I have stated before) and at each point, checking to see how things are going. If you are on track, move to the next step. If not, you might need to adjust some things. If this is the case, I strongly recommend you update your action plan and your measurements. You will have a higher degree of success that way.

Summary: Using the Taking-Action Tool

That was a lot to take in. Here is a brief summary of each step. Refer back to this until you get the hang of it. Trust me, it will come in handy.

1. Get clear: Everything starts here. You must be really clear on what you want to achieve. The more specific, the more likely you will achieve it. Remember to ask great questions

about the things you are working on achieving in your life. Keep asking those questions until you get really good answers. If you are struggling with getting clear on what you want to do, you can always review the section on getting clear, and it will walk you through the process.

2. Make the decision: You must put a stake in the ground and decide what direction you are going in. Better to decide and try something out rather than just to do nothing at all. Use the Decision Matrix tool I provided if you are struggling.

3. Create a plan: If you want to succeed at almost anything, you need a plan; otherwise you are just leaving things up to luck. Use my what, why, how, and when model, and you can't go wrong. Just define what it is you want to achieve, why you want to achieve it, how you plan to achieve it, and when you will achieve it. By laying out a good plan, you better ensure your success in achieving exactly what you want.

4. Blow away your roadblocks: There is no question you have some roadblocks standing in your way and making it difficult or impossible to take action. If you didn't have roadblocks, you would already be moving forward. Identify which roadblocks are in your way and come up with a strategy to deal with them. I have outlined many strategies in this section to help you blow them away.

5. Create momentum: It's time to supercharge our actions by creating momentum toward them. The best type of momentum is doing something that moves you closer to your goal. Momentum also comes from talking with people, finding a mentor to guide you, building a support team, and meditating. Make sure you add some momentum to your actions.

Measure and Adjust

And finally, the all-important measure of what you are achieving to see whether you are on track. Don't be afraid to adjust those plans as you are taking actions toward your goals. Measuring and adjusting as you go will not only make it easier for you to get to your destination but also make the journey much more pleasant.

STEP 5

Give Gratitude

CHAPTER 23

Gratitude Is the Key to Accelerating Your Happiness

I saved the best for last. Gratitude is the icing on the cake of life. It is such a befitting way to bring our journey together to an end. Gratitude pulls everything together and makes it all work. If you add a little dose of gratitude to everything you do, you will be amazed by how your life will change for the better.

Gratitude: The Missing Ingredient

As you know, I have spent more than twenty-five years studying and researching the topic of personal growth and development. For some reason, the topic of gratitude is either glossed over or skipped altogether. Moreover, there are very few books dedicated to the topic. It is puzzling to me because gratitude is the glue that holds a happy and fulfilling life together. It is one of the most powerful tools you have.

First, let's define *gratitude. Gratitude* is being thankful for *everything* in your life. It means giving thanks to the people in your life and also being grateful for all the situations that happen in your life — both good and bad. Wait, did I just say the good *and* the bad? How can you be grateful for the bad in life? We will talk lots about that in just a bit.

STEP 5 – GIVE GRATITUDE

Giving thanks sounds easy, doesn't it? But for many people, it is anything but. While some people learn gratitude at a very early age, others don't have very good role models growing up and miss this step. Have you ever noticed there are people who don't say thank you to a waiter at a restaurant? Or worse, maybe your partner doesn't say thank you to you. I see this all the time, and it drives me crazy. I'm not suggesting these people are mean and uncaring; rather, they just didn't learn about being grateful early in life. For me, being grateful is a habit. I just do it without thinking. I say thank you to everyone and in most every situation. It might even be a bit too much (if that is possible).

My thank-yous aren't usually your normal, under-your-breath thank you; rather, I raise my voice a bit, increase the pitch, put a big smile on my face, and look at people while I say thank you. And I will tell you, I see them respond positively. They can tell I really mean it and almost always smile back.

The Ingredients of Gratitude

Gratitude is made up of three important components: appreciation, love, and grace.

Appreciation

The first element of being grateful is appreciation. Appreciation is something that comes from deep in your heart and is something you feel. I think this adds the magic to gratitude. This is where the emotion comes from and people can sense that. I know when I am truly appreciative of something or someone that it takes being grateful to a new level.

Love

Being grateful is an expression of love. I think there needs to be a dose of love anytime you are grateful. Love is what opens the heart and allows you to give gratitude to yourself or others.

Grace

Grace is another word for God. I believe there is a spiritual component to gratitude, and grace is it. Gratitude isn't something you can see or touch necessarily, but you can feel it.

Gratitude is a bit complex and can be hard to define, but if you mix these three components together — appreciation, love, and grace — you will have a good idea what it means to give gratitude.

An Attitude of Gratitude

You may have heard the phrase "attitude of gratitude." It isn't just catchy but also very accurate. Gratitude is really an attitude you live with each and every day. It is something you incorporate into your life and embed into your brain cells. It governs all your interactions with people so much so that you don't even think about it. The cool thing is that you don't even need to think about it, though; it just happens because it is part of you.

I have incorporated gratitude into my everyday life, and it is the first thing that pops into my mind when I'm interacting with someone, whether I'm just buying a coffee or living in a very challenging business relationship that is driving me nuts. With the latter, I can always get back to center by giving a little gratitude to the situation. It is like taking a magic pill for me.

How do you build an attitude of gratitude? This is like most other things we have talked about in this book. Building an attitude of gratitude is just like building a muscle in your body. At first you have to think lots about it. In some cases, you even have to force yourself to be grateful for certain situations. It's easy to be grateful for the good things but much harder for the bad things. You must consciously stop yourself from reacting and ask yourself, "What can I be grateful for in this situation? How is this benefiting me?"

Use this same technique for the positive things in life as well. It might seem basic, but if you find that you don't thank people all that often, then look for opportunities to say thank you for things you wouldn't normally say thank you for. And try to do it just like I explained earlier, with a big, hearty, happy "Thank you!"

After a while, you will start to build your muscle memory for this. It will take a bit of time to get used to it, especially if you aren't already predisposed to it, but it will become more and more automatic. You won't even need to think about it. It will just become embedded in your soul.

STEP 5 – GIVE GRATITUDE

Gratitude: The Key to Accelerating Happiness

This is probably the biggest revelation I have had in my own life. The best way to truly feel happiness in your life is by giving gratitude. It works every time. It doesn't matter whether the situation or person is good or bad – the moment you are grateful, everything changes. It might seem crazy, but even in the worst situations, when I can find my path to become grateful for whatever is going on, suddenly my entire state changes. I go from sad or angry to happy. A smile crosses my face. It isn't always easy to change my state like this in an instant, but I have become very good at it, so for me, it happens almost automatically.

Let's say you get into a fight with your partner, and you are angry and hurt. You can teach yourself to easily and effortlessly be grateful for that person in your life because he or she is the one teaching you valuable lessons in life. It might seem hard to do at first, but you will get really good at it over time. By putting yourself in this state of gratitude, you will go from sad and angry to appreciative and reflective – appreciative for that person and reflective on what lessons you are learning.

At least, this is what happens to me, strange though it might seem. I also start getting even nicer and more appreciative to everyone around me. Sometimes I even have to stop and think, *Why do I react like this to a bad situation?* I hope you can let it happen to you as well because it is so much better than the alternative.

Try it out. Within the next twenty-four hours, find a situation or interaction that would usually frustrate you or cause you some negative emotions. At that moment, find a reason to be grateful for whatever is going on. Maybe your child or spouse is causing you to feel frustration and anger. In that situation, ask yourself, "What do I have to feel grateful for in this situation?" I assure you that your brain will come up with an answer. Maybe you are grateful for the amazing person he or she is and all the happiness the person brings into your life. If for some reason you can't come up with anything, my fallback position is figuring out what I am learning. No matter what the situation is, you most assuredly are learning something. In the situation with the kids or spouse, it might be how not to react from ego or possibly how not to react emotionally to situations like these. There is always something to learn and always something to be grateful for in every situation.

Interconnected Gratitude

I have been amazed to learn just how interconnected gratitude is to everything in our lives. Gratitude has a profound impact on whatever we are working on. Whether you are trying to lose weight, start a new business, work through challenges in a relationship, or become more spiritual, gratitude plays a role in making any life even better but also easier to manage. Because gratitude works as a cure-all for so many things, once you get good at it, you will find so many uses for it. Let's look at how gratitude connects to so many other elements.

Self-Acceptance

Gratitude can play a huge role in your ability to accept yourself. Remember, gratitude is all about love, and nothing is more important than the love you experience for yourself. It all starts right here. Gratitude for the amazing person you are can be a key that unlocks your self-love.

When you are grateful for yourself, it is very hard to beat yourself up at the same time. Instead, it will put you in a state of self-acceptance. Being grateful for who you are can help to reduce or eliminate any negative emotions around self-worth you might experience.

Take a situation where you often beat up on yourself. For example, maybe you're hard on yourself for your struggles with losing weight. Your internal voice tells you that you aren't good enough, not worthy of losing that weight, or maybe just not capable of doing it. Now, let's apply gratitude to the situation. Ask yourself, "What can I be grateful for, even though I am overweight?" Be grateful for the wonderful person you are inside. Be grateful for the opportunity to learn to lose weight in a healthy way. Be grateful for all the beauty in your soul that comes out and impacts everyone you touch, regardless of your weight.

Weight is just one example, but there are so many reasons why we don't accept ourselves for the perfect beings we are at this moment in time. Giving gratitude can open those pathways to be more kind and loving to yourself. Find those reasons to be grateful for who you are.

Clarity

The thing I love about gratitude is that it awakens the imagination. And as you know, your imagination is the starting point for the clarity in your life. I have found that gratitude relaxes me and opens up my mind to new possibilities. When my brain is relaxed, feeling that love and happiness, it sees the world from a positive perspective. And when you're positive and coming from a loving place, your imagination is ignited with new ideas.

Think of something you want to manifest in your life. Ask yourself, "Why should I be grateful for this idea, and how might this idea benefit me?" At the highest level, if you take action on this idea, it can help you grow and learn new lessons. Maybe this idea will allow you to manifest more money, a better relationship, or maybe even a new spiritual awareness. Giving gratitude to the idea will help you to expand it and develop it into something you can take action on; furthermore, it will give you extra motivation.

Remember, ideas don't just pop into your head; they are all part of your purpose. You wouldn't have the ideas in the first place if they weren't in alignment with your purpose and with those lessons you have to learn while you are here on earth. The ideas are all part of your growth plan.

Ego Busting

Gratitude is the ultimate ego buster. When you are coming from a place of true gratitude, it is also impossible to come from ego, because gratitude and ego are at opposite ends of the spectrum. Gratitude is all about giving love, and ego is about taking away love. Gratitude wants to build people (perhaps even yourself) up, and ego, through its judgments, wants to tear people (or yourself) down.

When you find yourself judging someone or yourself, try to express gratitude toward that person instead. You will find that it's impossible to do both. You have to pick one or the other. Choose to be grateful for that person and the lessons he or she is teaching you rather than judging him or her to make your ego feel good. And then watch what you get back. Instead of a negative experience, you will most likely get love and gratitude back — maybe even more than you gave.

Let's try another one. Catch yourself in a situation where you know you are coming from ego. Maybe you are competing at something and must win at all costs. Maybe you are comparing yourself against someone else. Stop yourself immediately and ask yourself, "What do I have to be grateful for in this situation?" This simple but powerful question will interrupt the pattern coming from ego and get your soul to experience true gratitude for whatever you are experiencing.

Taking Action

Taking action is never easy. It requires you to take a risk, face your fears, and maybe do something you aren't comfortable with. But it's so much easier to take action when you can do it from a place of gratitude. So be grateful for your vision. Be grateful for the opportunity to take action. And be grateful for the possible outcomes from the action you take. Gratitude can give you that extra motivation you need to move forward with your goals and initiatives. And giving gratitude just makes everything so much easier and more enjoyable.

When you are struggling with taking action on one of your goals or initiatives, it is a perfect time to apply some gratitude to the situation and to see whether you can break through. Identify something you want to take action on but can't seem to do so. Maybe you are having challenges with learning something new. Ask yourself, "What can I be grateful for when trying to learn how to do X?" The mere fact that you have the opportunity to learn this new thing is something to be hugely grateful for. The fact that you have the desire and capability to learn this new thing is a gift you should be grateful for. And going through the experience will open new doors you can't even imagine now. Go one step further and give some gratitude now for how this will make you a better person once you learn it.

Life Meaning

Whenever you feel a bit down or depressed, jump to that higher level and be grateful for your life and all you get to do during this lifetime. Be grateful for all you have. Be grateful for all your relationships, positive or negative. Be grateful for all you have accomplished and all you still have left to accomplish. Be grateful for all you have learned and all you still get to learn in this lifetime. You are a magnificent being, and for that alone you can give gratitude each day. I assure you this will lift your spirits up and out of whatever negative things you are feeling. Once you start doing this, you will find it easier each time you give gratitude for your magnificent life.

Practice giving gratitude for your life each day. Ask yourself, "What are all the things I have to be grateful for in my life today?" The list is very long, but even if you come up with only one or two things, you are making progress forward. Trust me that once you start doing this, your list will build over time. Soon you will have so many things to be grateful for, you'll have to write them all down. Won't that be a great thing?

STEP 5 – GIVE GRATITUDE

Other Principles of Gratitude

As I have learned more about gratitude and experienced it in my life, I have come across some fundamental principles I have found to always be true. Read through these principles, reflect on them, and think about how they apply to your experiences of gratitude.

Gratitude Comes from Love

It's hard to dispute this one. Gratitude is an expression of love for you or someone else. Love is what makes gratitude so powerful. Love is the ultimate positive emotion, and gratitude is just a derivative of it. When you are giving gratitude to yourself or others, you are really just giving a form of love to them. Check it out for yourself. When you are giving gratitude, have you found it hard or impossible to feel hate at the same time? I can safely say that when I am in a mind-set of gratitude, I can't be angry or experience negative emotions of any kind.

Gratitude Is Abundant

There is absolutely no shortage of gratitude. Just like love and money, you can have as much of it as you want. You will never run out. And others can take as much as they want from you, and you can always generate more. Give as much gratitude as you want. It is free and abundant.

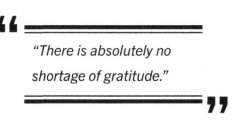

"There is absolutely no shortage of gratitude."

The More Gratitude You Give, the More You Get

Gratitude is like sunlight to flowers. The more sunlight you give a flower, the faster it will grow. Gratitude works exactly the same way. Gratitude begets more gratitude. As you start to give more gratitude in your daily life, you will soon see more gratitude coming back to you. Energy attracts like energy.

Gratitude Changes Energy

This fact can be very powerful. Give your gratitude freely, and you will see the energy change in the room in just about any situation. It's a really cool thing to watch. Just like love, gratitude is such a positive and powerful energy; it can't help but dramatically impact everyone around you. I know that when I am filled with joy and happiness and my energy is super high, I can watch the physical reactions of other people. The clerk at the store just can't help but smile when he is helping me. This happens to me all the time.

Gratitude Diminishes Fear

As you know, our lives are typically filled with lots of fear — much more than we even realize. And the side effects of fear can be devastating. Fear is what stops you from doing all those things you want to do but can't. Fear keeps you stuck in situations that frustrate you to no end. Go to battle with gratitude as your weapon of choice against fear. When you give gratitude, your fears disappear. Try it out for yourself. The next time you are feeling grateful, try to experience the emotion of fear. Gratitude is so much more powerful that it overwhelms those negative emotions.

Gratitude Is Infectious

I love this principle. When you are giving gratitude, other people will experience your gratitude and incorporate your example into their lives, even just a little bit. Planting the seed of gratitude into someone else through your actions is one of the greatest gifts you can give.

Have you ever had some random person be rude to you in some way? Maybe it was that person sitting next to you on an airplane. Maybe it was that person who cut you off while you were driving and then flipped you off in the process. When the person sitting next to me on the airplane is rude, I just look him or her in the eye and give the person a great big smile. I might even apologize. In most cases, these people immediately calm down and might even smile back. My grateful reaction changes their state to one that is more positive. For that aggressive driver, I just smile and wave at him or her while the person is flipping me off. You might be saying to yourself, "I couldn't do that." Well, if you are grateful that he didn't hit you, then you would be smiling all day. The gratitude you show that driver will most certainly change his or her state of mind, and it just might change his or her day. Using a more positive example, think of the friendly waiter you express your gratitude to with a great tip. Trust me, that gift will stick with that person more than you will ever know.

STEP 5 – GIVE GRATITUDE

Challenges with Gratitude

You might be saying to yourself, "All this sounds well and good, but how am I going to give gratitude to people I don't like or do harm to me? How do I give gratitude in situations that are negative or hurting me in some way?" It almost seems unnatural. But this is exactly what you need to do in these situations. It's easy to give gratitude when things are going well, and people are contributing positively to your life. But when things are challenging, it can be very powerful to find that love deep inside yourself to give gratitude.

As I have said over and over, your greatest lessons come from your biggest challenges. If you want to see where your life lessons are, you must look at the areas of your life where you are struggling the most. Since we are on this earth to learn our lessons, these are also your biggest gifts. These challenges come into your life for a reason, and once you overcome them, you learn their lessons. For this reason, it's so important to be grateful for these challenges. There is nothing more valuable, in fact. And once you learn their lessons, you can move forward. What once was a huge struggle in your life suddenly goes away. That process is worth some gratitude.

Furthermore, gratitude is actually the secret to learning your lessons in an easier and less painful manner. If you can give gratitude to the situation each night before you go to bed, you will find your perspective changing. Life's frictions fall away, and you'll find yourself coming from a more loving place. This creates a much higher likelihood that people will respond to you positively, and it makes your lessons far easier to learn.

Roadblocks to Giving Gratitude

We've already touched on some of the roadblocks that can prevent you from giving gratitude. Let's look at some others.

Roadblock 1: Your Ego

Your ego is probably your biggest roadblock when trying to give gratitude in challenging situations. Your ego doesn't come from a place of love and gratitude. Instead, it wants to compete, be the best at all costs, blame others, and be a victim. You must recognize the role your ego is playing when you are having problems giving gratitude. Just ask yourself, "How is my ego stopping me from giving gratitude?" The answer to this question will help you unleash the gratitude in your heart.

Roadblock 2: Misaligned Values

It's hard to give thanks and gratitude for something you don't value. Your brain will simply discard it as something that isn't important, and it will move on. You care about situations that are connected to your highest values, and you have no use for situations that seem to connect to things you value less. To help resolve this roadblock, you first need to understand what your highest and lowest values are. Next, reevaluate the situation. If you can take the current situation and understand how it relates to your highest values, then you will find it easier to give it gratitude.

Roadblock 4: Not Loving Yourself

It is hard to give love (and gratitude) when you don't have any love for yourself. If you are constantly beating yourself up in a situation and then turning around and trying to be grateful for it, you will most likely fail. If, however, you have love in your heart, you will find it so easy to give gratitude. The more you love yourself, the easier it is to give gratitude.

If you can't feel love for yourself in some area of your life, then try to find an area of your life where you can. For example, you might think, *I don't love my weight, but I love who I am when I am around my kids.* Allow this love to spread to other areas.

How to Give Gratitude in Challenging Situations

There is a very simple solution to giving gratitude in challenging situations. All you have to do is ask yourself, "How does this benefit me?" You can also ask the same question for challenging people in your life. "How is this person benefiting me?"

Search for the benefits in any challenging situation or with any challenging person, and you will be able to let the gratitude flow. Remember, you can always consider how this situation or person has moved you closer to learning your lessons. I know it's hard to give gratitude when you just don't feel like it, but you have to find space in your heart for this because it will make your life so much easier. This is probably the most valuable thing I can teach you. Let's check out a few challenging situations and see whether we can find some benefits in each.

Breaking Up with Your Lover or Spouse

This can be one of the hardest things we go through in life. The people we are closest to are also our greatest teachers, so it makes sense that a spouse or lover would teach us some great lessons. People come into your life for a reason, so figure out what that is. Be grateful for all those hard lessons they have taught you. You might also be grateful for the opportunity to move on and experience new lessons. Ending things is never easy, but it could open you up to an entirely new and amazing future relationship.

Losing Lots of Money

If you really value that money, there is no question you acquired some good skills while you were earning it. Be grateful for all those great skills you acquired along the way and know those skills will help you earn that money back again and probably lots more.

Challenging Business Relationships

Our feelings about other people are typically reflections of ourselves and what we don't like about ourselves. What is it about those coworkers or business partners you don't like? Maybe they are driving by their ego and always have to be right. Could this be something you need to work on? Usually what you don't like about someone else is inside you in some way. Find it, and your lesson might be revealed, so be grateful for this. Learning how to change the way you deal with these people could be the hidden gem of a lesson. They may be giving you your greatest gifts.

Failing Out of School

This can seem like a real setback in your life and a pretty embarrassing situation. But I assure you, there are things to be grateful for here too. Maybe school isn't part of your life plan. Maybe you are living your life through someone else's lens (doing what your parents want you to do rather than what you want to do). What lessons could be bundled up in this life event?

An Injury or Sickness

This is something we want to avoid at all costs. If you don't have your health, it makes other things in life so much more challenging. But what lessons can we learn from being sick or injured? Maybe you need to slow down and appreciate what you have, as opposed to being on the go all the time. Maybe this is a sign you need to simplify your life and focus on what is important, like love and your relationships.

Your House Burning Down

This would be a devastating event to just about everyone. What lessons could possibly come from this? Maybe your ego was running rampant and associating your worth with all your material things. There's nothing like losing much of what you own to teach you that lesson.

Death

This event, of course, is very hard. When someone has died, as my father did recently, I was so grateful for everything he taught me and for having such a loving person in my life. I was also grateful that he didn't have to suffer as he did while he was alive. Death is never easy but try to find love in your heart for all the love that person gave to the world.

Exercise: Gratitude in Challenging Situations

Now let's practice a bit. Think of a current situation or person you are struggling with. First, try to get clear as to why you feel you are struggling. Next, determine how this situation might be benefiting you. How is it helping you learn? List as many benefits as you can think of. Finally, make certain you give thanks for the situation and anyone involved in it, including yourself. Repeat this simple exercise with other challenging situations.

CHAPTER 24

The Ultimate Gratitude Toolkit

I am so excited to be able to share with you the absolute best toolkit for giving gratitude. Although you already have everything you need inside you, I have assembled several tools to help you experience gratitude daily. Read through all of them and pick the ones that resonate most with you. Even if you only adopt one of these, I will be thrilled. As you know, gratitude builds on itself, so even adding a little to your daily life can go a long way. Slowly you will find it gets easier to give gratitude, and more of it will pour into your life.

Gratitude Tool 1: Ask Gratitude Questions

Questions can help you pinpoint the things in any situation that will cause you to experience the highest degree of gratitude. The first rule in asking great questions is to try to be as specific as you can. For example, the question "What am I grateful for in my life?" is very general. While you can come up with some obvious answers, they are unlikely to focus your attention in a way that will really help you to grow. A much better question might be, "What are the three things I am grateful for while dealing with my boss at work?" That question will hone right into the core of the issue.

STEP 5 – GIVE GRATITUDE

Gratitude Tool 2: The Catch-All Gratitude Question

I have always found it helpful to have a go-to gratitude question that can be used in almost any situation. While it isn't as specific as I suggested earlier, it can start to get your brain working toward what you can be grateful for in any situation. Here are some possibilities:

- How has this situation, person, or experience benefited me?

- How has this situation, person, or experience shaped who I am?

- What has this situation, person, or experience taught me?

Use these questions whenever you need to. It's impossible not to experience gratitude after asking any one of these questions.

Gratitude Tool 3: Gratitude Journal

The gratitude journal has been a standby tool for gratitude seekers for many years. It isn't a lot of work to keep and will pay you dividends throughout your entire life. You can use it to record the people, situations, experiences, and lessons you're grateful for. I recommend you write at least a page each time; you want to have some depth to your writings.

I have been keeping a "gratitude" journal for about twenty years. (I put *gratitude* in quotes because my gratitude journal and regular journal are one and the same.) I like to use my journal to write about my life and work through whatever situations I'm faced with. Then after writing about my life, I always end with what I am grateful for. I also strongly believe that if your life is worth living, then it is worth documenting. I have a box of black college-rule Moleskine journals sitting in my house. While I may never go back through them, I have all my lessons there anytime I want to relive them.

I recommend that you make writing in your journal a regular habit. This has really worked well for me. My habit is to typically write in my journal while on airplanes. Since I usually fly once a week, this gives me the perfect opportunity to dedicate some time to writing. I always carry my journal in my briefcase, along with my favorite type of pen. I start writing as soon as I sit down to wait for the plane to take off. A habit helps get you in the swing of writing on a regular basis, so find a habit that makes sense for you. I suggest that if you can write once a week, that would be ideal. Whatever the schedule is, be consistent.

Don't let lots of time go by without writing in your journal. This is so important to your overall personal development, so please don't skip this one. It requires a little commitment, but hopefully you will become addicted to it, like I am.

Gratitude Tool 4: Gratitude List

This tool is an easy and quick one. All you have to do is keep an ongoing list of the situations, people, and experiences you are currently grateful for. Keep this list with you wherever you go or post it on the refrigerator or on your desk at work. Don't worry about someone else seeing it. I actually pray that someone will see it and get inspired to do the same. Or better yet, that someone will see his or her name on my gratitude list. I keep mine on a blue index card. (I love blue index cards for some reason; I have no idea why.) You might opt to keep it on your computer or phone. Just remember to look at this list from time to time. That is the important part.

Gratitude Tool 5: Gratitude Meditation

There is nothing better to still your mind and let the gratitude flow than meditation. It is super easy and can be done in fifteen minutes. I know we all have busy lives, but fifteen minutes a day (or even fifteen minutes a week if that is all you can do) can calm your brain down so your thoughts can flow more easily. This is essential to your growth. In fact, I have found that all the techniques I have outlined in this book can be enhanced through meditation.

Gratitude meditation is just answering a few easy questions at the end of your meditation. Remember, during your meditation you should do your best to relax your mind and not think of too much. But at the end, ask yourself the following:

- What do I have to be grateful for today or this week?

- Who am I grateful for?

- What situations am I currently grateful for?

- What lessons am I grateful for?

If you can ask questions that are more specific to you and your life, that's even better.

STEP 5 – GIVE GRATITUDE

Gratitude Tool 6: Dinner Table Gratitude

Often, family members give us some of our most challenging situations, because there is so much history and so many emotions bundled up in family dynamics. But this is even more reason to spend some time giving gratitude to your family. I love this simple but effective tool you can use in any family situation.

Try this: At an upcoming family dinner, before starting your meal, go around the table and have each person say one thing he or she is grateful for about every other person. I suggest you start with yourself first. Lead the way. The more specific the gratitude statement, the more the person receiving the gratitude will feel it.

Sometimes this might be hard because there could be people at the table you don't feel a whole lot of gratitude for. But that is the point of the exercise. Find the gratitude that might be hidden or buried. Remember, there is an abundance of gratitude, and you won't run out. And for those people whom you struggle with, you can always give gratitude for what they have taught you simply by being who they are. Even if you perceive this person has been a bad influence, you can still give gratitude for those lessons. Remember, your greatest struggles in life and your most challenging people are the ones who teach you the most and make you the person you are. Everyone has an impact on your life. If for no other reason, be grateful for that.

Once this exercise is over, can you imagine how much gratitude each person will feel? The love at the table will be higher than you probably have ever experienced. I have done this exercise before with friends, coworkers and business associates, and family, and I have to say that it is very moving. It will touch your heart and the heart of each person at the table.

There will be people who won't want to do this because they don't come from the same gratitude mind-set you come from, but lead them and encourage them to participate. Feel free to repeat this exercise with different groups as many times as you think appropriate. I would make it a habit with your immediate family at least once a year. For Americans, Thanksgiving is the perfect day to do this. This exercise goes much further than just a simple statement on what you are thankful for.

Gratitude Tool 7: Thank-You Letter

Writing a thank-you letter to those people responsible for who you are today can be an incredible way to give gratitude. First, take a look at your life and jot down a list of people (past or present) you feel have impacted you the most, either positively or negatively. Next, I would suggest you rank-order the list from the most impactful (again positive or negative) to the least impactful. Then make a selection of one or two people you want to write a letter to. You can choose as many people as you wish but just start with one or maybe two so as not to overwhelm yourself. Here are a few guidelines when writing your letter:

- Start out with the assumption that you might not actually send the letter. That will be your choice after you write it. Sometimes the mere act of writing the letter will be just what you need to give gratitude to the other person energetically. By approaching the writing process this way, it will help to lower or remove barriers that might stand in your way of saying exactly what you want to say.

- Make sure to include in the letter not only why you are grateful for this person but also how he or she has helped make you into the person you are today.

- Speak from the heart, not your brain.

- Length isn't important. Even one paragraph can make a world of difference.

Only after the letter is written will it be time to decide whether you should send it. I highly recommend sending it; just think how amazing you will make the other person feel once he or she receives it. I know it can be difficult for many people to expose themselves by sharing gratitude, but just think of all the good it will do for you and for the other people in your life. If you are struggling with this, remember it is your ego at work in worrying about the judgments of others. Don't let your ego take control of you.

Gratitude Tool 8: Gratitude Moments

I love gratitude moments because they are so easy to do. A gratitude moment is an opportunity to say thank you in whatever way fits the situation. Think of a time when you received a nice thank-you note or card from someone. How did that make you feel? It is hard not to feel happy when this happens. I am a big user of thank-you notes and cards. It brings me such joy just to write a handwritten note to someone to say thanks. And it really isn't a big production for me. I have incorporated it into my regular life. I always have a box of thank-you cards in my desk drawer, ready to send out. I know the temptation is to just send an e-mail, but a handwritten card for that special thank-you is much more meaningful. Trust me on that.

A gratitude moment can be anything. It can be a friendly smile to a waiter or waitress, an extra tip for someone who helps you out, or a brief e-mail. I recently purchased a house and sent a nice thank-you note to the lady at the title company who processed all the paperwork. She did all the work to make sure everything happened, but she was almost always behind the scenes and rarely received a thank-you from anyone. A nice little note can go a long way in a person's life.

One of my favorite ways of expressing gratitude is the thank-you on the check. When you are writing out your bills, just add the words "thank you" (and maybe the person's name) in the memo area of the check. I know this sounds a bit old-fashioned, but when you write a check to someone who has helped you, a simple thank-you in the memo section of the check can bring a smile.

Maybe you want to take your gratitude up a notch and say "thank you" with a small gift. It can be anything from a flower you picked from your garden to a Starbucks gift card or even a cupcake. It is a great way to express gratitude.

Keep gratitude moments at the top of your mind. Look for reasons to express gratitude for those who are helping you through life. If you aren't naturally inclined to do so, push yourself a bit at first and make it a habit. I am lucky because for me this comes naturally. I get so much joy from expressing my gratitude; I couldn't imagine not doing so.

Just think of all the positive energy you are generating. Your impact goes much further than just that small thank-you. Your thank-you spreads to the other person, who might well pick up on it and copy what you are doing. Spread the gratitude, and gratitude will take off around the world.

Exercise: Your Past and Gratitude

Most of us have people in our pasts for whom we have not expressed gratitude. Well, now is the time to change that. Whether you make it known to them or not, it is very important that you work through some of these past relationships. This has much more to do with you and how you hold that energy within yourself than anything else. Keep this exercise all about you. For this exercise, we'll focus on both your positive and negative relationships.

Positive Relationships

These are the people in your life who support you. They love you, even if it's conditionally. They are there when you are sick, when you need money, when you are sad, and when you are happy. They teach you great positive lessons in your life. With all your new knowledge about gratitude, you might realize you haven't expressed the level of gratitude you feel for them. Well, that is okay, because this is your opportunity to make it up to them. Show your gratitude to them directly, since it will make both of you feel amazing. Perhaps, some of these important people have passed, or you are no longer in touch with them. Or maybe you just don't feel comfortable expressing yourself to them in this manner. Don't let any of that stop you from expressing gratitude, either energetically or with your words. You can still speak to them or write them a letter, and this will help resolve this overlooked gratitude.

Negative Relationships

These relationships might be with a parent or loved one who didn't support you very well, a friend who betrayed you, a boss or coworker you conflicted with, or even a business partner who stole money from you. For these relationships, it will be difficult to find the space in your heart to give gratitude, but as I have said before, these are the relationships that have shaped who you are. They are incredibly valuable to you, and for that you need to be grateful. The important part of this part of the exercise is to change the energy both inside you and out there in the universe around these negative relationships. You will feel so much better after you rid yourself of this emotional baggage. Try this:

1. Select a positive relationship for which you feel you have not properly given gratitude. It might be one of your parents or maybe a teacher or friend who supported and inspired you. While you can select someone whom you currently interact with, it would be best for this exercise if you pick someone with whom you have little or no contact.

2. Take out a piece of paper or your journal and answer the following:

   a. How has this person impacted your life in a positive way?

   b. How has this person shaped who you are today?

    c.   How have you benefited from having this person in your life?

    d.   What lessons has this person contributed to you either directly or indirectly?

    e.   You are grateful for this person in your life because ...

3.   (Optional) If this person is still alive, you might want to give him or her a call or send him or her a note and express your gratitude for what the person have done for you. Even if it is as simple as staying "hi" and "thank you," it would still be a huge step toward giving gratitude. Trust me, that person will feel the gratitude just by you reaching out to him or her. If the person has passed away, then I suggest giving gratitude to him or her during a quiet time one evening before going to sleep or in your meditation.

4.   Now pick a person with whom you've had a negative relationship and for whom you haven't been grateful for. Again, I suggest you pick someone from your past with whom you have limited or no contact.

5.   Go to step two in this exercise and do the exact same thing you did for the person in your positive relationship.

6.   Unlike with the positive relationship, I am not encouraging you to reach out to this person. This exercise is all about you. If you want to reach out and say hi or even go so far as to express your gratitude for the person, great. This could help you with the healing process. But that is completely your call.

Exercise: Giving Gratitude to Yourself (Daily)

So often we forget to give ourselves the gratitude we deserve — and we deserve a ton of gratitude each and every day. Below are a series of gratitude questions. Read through them and answer one or all of them. But here is the trick: you must do so every day (or almost every day).

- What have you done today (or this week) to feel grateful for yourself?

- Have you helped someone today (or this week), and are you grateful for that ability?

- Whom did you inspire today (or this week), and how did that make you feel?

Don't forget to be grateful for all you are and your incredible magnificence. You will be amazed to see your level of happiness rise each time you do this, so make it a habit and do it every day.

CHAPTER 25

Practicing Gratitude

Think of this as a reference section — something you can come back to and review as needed and as many times as you want. Don't try to tackle every area at once; pick a section where you might be struggling and focus on that.

We are all given different challenges in life. Some people constantly struggle with money, while others have no problem with it. But for those who seem to effortlessly attract money, I assure you, they face other challenges, perhaps health or an out-of-control child. And that person with financial problems might have an incredible partner and family life.

I will admit, it does seem like some people have more challenges than others. Some people seem to just understand more about this game we call life. The more you understand and live the principles in this book, the more challenges you'll be able to free yourself from.

Mastering these principles is as easy as changing your perspective on how you see the challenges in your life. I have to say, I haven't really experienced too many challenges in my life since I changed my perspective.

For example, I have never really had challenges in the financial area. Since the age of ten, I've always found ways to make money. I had huge paper routes until I was sixteen and then went to work in the local hardware store. I saved enough to buy a brand-new sports car when I was seventeen, which seems a bit insane now. I paid for my undergraduate program at USC in cash. For my MBA, I took out a few loans but had it paid back within two years.

After that, I was off and running. I started my business one year out of grad school and self-funded the entire thing. I didn't take any money until nine years into the business, and that was from the same venture firm that funded companies like Google, Apple, LinkedIn, and YouTube. Over the next ten years, I raised millions of dollars with little effort and finally sold my company for a huge sum, as I've mentioned. However, I struggle with love relationships; they just aren't things I've managed to develop in my life yet. But don't be too sad for me, because despite my challenge area, I am very happy.

Below are several areas where you might be struggling. Take a look, find your own challenge area, and see if you might benefit from some of the specific advice.

Health and Fitness

So many people struggle with their body and fitness goals that this can be a very difficult area of your life to feel grateful for. Most of us don't like some aspect of our bodies. This can be a huge source of frustration, sadness, and dissatisfaction. So how is it possible to feel grateful for this?

Your body is such an emotional issue because it is connected to your appearance, and appearance is connected to your ego. We compare ourselves to others, judge ourselves and judge others. One of the best ways to fight your ego is by giving gratitude for exactly who you are at this moment in time. That doesn't mean you can't work on changing how fit and healthy you are, but you can love yourself in the process.

This means being grateful for the parts of you that are healthy but also for whatever health challenges you might be facing. While it might not seem like it when you are going through it, even healthy problems or diseases are part of your learning. Although this can be very difficult, gratitude will help you fight whatever you are dealing with and also provide a certain sense of calm as you go through these challenging situations.

Last year, I had a situation with my health that scared the living daylights out of me. I went in for my routine exam and found there were indicators for prostate cancer, which my father died from. My doctor decided to conduct a biopsy, and thank goodness, it came back negative. While the news was good, I was terrified for a few weeks as I waited for the results.

Through that entire ordeal, I became very good at giving gratitude each day for both my current situation and whatever the future would hold for me. As unpleasant as those months of worrying were, I always knew this was part of my life's path, and I was learning and growing while going through it. Gratitude was a huge help in getting through those months. I was much calmer and more relaxed about the situation because I knew there was a greater meaning to all of it.

Prior to that, I didn't spend much time giving gratitude for the healthy me. It wasn't until I was faced with a potentially serious condition that I became aware of my own health, both good and bad. So please learn from my mistake and be thankful for your health each day, whether good or bad.

Here are some questions to help guide you:

- What aspects of my body and fitness level can I be grateful for?
- How is my body's current fitness benefiting me right now?
- How is my healthy self-contributing to my life in a positive way?
- If I currently have an illness, how is it serving me in a positive way?
- How have my past illnesses benefited me in making me the person I am today?

Spirituality

We are all on a unique spiritual journey through life. I believe we are spiritual beings having a human experience, and our physical form is just a convenient way to experience this journey. Our spiritual journey is 100 percent about love — love for others and, even more importantly, for ourselves.

There is nothing more important than learning your lessons around love. For most of us, these are the hardest lessons to learn. Most of us spend time either beating ourselves up over not being good enough or beating other people up for not acting the way we think they should act.

I suggest to you that you can trace all your challenges in life back to either not loving yourself or not loving others. I encourage you to break out of this mode and finally learn the most important lesson of all, which is that everything is about love. It is the panacea that fixes most everything in life.

STEP 5 – GIVE GRATITUDE

There is no better way to tap into love than giving gratitude to both yourself and to those in your life. Here are some gratitude questions to help you on your spiritual journey for love:

- What is the love in my life I am grateful for?

- Who is my life is loving me?

- What love might I be resisting or rejecting that I want to express gratitude for?

- What situations in my life, where I am loving myself?

- What situations in my life, where I am not loving myself, do I also need to be grateful for?

- What am I grateful for in my spiritual life?

Career

For so many people, career is such an important part of a fulfilling life. Like me, some of us are doing the work we love to do and making money in the process, and it's easy to be grateful. Many others, however, are working to earn money, but their careers aren't in alignment with their mission in life. If this describes you and you struggle with gratitude, think about how millions of people struggle around the world because they don't have the opportunity to work and provide for their families, let alone develop careers they love. That itself is reason enough to give gratitude for whatever you do for work and for the opportunity to earn the money that helps propel you forward.

If you aren't yet building the career you dream of and are instead working in an uninspiring job just to make money, there is a pathway for you to change all that. In fact, that path you embark on might just be where some incredible lessons and growth come from.

I can't stress enough the importance of giving gratitude for wherever you are in the process of building your career. Even if you are doing exactly what you dreamed of doing for your career, usually you want to do more to fully realize your dream. Our brains tend to want to push forward to the next level of whatever we do, so you'll probably feel a certain level of discontent with where you are in your career. Make sure you appreciate whatever you are doing now because I guarantee you that it can lead you to whatever you ultimately want to do. Here are some questions for you to consider:

- What are the things I am grateful for in my work life?

- How is what I am doing in my career right now serving me to move me closer to my purpose or mission in life?

- Who has helped or inspired me in the development of my career?

- Who has helped or inspired me today?

- What opportunities did I have to help or inspire someone today?

Money and Finances

Money is a highly charged and emotional area of so many people's lives. We all seem to want more of it. Our egos love money for what it can buy us so we can be better than the next guy.

Like air, wealth is unlimited to everyone. You don't have to compete for it, because you can have as much as you want. I recently read a great book, *The One-Minute Millionaire*, by Mark Victor Hansen and Robert G Allen. They point out that if a man is walking down the street and takes a couple of extra breaths of air, would you go up to him and stay, "Stop that! You are taking up my air!"? Of course not. We all can have as much air as we want to consume. We don't compete with others for it. Well, money is similar to air. Money is unlimited. You don't need to take it away from the other guy or compete with him to get more. You can both have as much as you want.

I know this is a hard concept for many people to get their heads around. Money seems to be elusive to them. But the right perspective on money and the role it plays in your life will determine your happiness as it relates to your wealth. If you have a healthy perspective on what money means in your life, and if you appreciate the money you have, happiness will be there for you.

How you see money and the role it plays in your life will determine how much more money you have. If you are working for money so you can better serve others, then you are much more likely to see more money in your life. Money flows to those who are truly grateful for it, and true gratitude can't come from ego.

If you are fortunate to have the money you feel you need to lead a great financial life, then gratitude should be super easy for you. However, I have found that lots of wealthy people completely forget to give gratitude for their wealth and how it serves them. Usually this is the case because their egos want more. Just think how much more wealth might come to them if they could be grateful for all they have. I know some people who think that if they were grateful for their money, they would stop creating more wealth. But nothing is further from the truth.

If you are struggling with your lack of money, gratitude for your current situation seems like the farthest thing from your mind. But you know what I am going to say next: being grateful for your current situation is key to your financial future. Appreciate what you have today and be thankful for all it brings to you. Be grateful for all the capabilities you have inside you to earn more money whenever you want to. That's right. You can create a belief that money is unlimited, and you can have as much as you want. With a clear plan and a decisive action, there is no question you will create more money.

Acknowledge that the financial situation you are experiencing today is part of the lessons you are supposed to learn in this lifetime. Remember, your challenges are signposts for growth. Don't run from them or be frustrated about them — rather, embrace them, appreciate them, and be grateful for them. Change your attitude and perspective around money (and get your ego out of the way), and you'll discover that these challenges are huge opportunities. Here are some questions to help you increase the level of gratitude you have toward money.

- What can I be grateful for in my current financial situation?
- How has the wealth I have accumulated thus far served me in my life?
- What lessons have I learned about money that I can be grateful for?
- What lessons am I currently learning about money?
- How can I serve others with the wealth I currently have or the wealth I dream of getting?
- How can the wealth I dream of manifesting benefit me and others?
- How has my wealth made me a better person?

Relationships (Family and Friends)

Relationships are where some of our greatest lessons come from. Even in families and relationships where there is lots of love, everyone is continuously learning his or her lessons, so the result is a household where all the ups and downs are multiplied. Add to that a variety of differing expectations on what families should be and judgments about how each family member should behave. Of course, each family member thinks the others should act in accordance with his or her values. There's one little problem: it's pretty rare to find situations where everyone has the same values. And differing values, combined with close proximity, often create very dynamic situations that don't always seem filled with love and acceptance.

Since we know our biggest challenges are our greatest lessons, it's time we embraced our "dysfunctional" families with both arms. Always remember, each of our family members is in our lives for one purpose: to teach us our lessons. So instead of fighting and being angry at him or her, we should be so grateful the person is in our lives, teaching us these amazing lessons.

There's one thing to keep in mind: you actually picked your family before you came into this world. Your family is the team you are going to go through life with, and one of the things you get to do is pick your team before you begin it. I know some of you won't believe this to be true, but it is my belief. Like it or not, this is your team, and you are 100 percent responsible for it.

How about your friends? While you might be stuck with your family for your entire life, you choose your friends and can get rid of them anytime you want. Just like family, friends are also in your life to teach you all those good lessons as well. In some cases, your friends will teach you even more important lessons than your family will. And you really can't just dispose of friends that easily. The closer you are and the stronger your emotional connection to them is, the harder it is to just discard them.

Embrace your friends as you embrace your family members because they are part of your team. Give gratitude to your friends for being in your life and going on this journey with you. They are incredibly valuable. You have and will continue to run into struggles and challenges with friends, both close and distant, but remember they are in your life for a reason. The more challenging friends will teach you your best lessons. Those conflicts are valuable, so as hard as it sounds, be grateful for them.

I have a belief I share all the time: friends can be in your life for a day, a week, a month, a year, or forever, and no matter how long, they will have served their purpose. Sometimes we want to hold onto friends for longer than we should. It's just human nature. But it's okay to let friends go. Not all friends are intended to stay in your life forever, so don't hold that expectation. It's better to be grateful for whatever they give you for as long as they are present in your life. It can be sad to have friends grow distant, but this is normal, and even healthy. This allows you to bring new people in to form relationships based on all your growth.

Have you ever experienced growing apart from your friends, but you weren't sure why? I certainly have. As you grow and learn, your perspective on life and energy vibrations also changes. If certain friends fail to keep growing with you, then it can be challenging to keep them in your life. You might have seen the world the same as they do at one point, but then you grew, and maybe they didn't, or maybe they grew in a different way. As your view of life changes, the bond you used to share with friends also changes. Be grateful for the time you shared with them, for they played a part in that growth, whether they shared it or not. Here are some questions to help you increase your level of gratitude toward your family and friends.

- Which friends and family members bring me the love and acceptance I'm grateful for?
- Which friends and family members present me with challenges I'm grateful for?
- What lessons are my friends and family teaching me that I can be grateful for?
- Why am I grateful for my partner or spouse? What lessons have they taught me over the years, and what lessons are they currently teaching me?
- What am I most grateful for with the following people?
- Mother
  - Father
  - Each sibling
  - Grandparents
  - Children
  - Partner or spouse
  - Five of your most important friends

Learning and Growth

All roads lead back to your lessons and growth. This is why we are here, so nothing is more important than giving gratitude for the purpose of our existence. Wrap your lessons with love and be forever grateful for each and every one of them. Your lessons are the gems in your life and the keys to an incredible next life. I understand that not everyone believes we live multiple lives, but even if you are just focused on this life, with each lesson you learn, I assure you, your life will get easier, and you will become filled with more joy and fulfillment than before.

There is one law I am so certain of that I would stake my life on it. If you remember one thing from this book, remember this — it's the first irrefutable law of growth. *When you have a lesson to learn, you will relive it until you master it.* And if you don't learn all the lessons you came for in this lifetime, you will be back to learn whatever lessons you haven't mastered.

Have you seen this law at work in your life? What lessons have you been working on but never seem to learn? Do you keep attracting the same type of person in your love relationships? Have you been having the same fight with your mom or dad for years without resolution? Have you been struggling at work, never getting ahead, and you can't figure out why? I suggest the answers to all these questions are the same. You haven't yet learned what you are supposed to, so you repeat the same behaviors until you learn them. In fact, you will find yourself reliving these same nasty situations over and over until you master them. Maybe it's just a cruel trick the universe plays on us, but I assure you, there is no way around it. And you might think you are clever and can find a way around your lessons. Well, I am here to tell you there are no shortcuts. You get to go through this process just like everyone else in the world.

Here's the second irrefutable law of growth. *You have all the answers.* When you were given all these lessons to learn, you were also given the answers. God wouldn't give you the challenge without also giving you the ability to come up with the answers to them. It is just a matter of producing them and believing in them. That is the hard part.

Have you had situations where you were able to get quiet enough that a great solution to a problem or challenge you had been working on suddenly popped into your head? If so, this means that at some point, you asked yourself a good question to make that answer come to you. *The quality of your questions determines the quality of your life.* The better the questions you ask when working on your lessons, the faster you will get to the answers and to mastering the lesson. This is a core principle of growth. Get really good at asking great questions and be grateful for their power.

What about when you get stuck? This happens to all of us. You are working on one of your lessons, and you run into a brick wall and can't seem to make progress. It is possible that you don't realize you are actually working on a lesson. All you know is that you are stuck. We have all had the yucky feeling of being stuck. Maybe you are stuck in a bad relationship and are unsure what do you. Maybe you are trying to lose weight or get fit, but you just can't make any progress. Maybe you are in a job you hate but are fearful of making a change because you need the money and can't take the risk. Be grateful for this situation as well, because these are opportunities to learn some great lessons. Sometimes being stuck will make you take a step back and see things a new way or find help from somewhere you didn't expect it.

It's important to give gratitude to all lessons you encounter. Be grateful as you walk through the challenges and struggles of life. You will encounter easy lessons and hard lessons. You will encounter lessons that take an hour to learn and ones that take a lifetime. You will have small lessons and big lessons. You will have lessons that are less meaningful to you and ones that are incredibly meaningful. You will have lessons that are unemotional and ones that are extremely emotional. Regardless of the lessons at any given time, embrace them with both arms and give as much love and gratitude as you can to them. The more love and gratitude you give to them, the easier they will be to master. Life doesn't have to be difficult if you approach it from a loving and grateful place. Here are some questions to help you increase your gratitude toward your lessons and growth:

- What lessons am I currently learning that I am grateful for?

- What things have I learned in the past year that I am grateful for?

- Who has taught me the most valuable lessons in the last year (or currently), and why am I grateful for him or her?

- What growth over the past year should I be grateful for?

- How have I benefited from these lessons and growth?

- What lessons would I love to learn to help my current growth?

- What is my intuition telling me about my lessons?

- What did I learn today that I can be grateful for?

- Who has taught me something today I can be grateful for?

Get additional tools and resources on gratitude by visiting **KenBurke.com.**

CONCLUSION

CHAPTER 26

Bringing It All Together:
Practicing Happiness and Joy

Congratulations! You did it. I am going to assume you got through the entire book (unless you skipped ahead, which is okay too). That is a huge accomplishment in my eyes. I am super proud of you.

I know I'm not supposed to have a favorite chapter, but if I did, it would be this one. This isn't just a summary of the book but rather my attempt to put everything into perspective and give you a road map you can make actionable immediately.

To do this, I want to share with you a summary of the rituals and beliefs I use in my own life to practice joy and happiness daily. Please take whatever rituals resonate with you and mix them together with whatever rituals and beliefs you have found already work for you. This will move you forward on this incredible (and sometimes crazy) journey we call "life."

Practicing Happiness and Joy

Wait a minute — I am throwing out a new concept at the end of a book. I am supposed to be summarizing, not teaching new things. Well, as you will see in a moment, practicing happiness and joy incorporates all you have learned in this book.

STEP 5 – GIVE GRATITUDE

The entire premise of everything I have shared with you is that we are always growing and developing. Everything in the universe is in motion at all times and ever changing, and so are you.

If we are alive, we are moving our lives forward in some way. You might not notice it daily, but even the smallest experiences are providing you with new learning opportunities. It is your job to take advantage of all these life experiences and to learn as much as you can from them.

Because you are constantly growing, you are also changing constantly along with the situations you are facing. So just when you think you have everything figured out, the universe serves you up a new challenge. Therefore, you *must* learn how to practice joy and happiness daily.

What do I mean by practicing joy and happiness? Essentially, it means consciously working on your own happiness, joy, and (I will add) fulfillment each and every day. Yes, you need to work on this stuff all the time. If you think happiness is just supposed to happen to you organically, I hate to break it to you but you are misguided. It doesn't work that way. I have found that the way to be happy and fulfilled is to work (and work hard sometimes) at it. This is very similar to what people say about their love relationship. *If you are really in love, then you shouldn't have to work at it. It should just happen naturally.* Really? Anyone who has been in a love relationship (or a relationship of any kind) knows you have to work at it constantly. The same is true here.

> "In order to experience happiness and joy in your life on a consistent basis, you must consciously practice it daily."

Here's an important thing to remember: we aren't supposed to be happy, joyful, and fulfilled all the time. Growth is hard, and the bigger the lesson, the harder it is. Please don't hold yourself to an unreasonable standard of being happy 100 percent of the time. As long as you are growing (which you always are), there will be those times when practicing happiness and joy is a bit harder.

Here is a cool thing about practicing happiness and joy in your life. The more you practice them, the better you get, and the easier it becomes. Your muscle memory kicks in. I want you to get really good at this stuff, so please make sure you work at this.

Share Your Thoughts

I would love to know your rituals for practicing happiness and joy in your life. Go to my website at KenBurke.com and click on the "Share Your Thoughts" button.

My Rituals for Practicing Happiness and Joy

Are you ready to get started? I'm going to share with you the rituals I use to practice joy in my life. While I do all of them, I want you to take the ones that feel right for you. Start by incorporating one or two of these in your life and slowly add to your practice as you feel is appropriate. If you are already doing some, add a few more to your routine.

There is nothing revolutionary in my rituals for practicing happiness, so let this serve as a great checklist for you and a reminder to incorporate these rituals into your daily life. I find that most people are doing maybe one or two of these things but not on a consistent basis. For me, I have incorporated all these rituals into my life, and I practice them daily. And most importantly, I check in with myself daily to ensure I am working on my joy and happiness.

Make Time for Yourself

This might seem super simple, but it is probably the most difficult step for people to take. I know most of us lead very busy lives, but we must force ourselves to start this ritual. Honestly, being busy is no excuse. I suggest to you that if you did this regularly, you would be less busy and more effective with your time.

When I say to make time for yourself, there are three critical things you must incorporate. First, you must be alone. You can't be distracted by someone's energy. Second, you must change your environment. You must truly get away from your home or workplace. Third, the time you get away must be significant enough to have an impact. Getting away for one hour just isn't going to do it. You need time to let your brain relax and open up.

During your alone time, relax your brain and turn down the volume on that voice in your head. I know it will be hard to completely switch off, but quiet the thoughts in your head. Unlike meditation, I want you to think about your life and how you want to live it. Think about how you can be happier and more fulfilled. But to do that, you first need to slow down and get rid of those thoughts that clutter your mind.

I would love for you to create this into a ritual you do each month. I know this might be unrealistic for some of you but start small with maybe a long walk and build up from there. I assure you that the more time you can find for yourself, the better you will feel.

For me this means getting away for the weekend by myself. It doesn't need to be anything fancy; just a drive up the coast and an overnight at a B&B are perfect for me (preferably some quiet place in nature). The important thing for me is changing my environment. If I just stay home and lock myself away, that won't work. I need to be someplace different. This forces me to relax, contemplate, and open up my mind. Some people think going away alone is crazy, but it's one of my favorite things to do.

If you can't get away for an entire weekend, commit to taking a long drive alone (and I mean both long and alone). Crank up your favorite tunes and start driving. Make the trip a minimum of at least four hours. Watch your mind as it opens up the more you relax.

Can't take a long drive? Then go for a long (and I mean long) walk on the beach. Don't have a beach around? Then taking a long hike in nature (again alone) will do the trick.

Keep a Journal

I have been keeping a journal religiously for more than fifteen years. I am obsessed with it (sometimes a bit too obsessed), but it has been one of the best personal development tools I have ever used. I literally have boxes of my journals at my house.

Keeping a journal is all about the process of getting out what is in your head. I have found that the process of writing (which I absolutely love) really forces me to think things through. I am processing life's challenges and the lessons I am currently working through. The sheer act of writing it down is enough. Your brain will take care of the rest. Funny thing is, I have never reread my journals. I get all the benefit from just emptying my brain onto the paper.

No structure is required. Do whatever works for you. Just write. If you were to read my journal (God forbid), you would probably think I was a nutcase. Sometimes I write about the same thing for several years or more. Why? Because those are the things I am working though, and some of the bigger lessons take a long time to work through.

Keeping a journal is all about making a ritual out of it. For me, I mostly write in my journal while I am flying on a plane. I fly on planes a lot each year, so this gives me plenty of journal entries. As the plane is waiting to taxi to the runway, you will find my black Moleskine college-rule notebook out and me writing feverishly. Some days, I write one page, while on other days, I write twenty. And yes, you caught my obsession. I write only in the same black Moleskine journal. I have recently switched to Amazon's knock-off of the Moleskine. Not sure what I'll do if they stop making them!

Practice Meditation (and Yoga Too)

Okay, I'm guilty of not doing this as much as I would like, but I'm trying to get better. Some of you are great at this, so keep going. For others like me, listen up. Let's work on this together.

There are so many benefits to practicing meditation; it is unquestionably good for you. Meditation is all about quieting your brain, even for a few moments, which is impossible to do when you are living the craziness of our daily lives. Meditation is some of the best self-care you can do.

What I mostly care about for you is that you will give yourself a few hours a week (if possible) to relax and get in touch with yourself.

What has worked for me is making meditation a ritual I do regularly. Whether regular is every day or once a week, I don't care as long as you establish this practice and are consistent with it. I'm able to fit in about thirty minutes three to four days a week.

STEP 5 – GIVE GRATITUDE

I don't want to dictate how to medicate since there are many experts out there, but what works for me is listening to music that is specifically designed for meditating. The one I use was created by Wayne Dyer and is called "I Am: Wishes Fulfilled Meditation." But please use what works for you.

Check in on Your Ego

I have created a ritual where I routinely check in to see whether my actions are coming from ego. Whether I just wrapped up a sales meeting with a client or just spent a nice evening with friends or family, I quickly replay the encounter in my head to see whether my ego was in check. And if I find cases where I think my ego got the best of me, I will use that information to help modify my behavior with future encounters.

You might think this is crazy behavior, but I have to say it works really well. I'm always checking in on my ego in near real time and making adjustments as I go. I have been doing this for so long that it is automatic for me at this point.

So how can you create this ritual in your life? At first, you will need to check yourself on a regular basis for any ego outburst. As you do this, you will become better at spotting them and doing so more quickly. Once you are aware of them, your brain will go into action and work to modify your behavior around this (assuming you believe living from ego isn't a great thing for you). Slowly, you will start to weed out these ego manifestations, and joy will be more prevalent in your life. Ego manifestations are easy to spot. Just look for things like the following:

- Do I need to win this disagreement at all costs?
- Do I need to compete with this person?
- Am I constantly comparing myself to others?
- Am I passing judgment (or opinions) on people or situations I'm involved in?
- Am I constantly rendering opinions about myself?
- Am I talking way too much about myself with little concern for others?
- Am I easily offended by others' comments about me?
- Am I constantly defining myself to others based on how much money I have, what material goods I have, who my friends or family are, what my current status is, or what my status in the world is?

Be Aware When You Aren't Loving Yourself

It's so easy to fall into a funk with the chaotic lives that most of us live. We get so caught up in living our lives that we forget to pause and provide some love back to ourselves.

I am guilty of this more than I care to admit. There are so many things that can set me off like worry about money, frustration over not being able to achieve something, or something just not going my way. While it all seems silly as I reflect on it, at the time, these things are real-life issues. What are the real-life issues that set you off, make you mad, or cause you to get upset with yourself or others?

When this happens to me, I have a ritual that stops me in my tracks and changes my direction. I have gotten very good at recognizing when I'm not loving myself. I recognize when my negative thoughts are getting the better of me. I instantly become aware that I have stopped loving myself in that moment, and as fast as I can change my state, I use one (or more) of these four techniques.

First, as silly as it sounds, I tell myself that I love myself (yes, aloud). We have to remind ourselves of this all the time, and hearing it helps even more than just thinking about it.

Second, my brain goes straight to being grateful for something in my life. I pick from a huge list of things to be grateful for. I know you have a huge list too. It shouldn't be hard to come up with something, even if you're thoroughly in the process of beating yourself up. If you can't pick one thing, just be grateful you are alive and breathing. I sometimes think of all the people in the world who are less fortunate than I am, people who have real hardships that are worse than mine. This step generally kicks me in the butt to start thinking differently.

Third, I put whatever challenges I am having in perspective. Regardless of the reason I have gone into this funk, in the grand scheme of life, is it really that important? Maybe I didn't get that raise or recognition. Maybe there's a failure in one of my relationships, or maybe I lost a bunch of money. Looking at this situation through a different lens can make something that is seemingly big in the moment seem very small when you put it into the context of your entire life.

Forth, I sometimes change my physical state. Either I change my breathing patterns, usually by slowing down, taking some deep breaths, and remembering all the reasons I love myself, or I get up and start moving. Just getting up and going for a walk will allow you to reflect on the many good things in your life. I also have found that going to the gym (or going on a run) really helps me get focused on what is important.

I will admit that it was hard at first to remember to use this step, but the more I practiced it, the better I got. I want you to use it and even do better than I have. Just becoming aware that you aren't loving yourself in the moment (or you are beating yourself up for some reason) will help you snap out of it. Awareness is the starting point and the key to making this ritual work.

Give Yourself a Break

Are you being too hard on yourself? Are you using negative motivation (telling yourself you aren't good enough) to push yourself? Or are you just driving yourself hard at school, at work, or in your relationship? I have suffered from this problem for many years. I had to realize how to stop putting this incredible pressure on myself and to allow myself to pull back from the pressure I was putting on myself.

Become aware of when you are putting too much pressure on yourself and becoming stressed out. Being stressed will have the opposite effect on what you are trying to accomplish. You need to step back from the situation and regain perspective on things. Is what you are doing really that important to the grand plan of your life? Is the stress this is creating really helping you to achieve your objective? Give yourself permission to do nothing. It literally takes one second to change your perspective on a situation that has been stressing you out. Have you ever stressed out over making a hard decision in your life, and once you made that decision, you suddenly felt so much better? This happens to me all the time. Giving yourself a break is very similar to this. Just decide to give yourself a break and take the pressure off you.

You need to get good at this. The key is recognizing those situations that are causing you stress and having the strength to decide to take a breath for a while and reflect. When you take time to put things into perspective, life becomes so much better (and easier).

Plan Continuously to Help Fulfill Your Purpose

As I have said before, most people spend more time planning their summer vacation than planning their lives. I am always planning how my life can be better. And I'm not just thinking about what I want to do; I actually write it down and revise or update constantly. This ongoing planning pushes me forward with what I want to achieve in my life. Why is this important? When you are living a prosperous life, you are living a life of purpose. Living your purpose is one of the biggest contributors to your happiness. When you are fulfilled with working on your purpose, everything seems to come together. Sure, you will have challenges when you are pushing forward, but the satisfaction of living your purpose each day is an amazing feeling.

I am a bit fanatical about planning. Continuously planning what I want to do next keeps me on track with living my purpose. And there is no question you are happiest when you are living on purpose.

Here are a few things you can do to build continuous planning as a ritual. At a higher level, I recommend doing a yearly plan each January. This is exactly what most well-run businesses do to be successful. Create what I call your "key initiatives" for the year (all this is covered in the taking-action section of the book). Then I make more detailed plans each month on what I want to get done to move my dreams forward and to make them a reality. Next, I use my journal to further develop my planning in an informal and unstructured way. Finally, I keep to-do lists daily. If things don't get done, I carry them over to the next day's to-do list. Sometimes things will stay on my to-do list for months, and that is okay. I know this all sounds very tactical but see what fits you and how you can incorporate planning as a ritual that will help you continuously fulfill your purpose.

Take Action That Moves You toward Joy and Fulfillment

If you are living your purpose, planning isn't going to get you there. You actually have to do something that moves you forward with your purpose. When you are doing things that fill you up with joy inside (even if they are hard at times), you will know the happiness that comes from achieving or accomplishing something meaningful.

I want you to build taking action into a ritual. And yes, sometimes you need to push yourself a bit to overcome the fear that stops you from taking action and creating that momentum that pushes you forward so much more easily.

I'm constantly aware of what actions I'm taking on a continual basis that are moving me toward exactly what I want to create or achieve. And yes, sometimes I have to really push myself to take action, and that is okay. But I do it with grace and love for myself (not beating myself up). What ritual do you want to create around taking action? I make sure I monitor myself on this one. Awareness of your actions is key. It's easy to get off track, which is why you need this built into your rituals.

Be Grateful

I have found that anytime my brain goes to gratitude, I instantly feel better. All I have to do is think of something I'm grateful for and *boom,* I feel happier. And the great thing about this is that it can change your emotional state in literally a nanosecond. My ritual goes one step further. When something bad happens to me, like losing a bunch of money, I have trained my brain to instantly move to gratitude and to think about all the things I do have. Losing that money really wasn't all that important in the grand scheme of life.

I want you to build this easy-to-execute ritual into your overall practice of being happy. I have found it works well to give gratitude for something associated with the thing you are having challenges with. For example, if I lose a friend, then I give gratitude for all the amazing friends I do have.

Just like with all our other rituals, the more you do this, the easier it is to trigger automatically anytime you need it.

Give Back

Core to everything I believe is that we are here on earth to serve others. Period. Some are in professions that constantly serve others, like nursing or teaching, while others serve others by donating money or volunteering. Some give back day and night, and others do it every once in a while. You can define what serving others means to you. Some do more than others, but don't let that be your guide. Find a way to make this a ritual in your life. You already know that when you serve others, you unquestionably feel joy and fulfillment about what you are doing.

If you always seem to be taking, then consciously create a few things you can do to give back and execute them consistently. For me, giving back is working with people so they can live a better life. Now define what you can do to give back and integrate that into your life. Giving back is an important part of practicing joy and happiness.

My Hope for You

I'm so excited that you decided to take this journey with me. I truly hope this book has helped you as you continue your journey through life. Our journey together has been about looking at your life through a different lens. Even changing one of your thoughts, learning just one lesson, or better managing a limiting belief or fear you have can take your life in an entirely new direction.

I think most of us make life harder than it needs to be. I really want you to internalize practicing joy and happiness daily. Remember, your life is a masterpiece, and you are the artist. Like any artist, you have to work on your masterpiece daily. Your work is never really done. And remember to work on your masterpiece while loving yourself and practicing joy and happiness all the time.

One of the most important things you can do to live your prosperous life is to take action. To make meaningful change in your life and challenge yourself to learn your lessons, you need to do something. You have taken a great step forward by completing this book, but that isn't enough. To internalize the concepts I shared with you, you need to take action that moves your life in the direction you want to go. The more action you take, the more embedded these ideas become in your daily life.

Believe it or not, the more you practice this stuff, the better you become, and the easier it is. Trust me, I know. I have been practicing this plan for many years, and I can tell you it gets easier. Life gets easier and more fulfilling with each passing day. And I know this will happen to you!

Nothing would make me happier than knowing you are living your prosperous life. Feel free to drop me an e-mail at ken@kenburke.com or go to the website KenBurke.com and click on the feedback button. I would love to hear from you.

To enhance your experience with this book, make sure to get the Companion Guide, which contains valuable worksheets and other helpful resources.

Visit **KenBurke.com**